FreeRADIUS
Beginner's Guide

Manage your network resources with FreeRADIUS

Dirk van der Walt

BIRMINGHAM - MUMBAI

FreeRADIUS
Beginner's Guide

First published: September 2011

Production Reference: 1260811

Published by Packt Publishing Ltd.
Livery Place
35 Livery Street
Birmingham B3 2PB, UK.

ISBN 978-1-849514-08-8

www.packtpub.com

Cover Image by Asher Wishkerman (a.wishkerman@mpic.de)

Credits

Author

Dirk van der Walt

Reviewers

Ante Gulam

Atif Razzaq

Acquisition Editor

Chaitanya Apte

Development Editors

Kartikey Pandey

Alina Lewis

Technical Editor

Vanjeet D'souza

Copy Editor

Neha Shetty

Project Coordinator

Srimoyee Ghoshal

Proofreader

Chris Smith

Indexers

Hemangini Bari

Tejal Daruwale

Graphics

Nilesh Mohite

Production Coordinator

Adline Swetha Jesuthas

Cover Work

Adline Swetha Jesuthas

About the Author

Dirk van der Walt is an open source software specialist from Pretoria, South Africa. He is a firm believer in the potential of open source software. Being a Linux user for almost ten years, it was love at first boot. From then on Dirk spent his available time sharing his knowledge with others equally passionate about the freedom and affordability open source software gives to the community.

In 2003, Dirk started coding with Perl as his language of choice and gave his full attention to functional and aesthetic user interface design. He also compiled an online Gtk2-Perl study guide to promote the advancement of Perl on the desktop.

As Rich Internet Applications (RIA) became more popular, Dirk added the Dojo toolkit and CakePHP to his skills set to create an AJAX-style front-end to a FreeRADIUS MySQL database. His latest work is YFi Hotspot Manager. Today YFi Hotspot Manager is used in many localities around the globe. With many contributors to the project it proves just how well the open source software model can work.

I'd like to thank the Lord Jesus for life and light, my wife Petra and daughter Daniélle for all their support and understanding, my brother Karel for his interest and help. I would also like to thank the people involved with the FreeRADIUS project, from the coders to the commenters. Lastly I'd like to thank Packt Publishing for supporting Open Source software the way they do.

About the Reviewers

Ante Gulam is a 26-year-old software and system engineer with more than seven years of working experience in various segments of the IT industry. He has worked as a consultant and system engineer on POSIX-compliant systems (Linux, BSD, SCO, and others), and lately has focused mainly on security, design, and administration of Microsoft-based enterprise solutions. Ante is currently working as a system engineer and software developer, primarily on MS platforms (.NET) in Ri-ing d.o.o., a medium-sized software development company.

Being involved in security for several years Ante gained experience in the development of various security tools based on many different technologies and has written articles and co-edited *Phearless Security Ezine* actively for the last four years. Presently, he is working on large networking projects and enterprise environments; adopting them for standards like PCI-DSS enables him to stay in touch with security on the enterprise level.

I would like to thank my family, my friends, and my girlfriend for the their patience. Also all the guys from the "gn00bz" team for all the hours full of fun and knowledge while playing CTF for the past couple of years.

Atif Razzaq holds an MSc degree from Strathclyde University, Glasgow, UK in Communication, Control, and Digital Signal Processing, and a BSc degree in Computer Science from NUCES, Pakistan. After his MSc degree, he started his career as a software engineer in the area of Mobile Application Development in J2ME in Tricastmedia, Glasgow, UK. During this period he also published an article at Java.net titled *Getting Started with BlackBerry J2ME Development*.

He is currently working as the Development Manager at Terminus Technologies who specializes in telecom billing software development. His responsibilities include the development of the billing system and its integration with other applications both proprietary and open source (Asterisk, FreeSwitch, FreeRADIUS, and others). Prior to joining Terminus Technologies, he worked on telecom billing at Comcerto, Bahrain. He has been working on telecom billing and VoIP/SIP Telephony for about three years.

In his free time, he writes his own blog on different ICT topics available at `http://atif-razzaq.blogspot.com`. He can be contacted at `atif.razaq@googlemail.com`.

It has been a great experience working on this project. I'd like to thank the whole team working on this project: the author and all members from Packt Publishing. I'd like to thank my family for giving up their share of time which I gave to this project. Finally, I'd thank the Great Lord for everything and then my parents who taught me and made me what I am.

www.PacktPub.com

Support files, eBooks, discount offers, and more

You might want to visit www.PacktPub.com for support files and downloads related to your book.

Did you know that Packt offers eBook versions of every book published, with PDF and ePub files available? You can upgrade to the eBook version at www.PacktPub.com and as a print book customer, you are entitled to a discount on the eBook copy. Get in touch with us at service@packtpub.com for more details.

At www.PacktPub.com, you can also read a collection of free technical articles, sign up for a range of free newsletters, and receive exclusive discounts and offers on Packt books and eBooks.

http://PacktLib.PacktPub.com

Do you need instant solutions to your IT questions? PacktLib is Packt's online digital book library. Here, you can access, read, and search across Packt's entire library of books.

Why Subscribe?

- Fully searchable across every book published by Packt
- Copy and paste, print and bookmark content
- On demand and accessible via web browser

Free Access for Packt account holders

If you have an account with Packt at www.PacktPub.com, you can use this to access PacktLib today and view nine entirely free books. Simply use your login credentials for immediate access.

Table of Contents

Preface

FreeRADIUS Beginner's Guide contains plenty of practical exercises that will help you with everything from basic installation to the more advanced configurations like LDAP and Active Directory integration. This book will help you understand authentication, authorization, and accounting in FreeRADIUS using the most popular Linux distributions of today. Larger deployments with realms and fail-over configuration are also covered along with tips. A quiz at the end of each chapter validates your understanding.

What this book covers

The book can be divided into three sections:

1. Introduction and installation (Chapter 1 to Chapter 3)
2. AAA functions of FreeRADIUS (Chapter 4 to Chapter 7)
3. Advanced topics (Chapter 8 to Chapter 13)

Let's see what each chapter deals with:

Chapter 1, Introduction to AAA and RADIUS, introduces FreeRADIUS and the RADIUS protocol. It highlights some key RADIUS concepts, which help the user avoid common misunderstandings.

Chapter 2, Installation, describes how to build and install FreeRADIUS from source on popular Linux distributions. It also covers installing the FreeRADIUS packages included with popular Linux distributions. Ubuntu, SUSE, and CentOS will be used to ensure a wide coverage.

Chapter 3, Getting Started with FreeRADIUS, gives a brief introduction on the various components of FreeRADIUS. It also discusses the process of handling a basic authentication request.

Chapter 4, Authentication, teaches authentication methods and how they work. Extensible Authentication Protocol (EAP) is covered later in a dedicated chapter.

Chapter 5, Sources of Usernames and Passwords, covers various places where username/ password combinations can be stored. It shows which modules are involved and how to configure FreeRADIUS to utilize these stores.

Chapter 6, Accounting, discusses the need for accounting and the options available to record accounting data. It also discusses implementing a policy that includes limiting sessions and/or time and/or data.

Chapter 7, Authorization, discusses various aspects of authorization including the use of unlang.

Chapter 8, Virtual Servers, discusses various aspects of virtual servers and where they can potentially be used.

Chapter 9, Modules, discusses the various modules used by FreeRADIUS and how to configure multiple instances of a certain module.

Chapter 10, EAP, a dedicated chapter on EAP, is a one stop for EAP (802.11x and WiFi).

Chapter 11, Dictionaries, introduces dictionaries, which are used to map the names seen and used by an administrator, to the numbers used by the RADIUS protocol.

Chapter 12, Roaming and Proxying, deals with the RADIUS protocol, which allows the proxying of authorization and accounting requests. This makes roaming possible. This chapter covers various aspects of proxying in FreeRADIUS.

Chapter 13, Troubleshooting, works through many common problems, giving examples of what to look for, and how to fix the issue.

What you need for this book

You need to be familiar with Linux and have a solid understanding of TCP/IP. No previous knowledge of RADIUS or FreeRADIUS is required.

To get the most out of the practical exercises you will need a clean install of Ubuntu, SUSE or CentOS

Who this book is for

If you are an Internet Service Provider (ISPs) or a network manager who needs to track and control network usage, then this is the book for you.

Conventions

In this book, you will find a number of styles of text that distinguish between different kinds of information. Here are some examples of these styles, and an explanation of their meaning.

Time for action – heading

1. Action 1

2. Action 2

3. Action 3

Instructions often need some extra explanation so that they make sense, so they are followed with:

What just happened?

This heading explains the working of tasks or instructions that you have just completed.

You will also find some other learning aids in the book, including:

Pop quiz – heading

These are short multiple choice questions intended to help you test your own understanding.

Have a go hero – heading

These set practical challenges and give you ideas for experimenting with what you have learned.

Code words in text are shown as follows: "The `rlm_sqlcounter` module allows defining various counters (time or data based) to keep track of a user's usage."

A block of code is set as follows:

```
if(control:Auth-Type == 'PAP'){
    update reply {
        Reply-Message := `/bin/echo We are using %{control:Auth-Type}`
    }
}
```

When we wish to draw your attention to a particular part of a code block, the relevant lines or items are set in bold:

```
if(control:Auth-Type == 'PAP'){
    update reply {
        Reply-Message := `/bin/echo We are using %{control:Auth-Type}`
    }
}
```

Any command-line input or output is written as follows:

```
INSERT INTO radcheck (username, attribute, op, value) VALUES ('bob',
'Cleartext-Password', ':=', 'passbob');
```

New terms and **important words** are shown in bold. Words that you see on the screen, in menus or dialog boxes for example, appear in the text like this: "clicking the **Next** button moves you to the next screen".

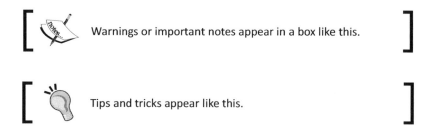

Warnings or important notes appear in a box like this.

Tips and tricks appear like this.

Reader feedback

Feedback from our readers is always welcome. Let us know what you think about this book—what you liked or may have disliked. Reader feedback is important for us to develop titles that you really get the most out of.

To send us general feedback, simply send an e-mail to feedback@packtpub.com, and mention the book title via the subject of your message.

If there is a book that you need and would like to see us publish, please send us a note in the **SUGGEST A TITLE** form on www.packtpub.com or e-mail suggest@packtpub.com.

If there is a topic that you have expertise in and you are interested in either writing or contributing to a book, see our author guide on www.packtpub.com/authors.

Customer support

Now that you are the proud owner of a Packt book, we have a number of things to help you to get the most from your purchase.

> **Downloading the example code for this book**
>
> You can download the example code files for all Packt books you have purchased from your account at http://www.PacktPub.com. If you purchased this book elsewhere, you can visit http://www.PacktPub.com/support and register to have the files e-mailed directly to you.

Errata

Although we have taken every care to ensure the accuracy of our content, mistakes do happen. If you find a mistake in one of our books—maybe a mistake in the text or the code—we would be grateful if you would report this to us. By doing so, you can save other readers from frustration and help us improve subsequent versions of this book. If you find any errata, please report them by visiting http://www.packtpub.com/support, selecting your book, clicking on the **errata submission form** link, and entering the details of your errata. Once your errata are verified, your submission will be accepted and the errata will be uploaded on our website, or added to any list of existing errata, under the Errata section of that title. Any existing errata can be viewed by selecting your title from http://www.packtpub.com/support.

Piracy

Piracy of copyright material on the Internet is an ongoing problem across all media. At Packt, we take the protection of our copyright and licenses very seriously. If you come across any illegal copies of our works, in any form, on the Internet, please provide us with the location address or website name immediately so that we can pursue a remedy.

Please contact us at copyright@packtpub.com with a link to the suspected pirated material.

We appreciate your help in protecting our authors, and our ability to bring you valuable content.

Questions

You can contact us at questions@packtpub.com if you are having a problem with any aspect of the book, and we will do our best to address it.

1

Introduction to AAA and RADIUS

It is my pleasure to present you a beginner's guide to FreeRADIUS. This book will help you to deploy a solid, stable, and scalable RADIUS server in your environment.

This chapter is used as an introduction to RADIUS and FreeRADIUS. We will be covering a fair amount of theory and recommend you pay special attention to it. This will supply you with a good foundation on the workings of the RADIUS protocol and will be of much help in subsequent chapters.

In this chapter we shall:

- ◆ See what AAA is, and why we need it
- ◆ Learn where RADIUS started and why it is so relevant today
- ◆ See why FreeRADIUS really shines as a RADIUS server
- ◆ Understand the relationship between AAA, RADIUS, and FreeRADIUS

Let's get started.

Authentication, Authorization, and Accounting

Users gain access to data networks and network resources through various devices. This happens through a wide range of hardware. Ethernet switches, Wi-Fi access points, and VPN servers all offer network access.

When these devices are used to control access to a network, for example a Wi-Fi access point with WPA2 Enterprise security implemented or an Ethernet switch with 802.1x (EAP) port-based authentication enabled, they are referred to as a **Network Access Server (NAS)**.

All these devices need to exercise some form of control to ensure proper security and usage. This requirement is commonly described as **Authentication, Authorization, and Accounting (AAA)**. AAA is also sometimes referred to as the Triple A Framework. AAA is a high-level architecture model, which can be used for specific implementations.

AAA is specified through various RFCs. **Generic AAA Architecture** is specified in RFC 2903. There are also RFCs that cover different AAA aspects.

Authentication

Authentication is usually the first step taken in order to gain access to a network and the services it offers. This is a process to confirm whether the credentials which Alice provided are valid. The most common way to provide credentials is by a username and password. Other ways such as one-time tokens, certificates, PIN numbers, or even biometric scanning can also be used.

After successful authentication a **session** is initialized. This session lasts until the connection to the network is terminated.

Who is Alice?

Alice and Bob are placeholder names. In fact there is a whole character set, each representing a specific role. We will use the following placeholder names:

Alice: A user who wants access to our network

Bob: Another user who wants access to our network

Isaac: The Internet Service Provider (ISP)/our network

You can read more about them on Wikepedia: `http://en.wikipedia.org/wiki/Alice_and_Bob`.

The following image illustrates an authentication process by using the common activity of drawing money from an ATM as an example. This in essence lets you gain access to the bank's network (although it is limited in the extreme).

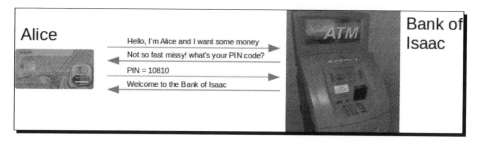

Authorization

Authorization is a means by which Isaac controls the usage of the resources. After Alice has authenticated herself, Isaac can impose certain restrictions or grant certain privileges. Isaac can, for instance, check from which device Alice accesses the network and based on this make a decision. He can limit the number of open sessions that Alice can have, give her a pre-determined IP Address, only allow certain traffic through, or even enforce Quality of Service (QoS) based on an SLA.

Authorization usually involves logic. *If* Alice is part of the student group *then* no Internet access is allowed during working hours. *If* Bob accessed the network through a captive portal *then* a bandwidth limit is imposed to prevent him from hogging the Internet connection.

Logic can be based on numerous things. Authorization decisions for instance can be based on group membership or the NAS through which you connect or even the time of day when you access our resources.

If we take the previous ATM example we can see that if Alice does not have an overdraft facility she will be limited on the amount of money she can withdraw.

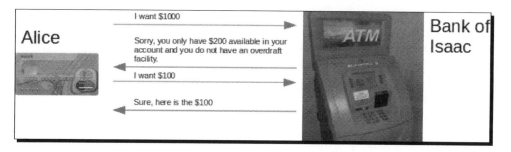

Accounting

Accounting is a means of measuring the usage of resources. After Isaac has established who Alice is and imposed proper control on the established session, he can also measure her usage. Accounting is the ongoing process of measuring usage.

This allows Isaac to track how much time or resources Alice spends during an established session. Obtaining accounting data allows Isaac to bill Alice for the usage of his resources. Accounting data is not only useful to recover costs but it allows for capacity planning, trend analysis, and activity monitoring.

When Alice wants to check her usage and availability of money the ATM offers this functionality. The Bank of Isaac can also monitor her account and discover if she is usually broke before the end of the month. They can then offer her an overdraft facility.

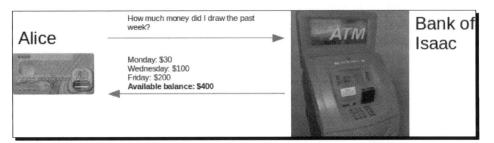

RADIUS is a protocol which is used to provide AAA on TCP/IP networks. The next section will continue with more on the RADIUS protocol.

RADIUS

RADIUS is an acronym for Remote Access Dial In User Service. RADIUS was part of an AAA solution delivered by Livingston Enterprises to Merit Network in 1991. Merit Network is a non-profit Internet provider, which required a creative way to manage dial-in access to various Points-Of-Presence (POPs) across it's network.

The solution supplied by Livingston Enterprises had a central user store used for authentication. This could be used by numerous RAS (dial-in) servers. Authorization and accounting could also be done whereby AAA was satisfied. Another key aspect of the Livingston solution included proxying to allow scaling.

The RADIUS protocol was then subsequently published in 1997 as RFCs, some changes applied, and today we have RFC2865, which covers the RADIUS protocol, and RFC2866, which covers RADIUS accounting. There are also additional RFCs which cover enhancements on certain RADIUS aspects. Having RFCs to work from allows any person or vendor to implement the RADIUS protocol on their equipment or software. This resulted in widespread adoption of the RADIUS protocol to handle AAA on TCP/IP networks. You will find the word RADIUS is used loosely to either mean the RADIUS protocol or the entire RADIUS client/ server system. The meaning should be clear from the context in which it is used.

Supporting the RADIUS protocol and standards became the de facto requirement for NAS vendors. RADIUS is used in a wide variety of places, from cellular network providers having millions of users to a small WISP start-up providing the local neighborhood with Internet connectivity to enterprise networks that implement Network Access Control (NAC) using 802.1x to ring fence their network. RADIUS is found in all these places and more!

ISPs and network administrators should be familiar with RADIUS since it is used by various devices that control access to TCP/IP networks. Here are a couple of examples:

- A firewall with VPN service can use RADIUS.

- Wi-Fi access points with WPA-2-Enterprise encryption involve RADIUS.

- When Alice connects through an existing Telco's infrastructure using DSL; the Telco's equipment will use RADIUS to contact Isaac's RADIUS servers in order to determine if she can gain Internet access through DSL (proxying).

The next section will summarize the RADIUS protocol as specified in RFC2865.

RADIUS protocol (RFC2865)

This section explores the RADIUS protocol on a technical level as published in RFC2865. RADIUS accounting is excluded. This is published as RFC2866 and explored in its own section.

The RADIUS protocol is a client/server protocol, which makes use of UDP to communicate. Using UDP instead of TCP indicates that communication is not strict on state. A typical flow of data between the client and server consists of a single request from the client followed by a single reply from the server. This makes RADIUS a very lightweight protocol and helps with its efficiency across slow network links.

Before successful communication between the client and server can be established, each has to define a shared secret. This is used to authenticate clients.

 An NAS acts as a RADIUS client. So when you read about a RADIUS client it means an NAS.

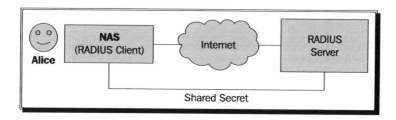

RADIUS packets have a specified format defined in the RFC. Two key components inside a RADIUS packet are:

- The **code**, which indicates the packet type
- Attributes, which carry the essential data used by RADIUS

Let's investigate the composition of a RADIUS datagram.

The data packet

Knowing the format of a RADIUS packet will greatly assist in understanding the RADIUS protocol. Let us look more closely at the RADIUS packet. We will look at a simple authentication request. A client sends an Access-Request packet to the server. The server answers with an Access-Accept packet to indicate success.

The RADIUS packets shown here are only the payload of a UDP packet. A discussion of the UDP and IP protocols is beyond the scope of this book.

The screenshots were obtained by capturing the network traffic between the RADIUS client and RADIUS server.

We used a program called Wireshark to capture and look at the content of the data packets. Wireshark is an open source tool that should be part of any serious network guru's arsenal. It can be found here:

http://www.wireshark.org

The screenshots here are the result of a simple Authentication request send to a RADIUS server. The obtaining of this data is commonly known as packet sniffing among IT geeks.

The following screenshot shows the Access-Request packet send from the RADIUS client:

```
+ Frame 1 (99 bytes on wire, 99 bytes captured)
+ Ethernet II, Src: 00:00:00_00:00:00 (00:00:00:00:00:00), Dst: 00:00:00_00:
+ Internet Protocol, Src: 127.0.0.1 (127.0.0.1), Dst: 127.0.0.1 (127.0.0.1)
+ User Datagram Protocol, Src Port: 33475 (33475), Dst Port: radius (1812)
- Radius Protocol
    Code: Access-Request (1)
    Packet identifier: 0x16 (22)
    Length: 57
    Authenticator: F7BCF35097153560CE87874B056AAB51
  - Attribute Value Pairs
    - AVP: l=7  t=User-Name(1): alice
        User-Name: alice
    - AVP: l=18  t=User-Password(2): Encrypted
        User-Password: k#{7 \312\270\220\025\322\226*\036\240\334\275
    - AVP: l=6  t=NAS-IP-Address(4): 127.0.0.1
        NAS-IP-Address: 127.0.0.1 (127.0.0.1)
    - AVP: l=6  t=NAS-Port(5): 0
        NAS-Port: 0
```

The following screenshot shows the RADIUS server responding to this request with an Access-Accept packet:

```
+ Frame 2 (62 bytes on wire, 62 bytes captured)
+ Ethernet II, Src: 00:00:00_00:00:00 (00:00:00:00:00:00), Dst: 00:00:00_00:
+ Internet Protocol, Src: 127.0.0.1 (127.0.0.1), Dst: 127.0.0.1 (127.0.0.1)
+ User Datagram Protocol, Src Port: radius (1812), Dst Port: 33475 (33475)
- Radius Protocol
    Code: Access-Accept (2)
    Packet identifier: 0x16 (22)
    Length: 20
    Authenticator: 71723CD1F8EDC25B4279788B3116D0C0
    [This is a response to a request in frame 1]
    [Time from request: 0.000199000 seconds]
```

Let's discuss the packets.

Code

Each packet is identified by a code. This field is one octet in size. The value of this code determines certain characteristics and requirements of the packet. The following table can be used as a reference to list some of the current defined codes for RADIUS packets:

RADIUS code (decimal)	Packet type	Sent by
1	Access-Request	NAS
2	Access-Accept	RADIUS server
3	Access-Reject	RADIUS server
4	Accounting-Request	NAS
5	Accounting-Response	RADIUS server
11	Access-Challenge	RADIUS server
12	Status-Server (Experimental)	
13	Status-Client (Experimental)	
255	Reserved	

Knowing these codes is beneficial when working with RADIUS.

Identifier

The second octet of each packet contains a unique identifier. It is generated by the client and used as an aid to match requests and replies. RADIUS packets are transported using connectionless UDP. This requires RADIUS to implement its own algorithm to submit retry requests from the client. When a client resends a request to the server the packet's identifier will remain unchanged. The server will respond to requests by matching the identifier in the response packet.

Length

This is the third and fourth octets in the datagram. It indicates up to where the useful data inside the packet is located. Octets outside the boundary indicated by this field are considered to be padding and silently ignored.

Authenticator

The manner in which this field, which consists of 16 octets, is formed differs depending on whether the packet is a request from the client or a response from the server. It also depends on the packet type, for example Access-Request or Accounting-Request. If it is a request, the field is referred to as a **Request Authenticator**. If it is a response, the field is referred to as a **Response Authenticator**.

The value of a Request Authenticator is a random number not to be repeated again. The value of a Response Authenticator is the MD5 hash of various fields in the reply packet along with the shared secret between the client and server.

If the request includes the User-Password attribute, then the value of this attribute will be encrypted. This encrypted value is typically generated by creating an MD5 hash from the shared secret combined with the authenticator and then XOR-ing the result with the user's password. This is why the shared secret has to be the same on the client and the server in order to decrypt the user's password.

Attributes

The rest of the RADIUS packet will contain zero or more attributes, which are referred to as Attribute Value Pairs (AVP). The end of these AVPs is indicated by the packet's length field, as mentioned before.

Conclusion

RADIUS packets are transported through UDP. The code field identifies the type of RADIUS packet. Attributes are used to supply specific information used for authentication, authorization, and accounting. To authenticate a user for instance, the User-Name and User-Password AVPs will be included along with some other attributes inside the Access-Request packet.

AVPs

AVPs are the workhorse of the RADIUS protocol. AVPs can be categorized as either check or reply attributes. Check attributes are sent from the client to the server. Reply attributes are sent from the server to the client.

Attributes serve as carriers of information between the client and server. They are used by the client to supply information about itself as well as the user connecting through it. They are also used when the server responds to the client. The client can then use this response to control the user's connection based on the AVPs received in the server's response.

The following sections will describe the format of an AVP.

Type

The first octet of the AVP is the type field. The numeric value of this octet is associated with an attribute name so that we humans can also understand. Assignment of these attribute names to numbers is controlled by IANA (http://www.iana.org/). The attribute names are usually descriptive enough to deduce their function, for example User-Name(1), User-Password(2), or NAS-IP-Address(4).

RADIUS also allows extending the protocol; attribute Type 26 (called Vendor-Specific) allows for this. The value of the Vendor-Specific attribute can in turn contain **Vendor Specific Attributes (VSAs)** which are managed by a vendor.

Length

The length field consists of the second octet in the AVP. This is used in the same manner as in the RADIUS packet itself to indicate the length of the AVP. This method allows one to have AVPs with different size values since the length field will mark the AVP's end.

Value

The value of an AVP can differ in size. The value field can be zero or more octets. The value field can contain one of the following data types: text, string, address, integer, or time.

Text and string can be up to 253 octets in size. Address, integer, and time are four octets long.

If we take the 'NAS-IP-Address' AVP in the Request packet we see the length is six. That is one octet for the type, one octet for the length, and four octets for the IP address, six octets in total.

The next section will discuss Vendor-Specific Attributes, which are an extension to the standard AVPs.

Vendor-Specific Attributes (VSAs)

VSAs allows vendors to define their own attributes. The format of the attribute definitions is basically the same as for normal AVPs with the addition of a vendor field. VSAs are sent as the value of AVP Type 26. This means that VSAs are an extension of AVPs and carried inside AVPs.

This makes RADIUS very flexible and allows a vendor to create extensions to customize their RADIUS implementation. CoovaChilli for instance has a VSA attribute called 'ChilliSpot-Max-Total-Octets'. When the CoovaChilli client receives this attribute in a reply from the RADIUS server it uses this value to restrict data through the captive portal.

The NAS will silently ignore any VSAs that are not meant for it. Some vendors publish their VSAs, but this is not required. Others simply list them on a website or document. This can then be consulted to determine the capabilities of the RADIUS implementation of their equipment.

Proxying and realms

The RADIUS protocol allows for scaling. Proxying allows one RADIUS server to act as a client to another RADIUS server. This can eventually form a chain.

A discussion on proxying also includes realms. Realms are names used to group users and form part of the username. A username is separated from the realm name with a specified delimiter character. The realm name can be prefixed or postfixed to the username. Today's popular standard uses domain names as a postfix and delimits it with the @ character, for example `alice@freeradius.org`. This is, however, just a convention. The realm can be any name and the delimiter can be any character. Windows users typically use a prefix notation specifying the domain first with a \ character as delimiter, for example `my_domain\alice`.

When the RADIUS server receives a request with a username containing a realm it can decide whether to process the request or to forward the request to another RADIUS server designated to handle requests for the specified realm. This would require that the second RADIUS server should have the forwarding RADIUS server defined as a client and that they also have a shared secret in common.

RADIUS server

The RADIUS protocol is client/server based. The RADIUS server will listen on UDP port 1812 and 1813. Port 1812 is used for authentication. This will involve Access-Request, Access-Accept, Access-Reject, and Access-Challenge packets. Port 1813 is used for accounting. This will involve Accounting-Request and Accounting-Response packets.

A client and the server require a shared secret in order to encrypt and decrypt certain fields in the RADIUS packet.

RADIUS client

RADIUS clients are usually equipment which supplies access to a TCP/IP data network. The client acts as a broker between the RADIUS server and a user or device that wants to gain network access.

The proxying functionality of RADIUS also allows one RADIUS server to be the client of another RADIUS sever, which eventually can form a chain.

The feedback from the RADIUS server not only determines if a user is allowed on the network (authentication), but can also direct the client to impose certain restrictions on the user (authorization). Examples of restrictions are a time limit on the session or limiting the connection speed.

The responsibility to impose the recommended adjustments to the user's session lies with the client though. Due to the stateless nature of the RADIUS protocol there is no way for the RADIUS server to know if the client is imposing the recommended restrictions. In order for the client to communicate successfully with the RADIUS server there should be a shared secret between the two. This is used to encrypt certain attributes.

Accounting is defined in a separate RFC. The next section will summarize RADIUS accounting as specified in RFC2866.

RADIUS accounting (RFC2866)

This section explores the accounting functionality of the RADIUS protocol. Accounting is a means of tracking usage of resources and typically used for billing.

Operation

The RADIUS accounting server runs on port 1813. When a user's session begins the NAS sends an Accounting-Request packet to the RADIUS server. This packet must contain certain AVPs. It is the first packet sent after successful authentication. The server will confirm reception by sending a matching Accounting-Response packet.

Throughout the session the NAS can send optional update reports on the time and data usage of a particular user. When the user's session ends the NAS informs the server about it. This puts closure to the accounting details recorded during the user's session.

The RADIUS client's functionality makes provision for instances when the server is down. The NAS will then, depending how it is configured, retry or contact another RADIUS server.

When a RADIUS server functions as a forwarding proxy to another RADIUS server, it will serve as a relay for the accounting data. It may also record the accounting data locally before forwarding it.

Packet format

Accounting involves RADIUS code 4 (Accounting-Request) and code 5 (Accounting-Response) packets. Accounting packets like authentication packets use the same RADIUS protocol. One unique feature of accounting packets is that the User-Password attribute is not sent in the request.

See the following output from Wireshark that shows a typical accounting transaction. It starts with an Accounting-Request from the client:

```
+ Frame 7 (186 bytes on wire, 186 bytes captured)
+ Ethernet II, Src: IntelCor_80:9b:0f (00:13:e8:80:9b:0f), Dst: CadmusCo_
+ Internet Protocol, Src: 192.168.1.103 (192.168.1.103), Dst: 192.168.1.1
+ User Datagram Protocol, Src Port: 44284 (44284), Dst Port: radius-acct
- Radius Protocol
      Code: Accounting-Request (4)
      Packet identifier: 0x44 (68)
      Length: 144
      Authenticator: D57C354DA8B7F8EC0E83005B39090B54
      [The response to this request is in frame 8]
   - Attribute Value Pairs
      + AVP: l=19  t=Acct-Session-Id(44): 4D2BB8AC-00000098
      + AVP: l=6   t=Acct-Status-Type(40): Start(1)
      + AVP: l=6   t=Acct-Authentic(45): RADIUS(1)
      + AVP: l=7   t=User-Name(1): alice
      + AVP: l=6   t=NAS-Port(5): 0
      + AVP: l=31  t=Called-Station-Id(30): 00-02-6F-AA-AA-AA:My Wireless
      + AVP: l=19  t=Calling-Station-Id(31): 00-1C-B3-AA-AA-AA
      + AVP: l=6   t=NAS-Port-Type(61): Wireless-802.11(19)
      + AVP: l=24  t=Connect-Info(77): CONNECT 48Mbps 802.11b
```

The server then replies to the client with an Accounting-Response:

```
+ Frame 8 (62 bytes on wire, 62 bytes captured)
+ Ethernet II, Src: CadmusCo_63:c2:83 (08:00:27:63:c2:
+ Internet Protocol, Src: 192.168.1.106 (192.168.1.106
+ User Datagram Protocol, Src Port: radius-acct (1813)
- Radius Protocol
      Code: Accounting-Response (5)
      Packet identifier: 0x44 (68)
      Length: 20
      Authenticator: A72D9494B5D5E987B9577C20AA5D965A
      [This is a response to a request in frame 7]
      [Time from request: 0.001801000 seconds]
```

Accounting-Request packets are also required to include certain AVPs. Let us take a look at important AVPs used in accounting.

Acct-Status-Type (Type40)

This packet indicates the status of the user or the NAS. An NAS may send interim updates on the usage of a certain session. in order to do this the NAS sets the type to Interim-Update. This allows us to follow usage trends in approximately real time.

The RADIUS server does not check up on an NAS. If an NAS has informed the RADIUS server about a newly connected user (status type Start) and thereafter the NAS breaks down completely, the records on the RADIUS server will still indicate that the user is connected to the NAS when in fact the user is not. These records are referred to as rogue entries. To reduce rogue entries, it is good practice for an NAS to send an Accounting-Off followed by an Accounting-On packet just after boot-up and also an Accounting-Off packet before shutting down. This action will cause RADIUS to close all open records for any user connected to the particular NAS allowing a clean start.

Rogue entries are particularly problematic when you limit the number of sessions a user can have. If the component limiting the sessions of a user makes use of data containing rogue entries the calculations will not be accurate.

The following decimal to type table can be used as reference for the possible status values:

Decimal value	Status type
1	Start
2	Stop
3	Interim-Update
7	Accounting-On
8	Accounting-Off
9-14	Reserved for tunnel accounting
15	Reserved for failed

Although the Acct-Status-Type AVP is not compulsory it is almost always included.

Acct-Input-Octets (Type42)

This indicates the octets received during the session and is used with Acct-Status-Type having a value of Interim-Update or Stop.

Take note of the value's limitation. Four octets limit it to 4,29,49,67,296. Most modern RADIUS implementations already cater for this.

Acct-Output-Octets (Type43)

This indicates the octets sent during the session and is used with Acct-Status-Type having a value of Interim-Update or Stop.

Take note of the value's limitation. Four octets limit it to 4,29,49,67,296. Most modern RADIUS implementations already cater for this.

Acct-Session-Id (Type44)

Compulsory for all Accounting-Request packets, this is a unique value that is used to match Start, Interim, and Stop records. All Start, Interim, and Stop records of a session should have the same value for Acct-Session-Id.

Acct-Session-Time (Type46)

The name is self explanatory. The time in seconds indicating the session's duration and is used with Acct-Status-Type having a value of Interim-Update or Stop.

Acct-Terminate-Cause (Type49)

This is accompanied by an Acct-Status-Type AVP with its value set to Stop. The value of this AVP is decimal. It is used in the same manner as Acct-Status-Type where a specific decimal value resolves to a termination cause.

Conclusion

This brings us to the end of RADIUS accounting. The next session will look at certain RFCs that add functionality and enhancements to the RADIUS definitions of RFC2865 and RFC2866.

RADIUS extensions

After the initial RFCs defining RADIUS in general and RADIUS accounting, various extensions were proposed to expand RADIUS usage or improve some weaknesses.

There is also an improved RADIUS protocol called Diameter (A word play—twice as good as RADIUS). The uptake of Diameter has been very slow though, and RADIUS still remains the de facto standard for the foreseeable future. A major reason for this is probably the fact that the many enhancements that Diameter was supposed to bring are already covered by the various RADIUS extensions. There is, for instance, the RadSec protocol that transports RADIUS over TCP and TLS. This makes RADIUS scale better in roaming environments.

Although there are more, we will only look at two important extensions likely to be used.

Dynamic Authorization extension (RFC5176)

This extension helps to create a feedback loop from the RADIUS server to the NAS. This in effect swaps the roles of the client and server. The RADIUS server becomes a client to the NAS.

Dynamic authorization allows for the RADIUS server to inform the NAS about changes that have to be made to a user's existing session on the NAS. There are two popular applications of this extension.

Disconnect-Message (DM)

Also known as a Packet of Disconnect (POD), this is used to disconnect an existing user's session. The RADIUS server sends the disconnect request and the NAS has to reply whether the disconnection was successful or not.

Change-of-Authorization Message (CoA)

This message supplies data to change the authorization of an existing user's session. We can now dynamically change the bandwidth limit per session for instance. This allows us to increase the per session bandwidth when load on our Internet link decreases. When load on our Internet link increases we can again decrease the per session bandwidth.

MikroTik RouterOS includes this functionality on some of the services that use RADIUS.

The following table lists the codes and names of the RADIUS packets involved:

Radius code (decimal)	Packet type	Send by
40	Disconnect-Request	RADIUS server
41	Disconnect-ACK	NAS
42	Disconnect-NAK	NAS
43	CoA-Request	RADIUS server
44	CoA-ACK	NAS
45	CoA-NAK	NAS

RADIUS support for EAP (RFC3579)

EAP stands for Extensible Authentication Protocol. It is mostly used for security on Ethernet switches and Wi-Fi access points.

EAP supports the use of an external authorization server. RADIUS can be such a server. EAP will then use the RADIUS protocol to wrap the EAP data inside AVPs in order to authenticate a connection.

This book has a dedicated chapter on EAP since it is such an important part of enterprise Wi-Fi security.

In the next section will look at the FreeRADIUS project. FreeRADIUS is an implementation of the RADIUS protocol and its various extensions including the two mentioned here.

FreeRADIUS

FreeRADIUS is an open source project supplying a very feature-rich implementation of the RADIUS protocol with its various enhancements (http://www.freeradius.org). When people refer to FreeRADIUS, they usually talk about the server software. This is the main component of the software suite included in a FreeRADIUS download.

History

FreeRADIUS development started in 1999 after the future of the original Livingston RADIUS server became uncertain. This allowed for the creation of a new RADIUS server that was open source and could include active community involvement.

FreeRADIUS managed to gain a solid reputation and was able to compete with and even beat most commercial equivalents. Their motto of "The world's most popular RADIUS Server" has been unchallenged for some time now, making it a very valid statement.

Strengths

FreeRADIUS has many strengths, which contributed to its popularity. Let us look at some of them:

- **Open source**: This is not just free as in beer; you are free to adapt, change, expand, and fix whatever is required. FreeRADIUS is released under the GNU General Public License (GPL).

- **Modular**: FreeRADIUS comes with lots of modules included. You can also create your own modules to be used by FreeRADIUS. Modules are included for LDAP integration or SQL back-ends. There are also Perl and Python modules, which allow you to unleash these two powerful scripting languages in FreeRADIUS.

- **Used by the masses**: Someone does not get fired for choosing FreeRADIUS. It is easy to get references from ISPs and large companies who have very large user counts in their FreeRADIUS deployments. FreeRADIUS conducted a survey to determine the usage and deployment size of FreeRADIUS. The detailed results of this survey are available on request from them.

- **Active community**: Because FreeRADIUS has such a large user base, chances are someone else has experienced the same hurdles as you. FreeRADIUS has active mailing lists with searchable archives.

- **Available info**: The information may not be in one locality, but it is available, and just has to be found. There are lots of Wiki pages full of detail. There are also man pages and configuration files, which are well written and easy to follow.

- **Active development**: FreeRADIUS follows the "release early, release often" motto. New developments around the RADIUS protocol are most likely to be supported first in FreeRADIUS. You can look forward to one or more new FreeRADIUS releases annually.

- **Commercial support**: The core developers of FreeRADIUS offer commercial support. There are also various people knowledgeable in FreeRADIUS who should be able to supply paid support. Network RADIUS SARL has a nice website with more details on paid support: `http://networkradius.com/`.

- **Availability**: FreeRADIUS is available for various operating systems. All of the popular Linux distributions include it as part of their available packages. It is even available for Windows! Under the downloads page of the FreeRADIUS website there are links to binary packages for various operating systems

Weaknesses

There is no such thing as a perfect piece of software; FreeRADIUS is no exception. Here are some of its weaknesses:

- **Complexity**: This is the only real weakness. FreeRADIUS offers an all-inclusive piece of software with many configuration options. If you are not careful you can end up with a broken system.

- **Vulnerabilities**: A few vulnerabilities were reported in the past but they have been fixed since then. You can read more about those vulnerabilities and what version of FreeRADIUS contained them at the following: `http://freeradius.org/security.html`.

The competition

When FreeRADIUS states that it is the most popular server, who it is competing with? There are competing RADIUS servers but also competing technologies. The competing RADIUS servers include Cisco's ACS, Microsoft's IAS, and Radiator. Competing AAA technologies include Diameter (mentioned earlier), TACACS+ (which is proprietary to CISCO, although also supported by other enterprise network equipment manufacturers), and LDAP (LDAP only supports authentication).

Summary

This chapter is the introduction and foundation on which we will build that. As a rehash on important points discussed, be sure to know the following facts:

Name	Stands for	Short description
AAA	Authentication, Authorization, and Accounting	The three components required for proper control of access and usage.
NAS	Network Access Server	A device controlling access to the network for example, a VPN server. Acts as the RADIUS client.
AVP	Attribute Value Pair	A three-field component inside a RADIUS packet used to contain a specified field and its data.
VSA	Vendor-Specific Attributes	An extension of the AVP managed by a specific vendor.

- ◆ AAA is a security architecture model.
- ◆ RADIUS is a specific implementation of AAA.
- ◆ FreeRADIUS is a practical application of RADIUS.
- ◆ Thus we have AAA → RADIUS → FreeRADIUS.
- ◆ RADIUS is all about central control and is the de facto standard supported by NAS vendors.
- ◆ RADIUS is a client/server protocol. It uses UDP and listens on port 1812 for authentication and port 1813 for accounting requests.
- ◆ RADIUS data packets have a code field, which specifies the type of RADIUS packet.
- ◆ RADIUS data packets have zero or more AVPs, which contain the data used in RADIUS.
- ◆ FreeRADIUS implements the RADIUS protocol along with its various extensions as specified in RFCs.
- ◆ FreeRADIUS is a very popular, widely used, and very flexible RADIUS server.

This chapter was a FreeRADIUS starter. The main course begins with the next chapter where we'll be installing FreeRADIUS and starting to use it.

Pop quiz – RADIUS knowledge

1. Explain the term NAS device.

2. What are the start and end points of a session?

3. Which protocol and ports does RADIUS use?

4. What do the RADIUS client and server require for successful communication?

5. What packet does the RADIUS client send when authenticating a user?

6. Who initiates a Disconnect Request packet and who receives it?

7. Name three components of an Attribute Value Pair (AVP).

8. Alice connects with username `alice@freeradius.org` to a network. What is the name of the realm to which Alice belongs?

2
Installation

There are two methods of installing FreeRADIUS on a Linux server. You can simply install pre-built binary packages or alternatively build and install FreeRADIUS from source code. This chapter will show you how to do both.

In this chapter we shall:

- ◆ Install FreeRADIUS from pre-built binary packages
- ◆ Build and install FreeRADIUS from source
- ◆ Investigate which programs FreeRADIUS installs
- ◆ Ensure FreeRADIUS is running correctly

So let's get on with it...

Before you start

There are a variety of Linux distributions to choose from. We will be covering three popular distributions to include an audience as wide as possible and to avoid a distro war.

 A **distro war** usually starts between two equal passionate GNU/Linux supporters. The problem is when they support different GNU/Linux distributions and believe their distribution is superior to all other available distributions or operating systems.

Based on the package management system they use, a majority of Linux distributions fall into one of two groups. One group uses Red Hat Package Manager (RPM) while the second group uses dpkg Package Manager. We chose two RPM-based distributions, CentOS and SUSE, which are popular in the enterprise. Instead of using Debian as a dpkg-based distribution, we chose Ubuntu because of its huge popularity among beginners. Since Ubuntu evolved out of Debian, the sections discussing Ubuntu should also apply on Debian without major changes.

The steps in this chapter require one of the following to be installed:

Distribution	Version
CentOS	5.5
SUSE	SLES 11
Ubuntu	10.4

A typical server install with root access will be used as a base. Use this chapter as a guideline if you do have a distribution with a version different from that specified.

Pre-built binary

Today's Linux distributions have lots of pre-build software, which can be installed with ease. A single command can be used to install FreeRADIUS from a software repository. This will resolve dependencies and install all the required packages in order to present a working system.

 Software repositories are used by the package management system that runs on Linux. If you are new to package management systems, refer to this URL for further reading: http://en.wikipedia.org/wiki/Package_management_system

The default installation of the three distributions will include repositories that contain the FreeRADIUS packages. If this is not the situation, consult the package management system's documentation in order to determine how to include the repositories that contain the FreeRADIUS packages.

Time for action – installing FreeRADIUS

Pre-build FreeRADIUS packages can be installed by using the following command on each distribution respectively:

- CentOS

  ```
  #> yum install freeradius2 freeradius2-utils
  ```

- SUSE

  ```
  #> zypper in freeradius-server freeradius-server-utils freeradius-
  server-doc
  ```

- Ubuntu

  ```
  $> sudo apt-get install freeradius
  ```

What just happened?

We installed the pre-build FreeRADIUS packages supplied for our Linux distribution to have a basic working RADIUS server installation.

Advantages

Using the pre-build FreeRADIUS package has the following advantages:

- Resolving dependencies is automatically taken care of. This includes taking care of future security updates, keeping track of all the optional packages that were required to be installed with our package, and also ensuring the correct version of a dependency package is installed.

- The Linux distributor's QA testing ensures properly working software.

- Updates are taken care of by the Linux distributor.

- Distribution-specific tweaks are already implemented.

One compromise you make using pre-built binary packages is that you will not have the latest version of FreeRADIUS on the machine.

Extra packages

FreeRADIUS is a feature-rich piece of software. Each distribution presents its FreeRADIUS differently by spreading it across multiple packages.

CentOS and Ubuntu include certain FreeRADIUS server modules as optional packages. This keeps the basic server installation package lean. Installing optional server module packages will also install required dependencies. This means, for instance, that when you install the `freeradius-mysql` package, all the required MySQL libraries will also be installed as dependencies.

SUSE divided their packages by functionality. You will find that the client and server each have their own set of packages. SUSE also has utilities and documentation packages for FreeRADIUS.

Available packages

This section lists available pre-built FreeRADIUS packages per distribution. Names in bold are recommended for a basic FreeRADIUS installation:

CentOS

Package name	Short description
freeradius2	Highly configurable RADIUS server
freeradius2-krb5	Kerberos 5 support for FreeRADIUS
freeradius2-ldap	LDAP support for FreeRADIUS
freeradius2-mysql	MySQL support for FreeRADIUS
freeradius2-perl	Perl support for FreeRADIUS
freeradius2-postgresql	PostgreSQL support for FreeRADIUS
freeradius2-python	Python support for FreeRADIUS
freeradius2-unixODBC	Unix ODBC support for FreeRADIUS
freeradius2-utils	FreeRADIUS utilities

SUSE

Package name	Short description
freeradius-client	FreeRADIUS client software
freeradius-client-libs	Shared library of FreeRADIUS client
freeradius-server	Highly configurable RADIUS server
freeradius-server-dialupadmin	Web management for FreeRADIUS
freeradius-server-doc	FreeRADIUS documentation
freeradius-server-libs	FreeRADIUS shared library
freeradius-server-utils	FreeRADIUS clients

Take note that the `freeradius-client` packages supplied by SUSE are used by software developers to utilize RADIUS for AAA. Client programs like `radtest` are included in the `freeradius-server-utils` package.

Ubuntu

Package name	Short description
freeradius	FreeRADIUS server package
freeradius-dbg	Contains detached debugging symbols for FreeRADIUS packages
libfreeradius2	FreeRADIUS shared library
freeradius-ldap	LDAP module for FreeRADIUS server
freeradius-common	FreeRADIUS common files, include dictionaries, and man pages
freeradius-iodbc	iODBC module for FreeRADIUS server
freeradius-krb5	Kerberos module for FreeRADIUS server
freeradius-utils	FreeRADIUS client utilities, including programs like radclient, radtest, smbencrypt, radsniff, and radzap
freeradius-postgresql	PostgreSQL module for FreeRADIUS server
freeradius-mysql	MySQL module for FreeRADIUS server
freeradius-dialupadmin	Web management add-on
libfreeradius-dev	FreeRADIUS shared library development files

Special considerations

Older versions of Ubuntu did not compile SSL library support into the pre-built binary packages. When installing FreeRADIUS on those versions, you need to build your own if you require SSL support on the EAP extensions.

SUSE also offers the `yast -i` command to install software; but instead use `zypper` because it has better decision making ability when installing packages and their dependencies.

The name of the FreeRADIUS package in CentOS is `freeradius2` instead of the expected `freeradius`. This is because the FreeRADIUS version that came out with CentOS 5 originally was 1.1.3. The changes in configuration files between the 1.x and 2.x releases of FreeRADIUS were, however, of such magnitude that it required a change in name.

Not all FreeRADIUS modules have their respective matching package in Ubuntu or CentOS. Modules without a matching package are simply included in the main FreeRADIUS package.

Remember the firewall

CentOS and SUSE install an active firewall by default. Please ensure UDP ports 1812 and 1813 are open for the outside world.

CentOS

There is a utility to configure the firewall on CentOS called `system-config-securitylevel-tui` that should be run as root. This will start a cursors-based program. Select the **Customize** option and press **Enter**. The **Allow incoming | Other Ports** list should include `1812:udp 1813:udp`. Select **OK** to return to the main screen and then select **OK** again to commit the changes.

Confirm the ports are now open by checking the output of the following command:

```
#> /sbin/iptables -L -n | grep 181*
ACCEPT      udp   --  0.0.0.0/0          0.0.0.0/0          state NEW
udp dpt:1812
ACCEPT      udp   --  0.0.0.0/0          0.0.0.0/0          state NEW
udp dpt:1813
```

Although not recommended you can disable the firewall by using the following commands:

```
#> /etc/init.d/iptables save
#> /etc/init.d/iptables stop
#> /sbin/chkconfig iptables off
```

To confirm whether the firewall is disabled, issue the following command:

```
#> /sbin/iptables -L -n
Chain INPUT (policy ACCEPT)
target      prot opt source            destination


Chain FORWARD (policy ACCEPT)
target      prot opt source            destination


Chain OUTPUT (policy ACCEPT)
target      prot opt source            destination
```

SUSE

Configuring the firewall on SUSE can be a bit of a catch-22 situation since the default firewall is so secure you cannot even SSH into the box! Log into the SLES server and start `YaST`. Select **Security and Users | Firewall**. Select **Allowed Services** on the left. I suggest you add **Secure Shell Server** to the **External Zone**. Click on the **Advanced** button and add `1812 1813` to the **UDP Ports**. Click **OK**. Click **Next** and **Finish** to commit these changes.

Confirm the ports are now open by checking the output of the following command:

```
#> iptables -L -n | grep 181
ACCEPT     udp  --  0.0.0.0/0          0.0.0.0/0          udp dpt:1812
ACCEPT     udp  --  0.0.0.0/0          0.0.0.0/0          udp dpt:1813
```

Although not recommended you can disable the firewall in the following way:

1. Use `YaST` and select **Security and Users | Firewall**.

2. Select **Start-Up** on the left. Select **Disable Firewall Automatic Starting** on the right. Also select **Stop Firewall Now** and press the **Enter** key to stop the currently running firewall.

3. Click **Next** and **Finish** to commit these changes.

Confirm the firewall is now disabled by checking the output of the following command:

```
#> iptables -L -n
Chain INPUT (policy ACCEPT)
target     prot opt source           destination


Chain FORWARD (policy ACCEPT)
target     prot opt source           destination


Chain OUTPUT (policy ACCEPT)
target     prot opt source           destination
```

Have a go hero – installing from source

Building software from source used to be synonymous with `configure, make, make install`. We will be using the distribution's package manager to build new software packages from source.

The following section is optional if you have already installed FreeRADIUS from pre-built binary packages.

Building from source

Sometimes there is a need to install the latest available version of software or to include support for a specific module not included with the pre-built binaries. This requires building the software from source. Most open source packages are distributed as compressed TAR files. TAR can actually refer to the program used to create the TAR file (the name is short for **tape archive**) or the file format of the resultant file. A TAR file is also typically compressed to reduce the size. The file name will indicate the compression format. A filename ending with `.tgz` or `.tar.gz` used `gzip`. A filename ending with `.tbz`, `.tb2`, or `.tar.bz2` used `bzip2`. To build the software we extract this file and then execute the commands `configure`, `make`, and `make install` inside the extracted directory.

There is, however, a preferred way by utilizing the Linux distribution's package management system when building the software. Not all TAR files facilitate doing this with ease, but FreeRADIUS is such a mature project that allows building packages from source on any of the three Linux distributions.

Advantages of building packages

The following are some of the advantages of building packages from source:

◆ Easy to install, upgrade, remove, or distribute software

◆ Easy to check which version of software is installed

◆ Ability to see which files are installed and see which distribution-specific changes were made

Now that you are convinced that building packages is the way to go, we will do it for each of our distributions.

Creating a build environment

It is good practice not to use production machines for development. This includes building software from source. Create a virtual machine on which you can build the packages. After testing simply copy and install the new packages on a production machine.

CentOS

CentOS is a Red Hat-style distribution. It is the community version of the enterprise version of Red Hat Enterprise Linux (RHEL). CentOS is not directly sponsored by Red Hat like the Fedora project. Although Red Hat's branding and logos are removed from CentOS, it is essentially the same as RHEL since the same source code is used to produce the distribution.

CentOS uses the RPM Package Manager to manage software. The software packages that are installed are known as RPMs.

Time for action – building CentOS RPMs

This section takes the recommendations and instructions from the following FreeRADIUS Wiki page to create the latest RPMs on CentOS:

```
http://wiki.freeradius.org/Red_Hat_FAQ#How_to_build_an_SRPM
```

You have to be the root user to execute most of these commands. Once that is done, follow these steps:

1. Install the `rpm-build` package. This creates the directory structure required for package building:

   ```
   #> yum install rpm-build
   ```

2. Allow write and execute rights for normal users on this directory structure:

   ```
   #> find /usr/src/redhat -type d | xargs chmod a+wx
   ```

3. The latest version of FreeRADIUS will be available for Fedora. We will use this version to build the RPMs on CentOS. Download the source RPM from the following URL:

   ```
   http://koji.fedoraproject.org/koji/packageinfo?packageID=298
   ```

   The source RPM package's name ends with `.src.rpm`.

4. Install this source package. Use the following command as an example. Your source package's name will be different:

   ```
   #> rpm -ihv --nomd5 freeradius-2.1.10-1.fc16.src.rpm
   ```

5. Issue the following command to determine the required dependencies. These dependencies have to be installed before the packages can be built:

   ```
   #> rpmbuild -ba /usr/src/redhat/SPECS/freeradius.spec
   ```

6. Use `yum` to install each of these dependencies. On my system it turned out to be the following:

   ```
   #> yum install autoconf gdbm-devel libtool libtool-ltdl-devel
   openssl-devel pam-devel zlib-devel net-snmp-devel net-snmp-utils
   readline-devel libpcap-devel openldap-devel krb5-devel python-
   devel mysql-devel postgresql-devel unixODBC-devel
   ```

7. Install a complier:

```
#> yum install gcc
```

8. Run `rpmbuild` again. Do this as a normal user and `tee` the output to a file for later investigation. This will start the build process, which takes some time to complete:

```
#> rpmbuild -ba /usr/src/redhat/SPECS/freeradius.spec | tee /tmp/
freeradius_build_out.txt
```

9. When it completes successfully there will be an indication that the RPMs are written. Lines like the following name the freshly built RPMs:

```
Wrote: /usr/src/redhat/RPMS/i386/freeradius-debuginfo-2.1.10-1.
i386.rpm
```

10. Install the newly build RPMs. Again use this as a pattern since your package names, especially the minor version number, may be different. The following command will result in a basic FreeRADIUS installation:

```
#> yum --nogpgcheck install /usr/src/redhat/RPMS/i386/
freeradius-2.1.10-1.i386.rpm /usr/src/redhat/RPMS/i386/freeradius-
utils-2.1.10-1.i386.rpm
```

If you get a message informing you `No package <path and package name>
available`, confirm that you specified the correct version.

What just happened?

We just created and installed RPMs for the latest version of FreeRADIUS on CentOS. Here's a breakdown of important points.

Installing rpm-build

The `rpm-build` package contains scripts and executable programs used to build RPM packages. It includes the `rpmbuild` program, which we will use to create the RPMs.

The source RPM package

We use Fedora's source RPM package as recommended on the FreeRADIUS wiki page. This results in a more stable and better working set of packages, which already contain distribution-specific tweaks and modifications.

The package name

Note that the package name is `freeradius` instead of `freeradius2`. This is because all the FreeRADIUS packages in Fedora are already on version 2.x.

There is not an issue of updating legacy FreeRADIUS version 1.x packages in Fedora as with CentOS.

Updating an existing installation

If you already have FreeRADIUS installed it may contain modules that you need to include when updating.

◆ Determine the FreeRADIUS version and packages currently installed by using the following command:

```
#> yum list freeradius\*
```

◆ When you have already installed `freeradius2` as pre-built binary packages, `yum` will complain when trying to install the new `freeradius` packages because of the clash in names. You can remove the `freeradius2` packages by using the following command:

```
#> yum erase freeradius\*
```

◆ The above assumes that you haven't made any configuration changes to the installation that you would like to preserve.

SUSE

SUSE also makes use of the RPM Package Manager for software management just like Red Hat distributions. Although both use RPM as the foundation for software management, SLES uses `zypper` to manage package repositories where CentOS uses `yum`.

SLES is a hardcore enterprise distribution. Use the pre-built binary packages if possible, but if you feel brave and would like to get your hands dirty, this section is for you.

Time for action – SUSE: from tarball to RPMs

Building RPMs for FreeRADIUS on SLES takes a little more effort compared to CentOS or Ubuntu.

Adding an OpenSUSE repository

To build FreeRADIUS from source requires various development libraries. The standard SLES repositories do not include them all, even when using the SDK DVDs that are part of SLES. We therefore need to add the OpenSUSE repository. This will satisfy all the development library requirements.

1. Locate your nearest OpenSUSE mirror from the following URL:

   `http://mirrors.opensuse.org/`

2. Start YAST as the root user.

3. Select **Software | Software Repositories** and then select **Add** to add a repository.

4. Add the OpenSUSE mirror that you chose at the start. The URL for my nearest OpenSUSE 11.3 is the following:

   `ftp://opensuse.mirror.ac.za/opensuse/distribution/11.3/repo/`
   `oss/suse/`

5. You might be asked to accept the importing of a GnuPG key for the new repository. Select **Import** to continue.

This sets the stage for building the FreeRADIUS RPMs. Now, follow these steps:

1. Download the latest version of FreeRADIUS in `tar.bz2` format from its website (`http://freeradius.org/download.html`).

2. SLES includes a directory structure that is used specifically to build RPMs. This is located under `/usr/src/packages`. Copy the original `bz2` source file to the SOURCES directory. Replace `x` and `y` with the downloaded version's numbers:

   `#> cp freeradius-server-2.x.y.tar.bz2 /usr/src/packages/SOURCES/`

3. Extract the SUSE RPM `.spec` file from the TAR file again replacing `x` and `y` with the correct version numbers:

   `#> cd /usr/src/packages/SOURCES/`

   `#> tar -xvjf freeradius-server-2.x.y.tar.bz2 freeradius-`
   `server-2.x.y/suse/freeradius.spec`

4. Copy the following file to the `/usr/src/packages/SPECS` directory:

   `#> cp freeradius-server-2.x.y/suse/freeradius.spec ../SPECS/`

5. Edit the following line in the `spec` file, changing `%{fillup_and_insserv -s freeradius START_RADIUSD }` to `%{fillup_and_insserv freeradius }`.

6. Run the following command to determine dependencies:

   `#> rpmbuild -ba /usr/src/packages/SPECS/freeradius.spec`

7. This will list the required development packages to install in order for the FreeRADIUS RPMs to be built. The list may be different on your system; on mine it is the following (use `zypper` to install them):

```
#> zypper in db-devel e2fsprogs-devel gcc-c++ gdbm-devel gettext-
devel glibc-devel ncurses-devel openldap2-devel openssl-devel pam-
devel postgresql-devel python-devel unixODBC-devel zlib-devel
apache2-devel cyrus-sasl-devel krb5-devel libapr1-devel
libmysqlclient-devel
```

8. Run the rpmbuild command again. If all the required dependencies are met, the building of the RPMs will commence. Tee the output to a file for later investigation:

```
#> rpmbuild -ba /usr/src/packages/SPECS/freeradius.spec | tee /
tmp/build_out.txt
```

9. When the build process is complete the RPMs will be located under the /usr/src/packages/RPMS/<architecture>/ directory.

10. Install the new FreeRADIUS packages using the following command where x and y are the specific version of FreeRADIUS:

```
#> cd /usr/scr/packages/RPMS/<architecture>/
```

```
#> zypper in freeradius-server-2.x.y-0.i586.rpm freeradius-server-
libs-2.x.y-0.i586.rpm freeradius-server-utils-2.x.y-0.i586.rpm
```

11. Take note that FreeRADIUS will run as the user radiusd by default. This user is created during the FreeRADIUS installation. Give this user ownership of the certs directory. Failing to do this will leave you with a broken FreeRADIUS installation.

```
#> chown -R radiusd. /etc/raddb/certs
```

12. Confirm that radiusd starts correctly by executing radiusd -X in a terminal.

13. *Ctrl* + *C* will stop the running FreeRADIUS. You can now start FreeRADIUS using the start-up script from the terminal:

```
#> /etc/init.d/freeradius start
```

What just happened?

We completed the build and installation of FreeRADIUS RPMs on SLES. Although not as elegant as CentOS it was still done without many problems.

zypper or yast -i

Use zypper to install the required dependencies. Using yast -i to install the required gettext-devel package will result in an error. zypper knows that the gettext-tools package will satisfy this dependency.

Using yast -i to install the dependencies also results in unwanted updates from the OpenSUSE repository. You have been warned.

Tweaks done by hand

There were some tweaks that we had to perform manually in order to get the latest FreeRADIUS packed and installed on SLES:

- ◆ Add the OpenSUSE repository as a source of development packages
- ◆ Install various development packages from OpenSUSE
- ◆ Edit the `freeradius.spec` file to remove legacy macros
- ◆ Change the ownership of the directory that contains the certificates

Ubuntu

Ubuntu is based on Debian Linux and uses the dpkg Package Manager to manage software packages known as debs.

The `apt` program is used to manage repositories for dpkg in the same way `zypper` and `yum` are used with RPM.

Time for action – Ubuntu: from tarball to debs

The following steps will show you how to install debs:

1. Install the `dpkg-dev` package. This package provides the development tools (including `dpkg-source`) required to unpack, build, and upload Debian source packages.

   ```
   $> sudo apt-get install dpkg-dev
   ```

   If this package does not install, check the list of sources used by the `apt` program. The repository sources are defined in the `/etc/apt/sources.list` file and updated with the `sudo apt-get update` command.

2. Install all the required development libraries for the `freeradius` package:

   ```
   $> sudo apt-get build-dep freeradius
   ```

   If you get a message that says: **Unable to find a source package for freeradius**, it is probably because the source repositories (`deb-src`) are not included in the `/etc/apt/sources.list` file.

3. Ensure the `fakeroot` program is installed:

   ```
   $> sudo apt-get install fakeroot
   ```

4. Ensure that the `ssl-cert` package is installed. Failing to install this package will cause trouble with the compiled EAP modules when FreeRADIUS starts up:

```
$> sudo apt-get install ssl-cert
```

5. Download the latest version of FreeRADIUS from its website. Use the `wget` program and replace x and y with actual version numbers:

```
$> wget ftp://ftp.freeradius.org/pub/freeradius/freeradius-server-
2.x.y.tar.gz
```

6. Extract the FreeRADIUS source TAR file. Replace x and y with the downloaded version's numbers:

```
$> tar -xzvf freeradius-server-2.x.y.tar.gz
```

7. Change to the extracted directory, again replacing x and y with the actual downloaded version's numbers:

```
$> cd freeradius-server-2.x.y
```

8. Make this current directory a `fakeroot` environment and build the package using the control file already included in the `debian` subdirectory. The build process will take a while and depends on the computing power of the machine on which it is executed. You can monitor the output of this command for fatal errors, although it should just work:

```
$> fakeroot dpkg-buildpackage -b -uc
```

9. This will create all the required debs and place them outside the `freeradius-server-2-x.y` directory.

10. Install the new debs by issuing the following commands (remember to substitute your version and architecture):

```
$> cd ../
```

```
$> sudo dpkg -i freeradius_2.x.y+git_i386.deb freeradius-
common_2.x.y+git_all.deb freeradius-utils_2.x.y+git_i386.deb
libfreeradius2_2.x.y+git_i386.deb
```

What just happened?

We just created and installed debs for the latest version of FreeRADIUS on Ubuntu. Here's a breakdown of important points.

Installing dpkg-dev

The dpkg-dev package installs all the tools required for building debs. This includes the autoconfig and make tools and also a compiler. It also includes the dpkg-buildpackage program, which we will use to create the debs.

Using build-dep

apt-get is followed by a command to instruct it what to do. When we are installing packages we use the install command. The build-dep command is used to install all the dependencies of the specified source package.

We are not using the source package that comes with Ubuntu, but rather use the latest source tarball from FreeRADIUS. This means that it is not a foolproof method especially if the latest source includes development libraries not used by the original Ubuntu source package. You will, however, be informed of that during the build process and can subsequently install those required libraries.

fakeroot

This command allows us to build debs as a normal user and is the recommended way. Fakeroot is followed by a command. The command which fakeroot calls will think it is run by a root user having root privileges for file manipulation. In our case we issue the dpkg-buildpackage command.

dpkg-buildpackage

This command is run inside the FreeRADIUS source folder. It will make use of the specified information inside the debian folder to compile the source and subsequently create the various FreeRADIUS packages. The -b option is for binary-only build and the -uc option is to skip the signing with a gpg key.

When compiling FreeRADIUS on some installations of Ubuntu 10.4 you may run into the following error:

undefined reference to 'lt_preloaded_symbols'

It happened on one of my machines, but the others compiled fine. Quick Googling led me to this reported bug:

https://bugs.launchpad.net/ubuntu/+source/freeradius/+bug/421005

Somehow it seems to be still present even in 10.4. YMMV but take note of the libltdl-related problem.

Installing the debs

We only install the debs required for a basic installation. When we require extra modules they can simply be installed as a package. Required dependencies can be installed by using the `apt` command.

For those preferring the old school

Although we encourage the building of packages there is nothing that stops you from using the `configure, make, make install` pattern. If you run `./configure --help`, a list of options will be shown that you can use to tweak the build of FreeRADIUS. You can for instance specify the location of certain directories (`--bindir=/usr/bin`), enable or disable certain features (`--enable-developer`), or include certain packages (`--with-openssl`).

Installed executables

FreeRADIUS has various executable files installed. When moving between distributions there are small differences to consider.

One such difference is the location of the configuration files. Another difference is the name of the FreeRADIUS server executable. In Ubuntu (and Debian) it is called `freeradius`. In CentOS and SLES it is called `radiusd`. The following table lists the important executables that are installed along with a brief description of their function:

Name	Description
`/usr/sbin/raddebug`	Shell script wrapper around `radmin` for debug output without having to run `radiusd` in debug mode.
`/usr/sbin/radiusd`	The RADIUS server.
`/usr/sbin/freeradius`	
`/usr/sbin/radmin`	Administration utility that connects to a running `radiusd` daemon.
`/usr/bin/radclient`	Utility program used to send various RADIUS packets to a RADIUS server and to show the reply.
`/usr/bin/radconf2xml`	Displays the current server configuration formatted in XML.
`/usr/bin/radcrypt`	Encrypts or checks a password in DES or MD5 format.
`/usr/bin/radeapclient`	Sends EAP packets to a RADIUS server.
`/usr/bin/radlast`	Front-end to the system's last command showing output from the accounting log file.
`/usr/bin/radsqlrelay`	Used to manage accounting detail recorded in a SQL log file. This file is created by the `rlm_sql_log` module.

Name	Description
`/usr/bin/radtest`	Sends Access-Request (code 1) packets to a RADIUS server and shows the reply. Front-end to `radclient`.
`/usr/bin/radwho`	Shows active sessions from the `radutmp` file
`/usr/bin/radzap`	Shell script wrapper used to remove rogue entries in the session database (file or SQL).
`/usr/bin/smbencrypt`	Gives `nt` password hash for a plaintext password required by MS-CHAP.

 Not all the listed commands will run by default. Commands like `radwho` and `radlast` depend on the existence of log files, which are used as input for these commands. Commands like `radmin` and `raddebug` require a special set up on the server before they can be run. Don't be discouraged if not all the commands are working on a new installation.

Running as root or not

FreeRADIUS should be running with as few privileges as possible in a production environment. A normal installation creates a dedicated user and group for this purpose.

On CentOS and SLES the user and group are called `radiusd`. On Ubuntu the user and group are called `freerad`. Only on special configurations will root privileges be required.

Dictionary access for client programs

On some installations (SLES) the FreeRADIUS client programs could not read the dictionary file. This only happens when you run the client programs as a normal user. Access to the `dictionary` file is required for the client programs to resolve the various RADIUS AVPs to numbers.

When this problem exists you will get a message like the following:

```
#> radclient: dict_init: Couldn't open dictionary "/etc/raddb/
dictionary": Permission denied
```

Fix this problem by running the following commands as the root user:

```
#> chmod o+xr /etc/raddb
```
```
#> chmod o+r /etc/raddb/dictionary
```

After this a normal user should be able to run the FreeRADIUS client programs without any rights issues.

Ensure proper start-up

Executing `radiusd -X` (or `freeradius -X` on Ubuntu) as root will start the FreeRADIUS server in debug mode and indicate if there are any problems.

To stop the server simply type *Ctrl + C*. This will stop the program.

 If you get an error message about port 1812 already in use, FreeRADIUS is already running. You can stop it through the startup script and try again.

We also need to make sure FreeRADIUS will start up with the rest of the services after a reboot. Unfortunately each distribution works differently here. The following tables can be used as a guideline for commands to manage FreeRADIUS startup.

Each of these scripts must be called with one of the listed arguments:

Start-up script	
CentOS	`#> /etc/init.d/radiusd start|stop|restart`
SLES	`#> /etc/init.d/freeradius start|stop|restart`
Ubuntu	`#> /etc/init.d/freeradius start|stop|restart`

Activate and de-activate	
CentOS	`#> /sbin/chkconfig radiusd on`
	`#> /sbin/chkconfig radiusd off`
SLES	`#> /sbin/chkconfig -a freeradius`
	`#> /sbin/chkconfig -d freeradius`
Ubuntu	`$> sudo update-rc.d freeradius defaults`
	`$> sudo update-rc.d -f freeradius remove`

Ensure FreeRADIUS running	
CentOS	`#> pidof radiusd`
SLES	`#> pidof radiusd`
Ubuntu	`#> pidof freeradius`

An alternative command can be used to check if FreeRADIUS is running:

```
#> ps aux | grep radius
```

The following command shows which interface and UDP ports FreeRADIUS is using:

```
#> netstat -unap | grep radius
```

Summary

This chapter was all about installing FreeRADIUS on your machine. Specifically, we covered:

- ◆ Installing pre-built binary packages. This is the quickest and surest way to have a working FreeRADIUS server.

- ◆ Building and installing FreeRADIUS from source code. This is a bit more involved, but allows you to run the latest release. This also allows you to boast about your ability to build packages from source code for your Linux distribution.

- ◆ FreeRADIUS installs various executables and contains various modules. Some of these modules are packed separately depending on the Linux distribution that you use. When you require the use of a separately packed module it first has to be installed along with its dependencies.

- ◆ You should also install client utility programs along with the FreeRADIUS server. This allows you to effectively test and troubleshoot.

- ◆ Running client utility programs as a normal user may result in file rights issues when trying to access the dictionary file. This can be fixed by tweaking the rights.

We also discussed how to ensure automatic start-up after reboots and running FreeRADIUS in debug mode to troubleshoot.

Now that FreeRADIUS is installed and running on our machine we can start using it. Getting started with FreeRADIUS is the topic of the next chapter.

Pop quiz – installation

1. Isaac is confused. He installed FreeRADIUS on Ubuntu in much the same way he used to install on CentOS but the `radiusd` binary is missing, why is this?

2. After you install the pre-built binary packages for FreeRADIUS, you reboot the server. You would like to run `radiusd` in debug mode but `radiusd` complains something about address already in use. What is wrong?

3. You would like FreeRADIUS to connect to a MySQL database on CentOS. What pre-built FreeRADIUS package is required for this?

4. A friend of you is asking for help. He wants to build FreeRADIUS on SLES 11 but when he tries to install the required build libraries it can not find all the required libraries. What can the problem be?

3

Getting Started with FreeRADIUS

After FreeRADIUS has been installed it needs to be configured for our requirements. This chapter will help you to get familiar with FreeRADIUS. It assumes that you already know the basics of the RADIUS protocol as discussed in Chapter 1.

In this chapter we shall:

- ◆ Perform a basic configuration of FreeRADIUS and test it
- ◆ Discover ways of getting help
- ◆ Learn the recommended way to configure and test FreeRADIUS
- ◆ See how everything fits together with FreeRADIUS

So let's get on with it.

Before you start

This chapter assumes that you have a clean installation of FreeRADIUS. You will need root access to edit FreeRADIUS configuration files for the basic configuration and testing.

A simple setup

We start this chapter by creating a simple setup of FreeRADIUS with the following:

◆ The localhost defined as an NAS device (RADIUS client)

◆ Alice defined as a test user

After we have defined the client and the test user, we will use the `radtest` program to fill the role of a RADIUS client and test the authentication of Alice.

Time for action – configuring FreeRADIUS

FreeRADIUS is set up by modifying configuration files. The location of these files depends on how FreeRADIUS was installed:

◆ If you have installed the standard FreeRADIUS packages that are provided with the distribution, it will be under `/etc/raddb` on CentOS and SLES. On Ubuntu it will be under `/etc/freeradius`.

◆ If you have built and installed FreeRADIUS from source using the distribution's package management system it will also be under `/etc/raddb` on CentOS and SLEs. On Ubuntu it will be under `/etc/freeradius`.

◆ If you have compiled and installed FreeRADIUS using `configure`, `make`, `make install` it will be under `/usr/local/etc/raddb`.

The following instructions assume that the FreeRADIUS configuration directory is your current working directory:

1. Ensure that you are root in order to be able to edit the configuration files.

2. FreeRADIUS includes a default client called `localhost`. This client can be used by RADIUS client programs on the localhost to help with troubleshooting and testing. Confirm that the following entry exists in the `clients.conf` file:

```
client localhost {
    ipaddr = 127.0.0.1
    secret = testing123
    require_message_authenticator = no
    nastype = other
}
```

3. Define Alice as a FreeRADIUS test user. Add the following lines at the top of the `users` file. Make sure the second and third lines are indented by a single tab character:

```
"alice" Cleartext-Password := "passme"
    Framed-IP-Address = 192.168.1.65,
    Reply-Message = "Hello, %{User-Name}"
```

4. Start the FreeRADIUS server in debug mode. Make sure that there is no other instance running by shutting it down through the startup script. We assume Ubuntu in this case.

```
$> sudo su
#> /etc/init.d/freeradius stop
#> freeradius -X
```

You can also use the more brutal method of `kill -9 $(pidof freeradius)` or `killall freeradius` on Ubuntu and `kill -9 $(pidof radius)` or `killall radiusd` on CentOS and SLES if the startup script does not stop FreeRADIUS.

5. Ensure FreeRADIUS has started correctly by confirming that the last line on your screen says the following:

```
Ready to process requests.
```

If this did not happen, read through the output of the FreeRADIUS server started in debug mode to see what problem was identified and a possible location thereof.

6. Authenticate Alice using the following command:

```
$> radtest alice passme 127.0.0.1 100 testing123
```

7. The debug output of FreeRADIUS will show how the `Access-Request` packet arrives and how the FreeRADIUS server responds to this request.

8. `Radtest` will also show the response of the FreeRADIUS server:

```
Sending Access-Request of id 17 to 127.0.0.1 port 1812
    User-Name = "alice"
    User-Password = "passme"
    NAS-IP-Address = 127.0.1.1
    NAS-Port = 100
rad_recv: Access-Accept packet from host 127.0.0.1 port 1812,
id=147, length=40
    Framed-IP-Address = 192.168.1.65
    Reply-Message = "Hello, alice"
```

What just happened?

We have created a test user on the FreeRADIUS server. We have also used the `radtest` command as a client to the FreeRADIUS server to test authentication.

Let's elaborate on some interesting and important points.

Configuring FreeRADIUS

Configuration of the FreeRADIUS server is logically divided into different files. These files are modified to configure a certain function, component, or module of FreeRADIUS. There is, however, a main configuration file that sources the various sub-files. This file is called `radiusd.conf`.

The default configuration is suitable for most installations. Very few changes are required to make FreeRADIUS useful in your environment.

Clients

Although there are many files inside the FreeRADIUS server configuration directory, only a few require further changes. The `clients.conf` file is used to define clients to the FreeRADIUS server.

Before an NAS can use the FreeRADIUS server it has to be defined as a client on the FreeRADIUS server. Let's look at some points about client definitions.

Sections

A client is defined by a `client` section. FreeRADIUS uses sections to group and define various things. A section starts with a keyword indicating the section name. This is followed by enclosing brackets. Inside the enclosing brackets are various settings specific to that section. Sections can also be nested.

Sometimes the section's keyword is followed by a single word to differentiate between sections of the same type. This allows us to have different client entries in `clients.conf`. Each client has a short name to distinguish it from the others.

The `clients.conf` file is not the only file where `client` sections can be defined although it is the usual and most logical place. The following image shows nested client definitions inside a server section:

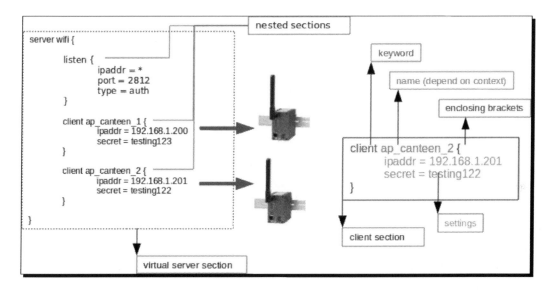

Client identification

The FreeRADIUS server identifies a client by its IP Address. If an unknown client sends a request to the server, the request will be silently ignored.

Shared secret

The client and server also require to have a shared secret, which will be used to encrypt and decrypt certain AVPs. The value of the `User-Password` AVP is encrypted using this shared secret. When the shared secret differs between the client and server, FreeRADIUS server will detect it and warn you when running in debug mode:

```
Failed to authenticate the user.
    WARNING: Unprintable characters in the password. Double-check the
shared secret on the server and the NAS!
```

Message-Authenticator

When defining a client you can enforce the presence of the `Message-Authenticator` AVP in all the requests. Since we will be using the `radtest` program, which does not include it, we disable it for `localhost` by setting `require_message_authenticator` to no.

Nastype

The `nastype` is set to `other`. The value of `nastype` will determine how the `checkrad` Perl script will behave. `Checkrad` is used to determine if a user is already using resources on an NAS. Since `localhost` does not have this function or need we will define it as `other`.

Common errors

If the server is down or the packets from `radtest` cannot reach the server because of a firewall between them, `radtest` will try three times and then give up with the following message:

```
radclient: no response from server for ID 133 socket 3
```

If you run `radtest` as a normal user it may complain about not having access to the FreeRADIUS dictionary file. This is required for normal operations. The way to solve this is either to change the permissions on the reported file or to run `radtest` as root.

Users

Users are defined in the `users` file under the FreeRADIUS configuration directory. The content of the `users` file is used for both Authorization and Authentication purposes. This file is not the only source of users but is a simple and effective way to begin. Let's look at some key points about users.

Files module

The `files` module (`rlm_files`) reads the contents of the `users` file to determine if the user specified in the `Access-Request` exists and is authorized to use the NAS. It also determines what attributes should be returned to the client.

The `files` module may set the `Auth-Type`. This will determine the authentication method to be used. If a user is defined with a `Cleartext-Password` check item it will set `Auth-Type = PAP`.

The `files` module also supplies other modules with a value of "known good password" if one is defined. In our example it supplied the `pap` module (`rlm_pap`) with the value specified in the `Cleartext-Password` check AVP.

PAP module

The pap module (rlm_pap) was used for authentication. If the Auth-Type is set to PAP it will look for a "known good password" and compare this with the User-Password AVP's value. If it is the same, the module will pass the authentication request.

The request may still fail because of other modules in the FreeRADIUS authentication chain.

Users file

The users file does not contain any sections like clients.conf. This is because it is specific to the files module and not directly related to the configuration of the FreeRADIUS server itself.

To add an entry in the users file you define a username followed by zero or more comma-separated check items. This is followed by zero or more tab-indented lines with comma-separated reply items.

We assume you are using the default setup without any changes to the sites-enabled/default virtual server. If you have, for instance, activated the unix module under the authorize section and Alice is also defined as a system user, the system user with its password will be the preferred user instead of the one defined in the users file. The result will be that an Access-Reject packet is returned in response to the Access-Request if the passwords differ between Alice the system user and Alice the user defined in the users file.

Check items

The following entry requires that the Access-Request packet contains an AVP for NAS-IP-Address with a value of 127.0.0.1.

```
"alice" Cleartext-Password := "passme", NAS-IP-Address == '127.0.0.1'
```

The radtest program will set the value of NAS-IP-Address by default to the IP of the hostname specified in the /etc/hosts file. Later in this chapter you will see how to change this value.

Some AVPs have a special meaning and are used internally by FreeRADIUS. Although the incoming Access-Request does not contain an AVP called Cleartext-Password, the files module uses it internally to adjust the value of Auth-Type and to create a known good password, which can be used by the pap module for authentication.

Another example of a special AVP is when you want to reject or accept a user based on the username, no matter what their password may be. The previous line will change to one of the following.

```
"alice" Cleartext-Password := "passme", Auth-Type := Reject
"alice" Cleartext-Password := "passme", Auth-Type := Accept
```

Although `Auth-Type` appears to be a standard AVP check item, it is internal to FreeRADIUS and used to control the way in which the authentication will be done.

Reply items

Reply items are preceded with a line containing a username and zero or more check items. Reply items are indented with a single tab. Multiple items can fit on a single line separated by commas. They can also span over multiple lines, but have to be separated by commas.

Operators

You may have noticed that we use different operators when assigning values to AVPs. There are various operators available, which determine the logical outcome of a check or reply action. Operators will be discussed in more detail in the chapter on Authorization. For now you can remember that all reply items contain = and check items that need to match incoming AVPs are == while others are := .

Substitution

The `users` file allows for substitution. The special sequence of `%{<AVP>}` will replace the AVP with its actual value. In our setup we return a message to the user by substituting the `User-Name` AVP with its value (`%{User-Name}`).

DEFAULT user

The `users` file has a special user called `DEFAULT`. This user can be defined multiple times with different checks and replies. This user matches any username.

Because of this you should always put `DEFAULT` entries at the end of the `users` file. You should also take note of the special reply value called `Fall-Through`. If `Fall-Through` is not defined it takes on the value of `no`.

If an entry matches and `Fall-Through` is set to `no` (default if not specified), the search process stops. This means that the default value of `no` will cause the `files` module to return on the first match of a specified requirement inside the `users` file.

When `Fall-Through` is set to `yes`, searching the `users` file for further matches continues after a match has been discovered. We will now discuss two commonly used internal check AVPs: Login-Time and Simultaneous-Use.

Login-Time

`Login-Time` is a very powerful internal check AVP. It allows flexible authorization and its value is used by the `logintime (rlm_logintime)` module to determine if a person is allowed to authenticate to the FreeRADIUS server or not. This value is also used to calculate the `Session-Timeout` reply value. `Session-Timeout` is subsequently used by the NAS to limit access time.

The following line will grant Alice access only between 08:00 and 18:00 each day.

```
"alice" Cleartext-Password := "passme", Login-Time := 'Al0800-1800'
```

The `logintime` module will calculate the reply value of `Session-Timeout` if Alice has logged in within the permitted timeslots to inform the NAS how long she is allowed to stay connected. If Alice tries to access the network when she is not permitted, the request will be rejected.

Simultaneous-Use

`Simultaneous-Use` is another internal AVP used to specify the number of concurrent logins a user is allowed to have.

```
"alice" Cleartext-Password := "passme", Simultaneous-Use := '1'
```

The `Simultaneous-Use` check is used by the session section, which is part of the FreeRADIUS configuration. The session section makes use of either flat files (`rlm_radutmp`) or SQL data (`rlm_sql`) to determine if a user is already logged into an NAS.

Framed-IP-Address

In our example we used the `Framed-IP-Address` as a return AVP. This attribute can, however, be used in both a request and a reply. If the NAS sends this along with the access request, it is a request to the RADIUS server that this IP address is preferred for the given client. The RADIUS server can then decide if it will allow the use of the requested IP address or suggest a different one to the NAS by including this AVP with the `Access-Accept` packet.

Radtest

Details of the `radtest` command will not be discussed here because the next section will show you how to find it yourself.

Helping yourself

Open source projects are sometimes criticized because they lack documentation and support. FreeRADIUS has done a great job in supplying proper documentation and ways to get help.

Installed documentation

There is plenty of documentation, which installs with FreeRADIUS. It is in the form of man pages, comments inside configuration files, various README files, and also rfc files.

Man pages

You may not always be sure which man pages are available as part of the FreeRADIUS installation. The following section will show you how you can find this out.

Time for action – discovering available man pages for FreeRADIUS

The following commands can be used as a guideline to first determine which FreeRADIUS packages are installed and subsequently determine which files are contained in the package.

dpkg systems

To list all the installed FreeRADIUS packages:

```
$> dpkg -l | grep radius
```

Use each of the listed packages as the package argument to the dpkg -L command. Let's take the freeradius-common package for instance:

```
$> dpkg -L freeradius-common
```

From the previous output we see that there are many man pages installed under the /usr/share/man directory.

rpm systems

To list all the installed FreeRADIUS packages:

```
$> rpm -qa | grep radius
```

Take each of the listed packages and use it as the argument to rpm -ql as shown:

```
$> rpm -ql <package name>
```

From the previous output we can locate the man pages installed with FreeRADIUS under the /usr/share/man directory.

radtest revisited

To get more details on radtest the following command will display its man page:

```
$> man radclient
```

The Synopsis section contains two handy options:

- ppphint: Adding a value greater than one will cause radtest to add the Framed-Protocol = PPP AVP to the Access-Request packet.

- nasname: Adding a hostname or IP address will cause radtest to add the NAS-IP-Address = <IP Address> to the Access-Request packet.

The following command adds the Framed-Protocol = PPP and NAS-IP-ADDRESS = 10.20.30.1 attributes to the Access-Request packet.

```
$> radtest alice passme 127.0.0.1 100 testing123 1 10.20.30.1
```

Now that you know where the man pages are located, let's explore the radclient command's man page.

Radclient

Radclient is the real thing since the radtest man page mentions that it is simply a front-end to radclient. Let's see what radclient is all about:

```
$> man 1 radclient
```

From the man page we can see that radclient gives us much more power as compared to radtest. The following command can be used as an equivalent to the radtest command used at the start of this chapter:

```
$> echo "User-Name=alice,User-Password=passme" | radclient 127.0.0.1 auth testing123
```

The response from radclient returns a code number and does not clearly indicate a pass or fail for an Access-Request. This is where you need to know the RADIUS packet codes as discussed in **Chapter 1**.

Here is the response of an Access-Accept packet (Code 2):

```
Received response ID 32, code 2, length = 40
Framed-IP-Address = 192.168.1.65
Reply-Message = "Hello, alice"
```

Here is the response of an Access-Reject packet:

```
Received response ID 59, code 3, length = 34
Reply-Message = "Hello, alice"
```

Radclient also offers us the opportunity to send accounting, status, and disconnect packets. We will use these features in subsequent chapters.

What just happened?

You have just learned how to find and use the man pages, which are part of the FreeRADIUS installation on your server.

Have a go hero – adding more AVPs to the auth request

Try some of these tasks as a further challenge:

- ◆ The number of AVPs received by FreeRADIUS is fewer when we use `radclient` instead of `radtest`. See if you can add those missing ones to the standard input for the `radclient`.

- ◆ `Radtest` also offers the option to read AVPs from a file. Create a file with the required AVPs and use it with `radclient`. Use the `Packet-Type` attribute in the file to specify the packet type inside the file.

- ◆ If you use the `Packet-Type` inside a file remember the following important points:
  - ❑ Specify the packet type as `auto` on the command line.
  - ❑ The `Packet-Type` value is the numeric of the RADIUS packet code. This means that an `Access-Request` packet will have a value of `1`.
  - ❑ You also need to specify an AVP for the destination port. Failing to do so will cause it not to be sent. `Access-Request` requires the following entry. `Packet-Dst-Port=1812`.

The following can be used as an example to work from:

```
User-Name = alice
User-Password = passme
NAS-IP-Address = 127.0.0.1
NAS-Port = 100
Packet-Type = 1
Packet-Dst-Port = 1812
```

Man pages are not the only source of information in the FreeRADIUS installation. The FreeRADIUS configuration files have many comments. This makes the configuration much easier.

Configuration file comments

The configuration files are filled with guidelines, tips, and pointers to more information. All this is contained in comments inside the configuration files.

Pop quiz – clients.conf

As an exercise read through the `clients.conf` file and answer the following questions on the comments inside the file.

1. How do we distinguish between various client sections?

2. True or false: Using a `netmask` other than 32 is recommended.

3. If a client connects with an IP Address that you cannot determine beforehand, what will be the recommended way to handle this?

4. You have an old legacy NAS that will contact the FreeRADIUS server. What required attribute may be missing in the `Access-Request` packet and how will you compensate for this?

5. Does FreeRADIUS support clients using the IPv6 protocol?

6. True or false: The shared secret does not need to be more than 8 characters because only the first 8 characters are used.

7. What may happen if the `nastype` is identified incorrectly?

As you can see there is valuable information inside the comments of a configuration file. This information should be considered when you set up FreeRADIUS.

Online documentation

There are many sources of information on FreeRADIUS available on the Internet. Some of this information is outdated or simply not correct. FreeRADIUS develops at a fast pace. Using outdated documentation can cause unexpected results leading to a lot of frustration.

The following is a list of recommended URLs to visit:

URL	Description
`http://freeradius.org/`	This is the homepage of the FreeRADIUS project and contains links to documentation sources. This should be your first stop.
`http://wiki.freeradius.org/`	Although there is also a link to the Wiki on the FreeRADIUS homepage, it is listed here to emphasize its importance.
`http://deployingradius.com/`	Contains practical documentation.
`http://google.com`	Google is your friend!

Online help

If you have tried all the available documentation and still have problems you can make use of the FreeRADIUS mailing lists. This is a very effective way to get help, but you have to abide by a few basic rules for the benefit of everyone.

The FreeRADIUS home page has a **Mailing Lists** link, which you can follow for further instructions.

Once you have obtained the new knowledge it's time to apply it. The following section looks at recommended practices when configuring FreeRADIUS.

Golden rules

These golden rules are not my own, but the recommendations from the online documentation listed above. For best results follow them!

◆ Do *as little as possible—the default configuration should work as is.*

◆ *Do not edit the default configuration files unless you understand what they do.*

◆ When you make changes, keep them small and make backups.

◆ Confirm that the changes work as intended by running FreeRADIUS in debug mode and carefully observing the output during various scenarios.

Inside radiusd

This section gives a general overview on the workings of the FreeRADIUS server program called `radiusd`.

Configuration files

We've already said that the behavior of `radiusd` is determined by configuration files. The main configuration file for the FreeRADIUS server is `radiusd.conf`, which resides in the configuration directory. The location and name of the configuration directory depends on the Linux distribution and the manner in which FreeRADIUS was compiled and installed.

The `radiusd.conf` file consists of general items and various sections. Contents of other files and directories are included by using the special keyword `$INCLUDE` inside the `radiusd.conf` file.

Important includes

The following table lists important inclusions and their descriptions:

Include	Description
$INCLUDE proxy.conf	Used to define realms for which requests will be proxied. This turns the FreeRADIUS server into a client that forwards requests for certain users to other RADIUS servers.
$INCLUDE clients.conf	Used to define various clients (NAS) with their IP address and shared secrets.
$INCLUDE ${confdir}/modules/	Configuration settings specific to a module are inside this directory. We configure a module by changing the corresponding file in this directory. The ldap module (rlm_ldap) for instance will have a corresponding ldap file that configures the ldap module.
#$INCLUDE sql.conf	The configuration of the sql module (rlm_sql) bends the rules a little bit by not sitting under the modules directory. The # at the start means it is excluded by default.
$INCLUDE eap.conf	EAP can be quite complex. For this reason it is logically separated and inside a dedicated file
$INCLUDE policy.conf	Policies are virtual modules, which can be used in the same way as modules
$INCLUDE sites-enabled/	FreeRADIUS uses virtual servers in the same way Apache uses them. A virtual server is created in the sites-available directory and activated by linking it to the sites-enabled directory. By default two virtual servers are active upon installation, namely default and inner-tunnel. Default is for general usage and inner-tunnel for EAP requests.

Libraries and dictionaries

FreeRADIUS has many modules. Module file names are in the form of rlm_<module name>.

A module is a form of a library. All modules are libraries, but not all libraries are modules. These modules are located under a library directory, which is specified as libdir in radiusd.conf. Multiple locations can be listed by separating them with a colon character, for example:

```
libdir = /usr/lib/freeradius:/usr/local/my_freeradius
```

FreeRADIUS needs to resolve AVP names to numbers. This requirement is not only for AVPs, but also for VSAs. For this FreeRADIUS uses dictionary files. Dictionary files are text files which describe AVPs and VSAs.

There is a master dictionary file, which is used by both `radiusd` and client programs like `radtest` and `radclient`. This file is located under the configuration directory and called `dictionary`. This file has a `$INCLUDE` statement pointing to a directory, that contains many dictionary files. Files inside this dictionary directory are of the form `dictionary.<vendor name>`.

FreeRADIUS-specific AVPs

FreeRADIUS has its own special dictionary called `dictionary.freeradius.internal`. The AVPs in this dictionary are used internally by FreeRADIUS during operation. Internal AVPs that we have used up to now include `Cleartext-Password`, `Auth-TypeX`, and `Login-Time`. The usage of dictionaries and internal AVPs will be discussed in more detail throughout the book.

Running as ...

FreeRADIUS runs on *non-privileged ports* (N>1023), which means you do not have to be root to run it.

The FreeRADIUS authors highly recommend that you run FreeRADIUS with as few permissions possible. The only reason for you to run FreeRADIUS as a root user is when you need access to files that only root can access. This is for instance when you want to use the system users on the Linux server as a user store (`rlm_unix` and `rlm_pam`) instead of the `users` file used by the `files` module. There are, however, ways around this by changing permissions on those files.

The `radiusd.conf` file has two directives that are set to specify the name of the user and group under which FreeRADIUS will run. They are `user` and `group`. If you comment these values out, FreeRADIUS will run as the user who started it.

Listen section

FreeRADIUS listens on all the available interfaces by default. You can, however, change this by specifying that it should only listen on a particular NIC or even a VPN tied to TUN/TAP interface. Alternatively you can specify that it should only listen on a specified IP address. There are various possibilities that allow you to tie interface and IP address combinations to virtual servers or request types. This feature in itself makes the FreeRADIUS server incredibly versatile.

If you have a multihomed server there is usually one interface that runs a very strict firewall. If clients connect through this interface, make sure that they are allowed through the firewall.

If you are running FreeRADIUS on a VPN interface, confirm that the VPN is already up and running during start-up before FreeRADIUS is started.

Log files

Production environments do not allow FreeRADIUS to run in debug mode all the time. When we run FreeRADIUS as a normal daemon it writes certain data to log files.

Inspecting these log files at regular intervals is very important to detect potential problems in your environment. Let's have a look at them.

radiusd

The usual location for the `radiusd` log file is `/var/log/radius/radius.log`. You can also specify what should be logged to this file in the `radiusd.conf` file. There is a dedicated `log` section to fine tune the logging.

Who was logged in and when?

The command `last` in Linux gives a history of who has logged into the machine as well as the duration of the session. This is done by reading the file `/var/logwtmp`.

FreeRADIUS has a similar feature where the `radlast` command will read the `/var/log/radius/radwtmp` file to show all the users that were logged in through an NAS using FreeRADIUS. For this to work `unix` must be listed in the accounting section of the virtual server (enabled by default).

Who is logged in right now?

The `who` command lists all the users that are logged in at a specific time. This is done by reading the `/var/run/utmp` file.

FreeRADIUS has a similar feature where the command `radwho` will read the `/var/log/radius/sradutmp` file to show the users with active sessions right now. The `sradutmp` file is not present by default and has to be activated by uncommenting the `sradutmp` line in the `accounting` section of the virtual server (disabled by default).

You may think that `radwho` should read a file called `/var/log/radius/radutmp`. This file does exists, but it contains sensitive information. You can read about the difference between the two on this Wiki page:

`http://wiki.freeradius.org/Rlm_radutmp`

Knowing these log file locations and commands to extract important information will give you the edge in times of trouble.

Summary

This chapter gave us initial hands-on experience of FreeRADIUS. We have also learned more on documentation and the workings of the FreeRADIUS server called `radiusd`.

Specifically, we have covered:

- **Configuring FreeRADIUS**: FreeRADIUS has a primary configuration file called `radiusd.conf`. Various other configuration files get sourced through the primary configuration file using the `$INCLUDE` keyword.

- **NAS devices**: An NAS device is a RADIUS client and shares a secret with the RADIUS server. NAS devices are defined in the `clients.conf` file. The localhost is by default defined as a client. This enables us to do various tests with RADIUS client programs like `radclient` and `radtest`.

- **Defining users**: The `users` file is a quick and simple way to define users and is used by the `files` module. Users defined in the `users` file have check and reply AVPs. Some of these AVPs have special meaning to FreeRADIUS and influence the behavior of the authentication and authorization outcomes.

- **Finding documentation**: FreeRADIUS has local and online documentation. On our own machine we can use man pages and also read comments inside configuration files for guidance. There is also documentation available on the Internet specifically on the FreeRADIUS home page. There are also mailing lists to which we can post questions.

- **When we configure**: There are a few rules to stick by when changing the configuration. Backup, make small changes, run in debug mode, and test.

We have also looked at various components and aspects of the `radiusd` program. This includes configuration files that are sourced, modules, dictionaries, AVPs specific to FreeRADIUS, log files, and running it with minimum rights.

Now that we know the basics of FreeRADIUS, we're ready to zoom in on authentication—which is the topic of the next chapter.

4
Authentication

This chapter zooms in on authentication. Authorization and accounting will follow later in the book.

Authentication is a process where we establish if someone is who he or she claims to be. The most common way is by a unique username and password.

In this chapter we shall:

- ◆ Discuss PAP, CHAP, and MS-CHAP authentication protocols
- ◆ See when and how authentication is done in FreeRADIUS
- ◆ Explore ways to store passwords
- ◆ Look at other authentication methods

So let's get on with it...

Authentication protocols

This section will give you background on three common authentication protocols. These protocols involve the supply of a username and password.

The `radtest` program uses the **Password Authentication Protocol (PAP)** by default when testing authentication. PAP is not the only authentication protocol but probably the most generic and widely used. Authentication protocols you should know about are PAP, CHAP, and MS-CHAP. Each of these protocols involves a username and password. The **Extensible Authentication Protocol (EAP)** protocol has its own dedicated chapter later in this book and will introduce us to more authentication protocols.

An authentication protocol is typically used on the `data link layer` that connects the client with the NAS. The `network layer` will only be established after the authentication is successful. The NAS acts as a broker to forward the requests from the user to the RADIUS server.

The `data link layer` and `network layer` are layers inside the **Open Systems Interconnect model (OSI model)**. The discussion of this model is almost guaranteed to be found in any book on networking:

`http://en.wikipedia.org/wiki/OSI_model`

PAP

PAP was one of the first protocols used to facilitate the supply of a username and password when making point-to-point connections. With PAP the NAS takes the PAP ID and password and sends them in an `Access-Request` packet as the `User-Name` and `User-Password`. PAP is simpler compared to CHAP and MS-CHAP because the NAS simply hands the RADIUS server a username and password, which are then checked. This username and password come directly from the user through the NAS to the server in a single action.

Although PAP transmits passwords in clear text, using it should not always be frowned upon. This password is only in clear text between the user and the NAS. The user's password will be encrypted when the NAS forwards the request to the RADIUS server.

If PAP is used inside a secure tunnel it is as secure as the tunnel. This is similar to when your credit card details are tunnelled inside an HTTPS connection and delivered to a secure web server.

HTTPS stands for **Hypertext Transfer Protocol Secure** and is a web standard that uses **Secure Socket Layer/Transport Layer Security** (SSL/TLS) to create a secure channel over an insecure network. Once this secure channel is established, we can transfer sensitive data, like credit card details, through it. HTTPS is used daily to secure many millions of transactions over the Internet.

See the following schematic of a typical captive portal configuration.

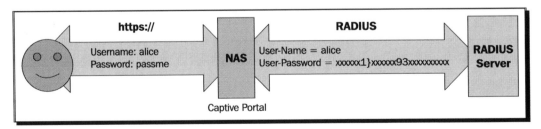

The following table shows the RADIUS AVPs involved in a PAP request:

AVP	Typical value
User-Name	alice
User-Password	\xbe\xd1}r\xc8vc/\x93*\x8f\xa0$\xa4gz

As you can see the value of User-Password is encrypted between the NAS and the RADIUS server. Transporting the user's password from the user to the NAS may be a security risk if it can be captured by a third party.

CHAP

CHAP stands for **Challenge-Handshake Authentication Protocol** and was designed as an improvement to PAP. It prevents you from transmitting a cleartext password.

CHAP was created in the days when dial-up modems were popular and the concern about PAP's cleartext passwords was high.

After a link is established to the NAS, the NAS generates a random challenge and sends it to the user. The user then responds to this challenge by returning a one-way hash calculated on an identifier (sent along with the challenge), the challenge, and the user's password. The user's response is then used by the NAS to create an Access-Request packet, which is sent to the RADIUS server. Depending on the reply from the RADIUS server, the NAS will return CHAP Success or CHAP Failure to the user.

The NAS can also request at random intervals that the authentication process be repeated by sending a new challenge to the user. This is another reason why it is considered more secure than PAP.

One major drawback of CHAP is that although the password is transmitted encrypted, the password source has to be in clear text for FreeRADIUS to perform password verification.

The FreeRADIUS FAQ discuss the dangers of transmitting a cleartext password compared to storing all the passwords in clear text on the server.

The following table shows the RADIUS AVPs involved in a CHAP request:

AVP	Typical value
User-Name	alice
CHAP-Password	4A2578ED8C1A747AFED86EB96F024ADFF8

User challenge response NAS request CHAP reply

MS-CHAP

MS-CHAP is a challenge-handshake authentication protocol created by Microsoft. There are two versions, MS-CHAP version 1 and MS-CHAP version 2.

The challenge sent by the NAS is identical in format to the standard CHAP challenge packet. This includes an identifier and arbitrary challenge. The response from the user is also identical in format to the standard CHAP response packet. The only difference is the format of the `Value` field. The `Value` field is sub-formatted to contain MS-CHAP-specific fields. One of the fields (`NT-Response`) contains the username and password in a very specific encrypted format. The reply from the user will be used by the NAS to create an `Access-Request` packet, which is sent to the RADIUS server. Depending on the reply from the RADIUS server, the NAS will return `Success Packet` or `Failure Packet` to the user.

> The RADIUS server is not involved with the sending out of the challenge. If you sniff the RADIUS traffic between an NAS and a RADIUS server you can confirm that there is only an `Access-Request` followed by an `Access-Accept` or `Access-Reject`. The sending out of a challenge to the user and receiving a response from her or him is between the NAS and the user.

MS-CHAP also has some enhancements that are not part of CHAP, like the user's ability to change his or her password or inclusion of more descriptive error messages.

The protocol is tightly integrated with the LAN Manager and NT Password hashes. FreeRADIUS will convert a user's cleartext password to an `LM-Password` and an `NT-Password` in order to determine if the password hash that came out of the MS-CHAP request is correct. Although there are known weaknesses with MS-CHAP, it remains widely used and very popular.

> Never say never. If your current requirement for the RADIUS deployment does not include the use of MS-CHAP, rather cater for the possibility that one day you may use it. The most popular EAP protocol makes use of MS-CHAP. EAP is crucial in Wi-Fi authentication.

Because MS-CHAP is vendor specific, VSAs instead of AVPs are part of the `Access-Request` between the NAS and RADIUS server. This is used together with the `User-Name` AVP.

VSA	Typical value
MS-CHAP-Challenge	CF702D195889B225
MS-CHAP-Response	:00:00:00:00:00:00:00:00:00:00:00:00:00:00:00:00:00:00:00:e6:3e:d6:be:b8:90:b4:88:84:bc:b3:71:c0:ce:b8:d3:1d:1a:06:35:32:c5:f1:85

Now that we know more about the authentication protocols, let's see how FreeRADIUS handles them.

FreeRADIUS—authorize before authenticate

It's time to see how FreeRADIUS handles incoming `Access-Request` packets.

Time for action – authenticating a user with FreeRADIUS

We continue with our exercise from the previous chapter where we authenticate a user defined in the `users` file. Instead of looking at the feedback of the `radtest` command, we will now look at the output of the FreeRADIUS server running in debug mode.

1. Ensure you are root in order to edit the `users` file.

2. Define Alice as a FreeRADIUS test user. Add the following lines at the top of the `users` file. Make sure the second line is indented by a single tab character.

   ```
   "alice" Cleartext-Password := "passme"
       Reply-Message = "Hello, %{User-Name}"
   ```

3. Start the FreeRADIUS server in debug mode. Ensure there is not already an instance running by shutting it down through the start-up script. We assume Ubuntu in this instance.

   ```
   $> sudo su
   #> /etc/init.d/freeradius stop
   #> freeradius -X
   ```

4. Authenticate Alice using the following command:

   ```
   $> radtest alice passme 127.0.0.1 100 testing123
   ```

5. The debug output of FreeRADIUS will show how the `Access-Request` packet arrives and how the FreeRADIUS server responds to this request.

What just happened?

You have sent an `Access-Request` packet to FreeRADIUS. You have received an `Access-Accept` packet back. Nothing exciting really, but it is quite interesting to observe the debug output of FreeRADIUS. This shows what is involved to return an `Access-Accept` packet.

If you want to make use of the terminal where FreeRADIUS runs in debug mode, while keeping it alive you can use *Ctrl+Z* to suspend the current job (radiusd -X) then execute the bg command to run it in the background. The terminal should now be available to you. To run FreeRADIUS again in the foreground simply execute the fg command.

Let's explore the debug output.

Access-Request arrives

When the packet arrives at the FreeRADIUS server it is indicated by the following part:

```
rad_recv: Access-Request packet from host 127.0.0.1 port 48698, id=73,
length=57
    User-Name = "alice"
    User-Password = "passme"
    NAS-IP-Address = 127.0.1.1
    NAS-Port = 100
```

We see that the incoming request contains four AVPs.

Although the AVP User-Password is shown here in clear text, it was not transmitted to the server in clear text. FreeRADIUS uses the shared secret to encrypt and decrypt the value of the User-Password AVP.

Authorization

After the request is received, the authorize section takes care of the request:

```
# Executing section authorize from file /etc/freeradius/sites-enabled/
default
 +- entering group authorize {...}
 ++[preprocess] returns ok
 ++[chap] returns noop
 ++[mschap] returns noop
 ++[digest] returns noop
 [suffix] No '@' in User-Name = "alice", looking up realm NULL
 [suffix] No such realm "NULL"
 ++[suffix] returns noop
 [eap] No EAP-Message, not doing EAP
 ++[eap] returns noop
 [files] users: Matched entry alice at line 137
 [files]   expand: Hello, %{User-Name} -> Hello, alice
 ++[files] returns ok
 ++[expiration] returns noop
```

```
++[logintime] returns noop
++[pap] returns updated
Found Auth-Type = PAP
```

The `authorize` section is defined inside a virtual server. Let's first look at some points about virtual servers in FreeRADIUS:

- Virtual servers are defined under the `sites-available` directory, which resides under the configuration directory of FreeRADIUS.
- Each virtual server is represented by a single text file.
- Virtual servers are activated by creating a soft link from the file in the `sites-available` directory to a file in the `sites-enabled` directory with the same name.
- This method is similar to that used by the Apache web server.
- The virtual server named `default` handles all the typical requests.
- Virtual servers are basically like having several RADIUS servers. One virtual server can even forward a request to another virtual server. This makes a FreeRADIUS installation extremely versatile and powerful.
- Each virtual server, including `default`, has various sections. A virtual server can contain the following sections nested inside the virtual server definition: `listen`, `client`, `authorize`, `authenticate`, `post-auth`, `pre-proxy`, `post-proxy`, `preacct`, `accounting`, and `session`.
- The `Access-Request` is first handled by the `authorize` section.

Authorize set Auth-Type

When the request is handled by the `authorize` section, various FreeRADIUS modules look at the AVPs contained in the `Access-Request`. These modules try to determine the mechanism and module to be used for authenticating the user. In our example `authorize` sets the `Auth-Type` to PAP.

If the `Access-Request` contained MS-CHAP attributes instead of the `User-Password` for instance, the `mschap` module would have detected this and set `Auth-Type = MS-CHAP`.

Authorization in action

The `authorize` section may decide to reject a request outright based on a decision on the presence or the value of a specified AVP. This will result in an `Access-Reject` packet returned to the client. There would then be no need for authentication.

Authentication

After the value of `Auth-Type` is set, the request is passed to the `authenticate` section:

```
# Executing group from file /etc/freeradius/sites-enabled/default
 +- entering group PAP {...}
 [pap] login attempt with password "passme"
 [pap] Using clear text password "passme"
 [pap] User authenticated successfully
 ++[pap] returns ok
```

Here we see that the `pap` subsection in the `authenticate` section is taking care of this request and returns `ok`.

Post-Auth

The `post-auth` section is done after authentication. You may use it to execute something:

```
# Executing section post-auth from file /etc/freeradius/sites-enabled/
default
 +- entering group post-auth {...}
 ++[exec] returns noop
```

Finish

The result is now sent back to the client:

```
Sending Access-Accept of id 73 to 127.0.0.1 port 48698
    Reply-Message = "Hello, alice"
Finished request 3.
```

Conclusion

Remember the following points when looking at the debug output:

◆ Main sections like `authorize`, `authenticate`, and `post-auth` start with a `# Executing`.

◆ These sections also indicate in which virtual server they reside.

◆ The `authorize` section sets the value of `Auth-Type`. This in turns determines which module inside the `authenticate` section will be used.

◆ The debug output of FreeRADIUS modules can be divided in two types. They are debug messages and return values.

◆ Debug messages are preceded by the module name, for example `[files] users: Matched entry alice at line 137`.

♦ Return values are preceded by ++[module_name] for example ++[files]
returns ok.

Have a go hero – using other authentication protocols

Since version 2.1.10 of FreeRADIUS the radtest client program allows you to specify an
authentication protocol to use.

If your FreeRADIUS installation is newer than 2.1.10 you can use the -t option to specify
chap and mschap and do the authenticate request again. Note how the debug feedback
from FreeRADIUS is now different when using the other authentication protocols.

The next section will look at different formats in which we can store a user's password.

Storing passwords

Username and password combinations have to be stored somewhere. The following list
mentions some of the popular places:

♦ **Text files**: You should be familiar with this method by now.

♦ **SQL databases**: FreeRADIUS includes modules to interact with SQL databases.
   MySQL is very popular and widely used with FreeRADIUS.

♦ **Directories**: Microsoft's Active Directory or Novell's e-Directory are typical
   enterprise-size directories. OpenLDAP is a popular open source alternative.

The users file and the SQL database that can be used by FreeRADIUS store the username
and password as AVPs. When the value of this AVP is in clear text, it can be dangerous if the
wrong person gets hold of it. Let's see how this risk can be minimized.

Hash formats

To reduce this risk, we can store the passwords in a hashed format. A hashed format of a
password is like a digital fingerprint of that password's text value. There are many different
ways to calculate this hash, for example MD5 or SHA1. The end result of a hash should be a
one-way fixed-length encrypted string that uniquely represents the password. It should be
impossible to retrieve the original password out of the hash.

To make the hash even more secure and more immune to dictionary attacks we can add a salt to the function that generates the hash. A salt is randomly generated bits to be used in combination with the password as input to the one way hash function. With FreeRADIUS we store the salt along with the hash. It is therefore essential to have a random salt with each hash to make a rainbow table attack difficult. The `pap` module, which is used for PAP authentication, can use passwords stored in the following hash formats to authenticate users:

Hash format	AVP name
Unix-style crypted password	`Crypt-Password`
MD5 hashed password	`MD5-Password`
MD5 hashed password with a salt	`SMD5-Password`
SHA1 hashed password	`SHA-Password`
SHA1 hashed password with a salt	`SSHA-Password`
Windows NT hashed password	`NT-Password`
Windows Lan Manager (LM) password	`LM-Password`

Both MD5 and SSH1 hash functions can be used with a salt to make it more secure.

Time for action – hashing our password

We will replace the `Cleartext-Password` AVP in the `users` file with a more secure hashed password AVP in this section.

There seems to be a general confusion on how the hashed password should be created and presented. We will help you clarify this issue in order to produce working hashes for each format.

A valuable URL to assist us with the hashes is the OpenLDAP FAQ:

> `http://www.openldap.org/faq/data/cache/419.html`

There are a few sections that show how to create different types of password hashes. We can adapt this for our own use in FreeRADIUS.

Crypt-Password

Crypt password hashes have their origins in Unix computing. Stronger hashing methods are preferred over crypt, although crypt is still widely used.

1. The following Perl one-liner will produce a crypt password for `passme` with the salt value of 'salt':

```
#> perl -e 'print(crypt("passme","salt")."\n");'
```

2. Use this output and change Alice's check entry in the `users` file from: `"alice"` `Cleartext-Password := "passme"` to: `"alice" Crypt-Password := "sa85/ iGj2UWlA"`

3. Restart the FreeRADIUS server in debug mode.

4. Run the authentication request against it again.

5. Ensure that `pap` now uses the crypt password by looking for the following line in the FreeRADIUS debug feedback:

```
[pap] Using CRYPT password "sa85/iGj2UWlA"
```

MD5-Password

The MD5 hash is often used to check the integrity of a file. When downloading a Linux ISO image you are also typically supplied with the MD5 sum of the file. You can then confirm the integrity of the file by using the `md5sum` command.

We can also generate an MD5 hash from a password. We will use Perl to generate and encode the MD5 hash in the correct format that is required by the `pap` module. The creation of this password hash involves external Perl modules, which you may have to install first before the script can be used. The following steps will show you how:

1. Create a Perl script with the following contents; we'll name it `4088_04_md5.pl`:

```perl
#! /usr/bin/perl -w
use strict;
use Digest::MD5;
use MIME::Base64;
unless($ARGV[0]){
  print "Please supply a password to create a MD5 hash from.\n";
  exit;
}
my $ctx = Digest::MD5->new;
$ctx->add($ARGV[0]);
print encode_base64($ctx->digest,'')."\n";
```

2. Make the `4088_04_md5.pl` file executable:

```
chmod 755 4088_04_md5.pl
```

3. Get the MD5 password for `passme`:

```
./4088_04_md5.pl passme
```

4. Use this output and update Alice's entry in the user's file to:

```
"alice" MD5-Password := "ugGBYPwm4MwukpuOBx8FLQ=="
```

5. Restart the FreeRADIUS server in debug mode.

6. Run the authentication request against it again.

7. Ensure that pap now uses the MD5 password by looking for the following line in the FreeRADIUS debug feedback:

```
[pap] Using MD5 encryption.
```

SMD5-Password

This is an MD5 password with salt. The creation of this password hash involves external Perl modules, which you may have to install first before the script can be used.

1. Create a Perl script with the following contents; we'll name it 4088_04_smd5.pl:

```perl
#! /usr/bin/perl -w
use strict;
use Digest::MD5;
use MIME::Base64;
unless(($ARGV[0])&&($ARGV[1])){
   print "Please supply a password and salt to create a salted MD5
hash from.\n";
   exit;
}
my $ctx = Digest::MD5->new;
$ctx->add($ARGV[0]);
my $salt = $ARGV[1];
$ctx->add($salt);
print encode_base64($ctx->digest . $salt ,'')."\n";
```

2. Make the 4088_04_smd5.pl file executable:

```
chmod 755 4088_04_smd5.pl
```

3. Get the SMD5 value for passme using a salt value of 'salt':

```
./4088_04_smd5.pl passme salt
```

Remember that you should use a random value for the salt. We only used salt here for the demonstration.

4. Use this output and update Alice's entry in the user's file to:

```
"alice" SMD5-Password := "Vr6uPTrGykq4yKig67v5kHNhbHQ="
```

5. Restart the FreeRADIUS server in debug mode.

6. Run the authentication request against it again.

7. Ensure that `pap` now uses the SMD5 password by looking for the following line in the FreeRADIUS debug feedback.

```
[pap] Using SMD5 encryption.
```

SHA-Password

SHA stands for **Secure Hash Algorithm**. SHA1 is most commonly used from the SHA series of cryptographic hash functions. It was designed by the **National Security Agency (NSA)** and published as their government standard. SHA-1 produces a 160-bit hash value. There was SHA-0 that had been withdrawn by the NSA shortly after publication and was superseded by SHA-1. There is also the SHA-2 series that features significant changes from SHA-1. SHA-2 includes the SHA-224, SHA-256, SHA-384, SHA-512 cryptographic functions. A new hash standard called SHA-3 is currently under development.

The creation of this password hash involves external Perl module, which you may have to install first before the script can be used.

1. Create a Perl script with the following contents; we'll name it `4088_04_sha1.pl`:

```perl
#! /usr/bin/perl -w
use strict;
use Digest::SHA1;
use MIME::Base64;
unless($ARGV[0]){
  print "Please supply a password to create a SHA1 hash from.\n";
  exit;
}
my $ctx = Digest::SHA1->new;
$ctx->add($ARGV[0]);
print encode_base64($ctx->digest,'')."\n";
```

2. Make the `4088_04_sha1.pl` file executable:

```
chmod 755 4088_04_sha1.pl
```

3. Get the SHA value for `passme`:

```
./4088_04_sha1.pl passme
```

4. Use this output and update Alice's entry in the user's file to:

```
"alice" SHA-Password := "/waczsxHgPn1JIkpJENLNV5Jp5k="
```

5. Restart the FreeRADIUS server in debug mode.

6. Run the authentication request again against it.

7. Ensure that pap now uses the SHA password by looking for the following line in the FreeRADIUS debug feedback:

```
[pap] Using SHA encryption.
```

SSHA-Password

This is an SHA password with salt. The creation of this password hash involves external Perl modules, which you may have to install first before the script can be used.

1. Create a Perl script with the following contents; we'll name it 4088_04_ssha1.pl:

```
#! /usr/bin/perl -w
use strict;
use Digest::SHA1;
use MIME::Base64;
unless(($ARGV[0])&&($ARGV[1])){
print "Please supply a password and salt to create a salted SHA1
hash from.\n";
exit;
}
my $ctx = Digest::SHA1->new;
$ctx->add($ARGV[0]);
my $salt = $ARGV[1];
$ctx->add($salt);
print encode_base64($ctx->digest . $salt ,'')."\n";
```

2. Make the 4088_04_ssha1.pl file executable:

```
chmod 755 4088_04_ssha1.pl
```

3. Get the SSHA value for passme using a salt value of 'salt':

```
./4088_04_ssha1.pl passme salt
```

Remember that you should use a random value for the salt. We only used salt here for the demonstration.

4. Use this output and update Alice's entry in the user's file to:

```
"alice" SSHA-Password := "bXUygZ+GToKwJysZyzghIEwf9tJzYWx0"
```

5. Restart the FreeRADIUS server in debug mode.

6. Run the authentication request against it again.

7. Ensure that pap now uses the SSHA password by looking for the following line in the FreeRADIUS debug feedback:

```
[pap] Using SSHA encryption.
```

NT-Password or LM-Password

The LM-Password AVP is used to store the LM hash of a user's password. The NT-Password AVP is used to store the NTLM hash of a user's password. The LM hash is the password hash that was used by Microsoft LAN Manager prior to Windows NT. The NTLM hash was introduced with Windows NT.

Due to their known flaws it is now recommended not to use them anymore. The flaws include vulnerability to pre-computed attacks because they do not use a salt. The password is also split up. This allows for fewer possibilities per chunk of the password, making it easier to guess.

Despite the flaws the LM hash and NTLM hash are still widely used because of the many legacy third-party CIFS implementations. Although not enabled, Windows Server 2008 still includes support for the LM hash.

To create an NT-Password or LM-Password hash we use the smbencrypt program, which is installed with FreeRADIUS. Because the NT-Password hash is more secure than the LM-Password hash we will use it here.

1. Get the NT-Password for passme by using the following command:

   ```
   smbencrypt passme
   ```

2. Use this output and update Alice's entry in the user's file to:

   ```
   "alice" NT-Password := "CED46D3B902D60F779ED78BFD90ED00A"
   ```

3. Restart the FreeRADIUS server in debug mode.

4. Run the authentication request against it again.

5. Ensure that pap now uses the NT password by looking for the following line in the FreeRADIUS debug feedback:

   ```
   [pap] NT-Hash of passme = ced46d3b902d60f779ed78bfd90ed00a
   ```

What just happened?

We have created and tested different hash formats for storing a user's password inside the users file.

Hash formats and authentication protocols

Hashing a password imposes limitations on the available authentication protocols that can use this password. As you have seen, PAP can be used with all of them. CHAP requires that the password be stored in clear text. MS-CHAP can only use clear text or NT-Password.

There is a nice authentication protocol and password encryption lookup grid at the following URL:

`http://deployingradius.com/documents/protocols/`
`compatibility.html`

Other authentication methods

There are two other authentication methods that are worth mentioning here. They are one-time passwords and certificates.

One-time passwords

FreeRADIUS includes a module called `rlm_otp` that can be used to handle OTP (one-time password) tokens. This module should be used in conjunction with additional programs. Unfortunately the company that contributed the code for the additional programs, Tri-D Systems, does not exist anymore. However, the code was forked and is now available from Google Code (`http://code.google.com/p/otpd/`).

If you want to implement your own one-time password functionality you can use a module like `rlm_perl` or `rlm_python` to handle the logic behind a one-time password. The NAS may still send `User-Name` and `User-Password` attributes to FreeRADIUS, but the way the `User-Password` is managed will be unique in order to handle a one-time password.

Certificates

Certificates do not involve the presentation of a username and password combination. EAP can use this as a sub-method. Certificates will be discussed in more detail in the EAP chapter.

Summary

This chapter looked at authentication in FreeRADIUS. Specifically, we have covered:

- **Authentication protocols**: There are three popular authentication protocols, namely, PAP, CHAP, and MS-CHAP. PAP is the least secure in certain situations but also the most versatile.

- **How FreeRADIUS handles Access-Requests**: When an `Access-Request` reaches the FreeRADIUS server the `authorize` section defined in the virtual server determines which authentication method will be used. The value of `Auth-Type` indicates which authentication section will be used.

◆ **Password storing**: Passwords do not need to be stored in clear text and it is better to store them in a hashed format. There are, however, limitations to the kind of authentication protocols that can be used when the passwords are stored as a hash.

Now that we've learned more about authentication, especially about the storing of usernames and passwords in the users file, we're ready to connect to alternative sources of usernames and passwords—which is the topic of the next chapter.

Pop quiz – authentication

1. You plan to implement EAP-TTLS-PAP for security on your Wi-Fi network. One of your fellow workers says PAP is a huge security risk. Is this true?

2. After you have decided to change all the cleartext passwords in the users file to SHA1 encrypted values, some dial-up users are complaining that they can no longer authenticate to the RAS server. What can be the problem?

3. Users are connecting to FreeRADIUS using PAP and MS-CHAP authentication protocols. State what password hash can you use to encrypt the user's password and name the program used to create it.

5
Sources of Usernames and Passwords

In the chapters up to now user details were kept in the `users` *file. The contents of this file were then used by FreeRADIUS to validate credentials during the authentication process. FreeRADIUS will most likely be part of an enterprise setup with existing users already created somewhere else. This chapter will look at ways to utilize existing user stores.*

In this chapter we shall:

- ◆ Look at user store options
- ◆ Use Linux system users as a user store for FreeRADIUS
- ◆ Use MySQL as a user store for FreeRADIUS
- ◆ Use LDAP as a user store for FreeRADIUS
- ◆ Use Microsoft Active Directory as a user store for FreeRADIUS

So let's get on with it...

User stores

A user store is a place where user details are kept. It is ideal to have a single user store with different systems making use of this single source. The need in the enterprise for such a store resulted in the directory. Novell's eDirectory, Microsoft's Active Directory, and OpenLDAP are all examples of directories.

In the WWW space popular web environments like Google and Facebook allow third parties to use their user stores through web services. This enables external web applications to use them for authentication.

FreeRADIUS allows us to incorporate external user stores. This reduces the administrative overheads involved with managing users and passwords. The following schematic shows different possibilities when configuring FreeRADIUS:

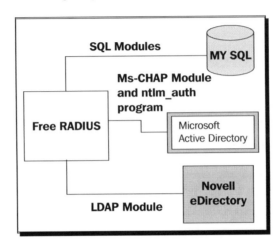

There are two ways in which FreeRADIUS can utilize user stores for authentication:

- By reading the contents of the store with the help of a FreeRADIUS module. The contents can then be used by other FreeRADIUS modules. The pap module for example uses information provided by the sql module for password verification.

- Interacting with the store by sending a user's credentials to a FreeRADIUS module or program to authenticate the user. The ldap module does this with Novell eDirectory. The mschap module uses the ntlm_auth program to interact with Microsoft Active Directory.

The rest of this chapter will be hands-on, to see how different user stores can be incorporated into FreeRADIUS.

System users

System users located on the server where FreeRADIUS is running can be used as a user store.

System users are traditionally associated with the /etc/password, /etc/shadow, and /etc/group files.

Linux machines can also use other means like NIS and LDAP, which allow a more central location of system users. This section, however, will focus on using system users defined locally on the server.

Time for action – incorporating Linux system users in FreeRADIUS

The FreeRADIUS documentation recommends that it runs as a non-privileged user. When we include the system users as a user store, this non-privileged user will need access to the /etc/shadow, file. Each of the three distributions has different default configurations with regards to the permissions and ownership of the /etc/shadow file.

Preparing rights

Ubuntu has the correct rights for the /etc/shadow file by default. In Ubuntu the /etc/shadow file is owned by the group called shadow which has read rights to the file. When FreeRADIUS installs, it adds a user and group called freerad. The user freerad is added to the shadow group, which allows freerad read access to /etc/shadow.

You can confirm this on Ubuntu by using the following commands. To check the ownership of the /etc/shadow file:

```
$> ls -l /etc/shadow
-rw-r----- 1 root shadow 743 2012-06-06 18:32 /etc/shadow
```

Confirm to which groups the freerad user belongs by using the following command:

```
$> getent group | grep freerad
shadow:x:42:freerad
freerad:x:112:
ssl-cert:x:113:freerad
```

SUSE is different

The SUSE README file distributed with FreeRADIUS recommends that you change the value of user and group in the radiusd.conf file to the following:

```
user = root
group = root
```

Although the /etc/shadow file in SUSE is owned by the shadow group, adding the non-privileged user under which FreeRADIUS runs to the shadow group does not yield the expected results. The README is there for a reason.

When user and group's values change

After you have changed the value of user and group in `radiusd.conf`, the following message will appear when restarting the server:

we do not own /var/run/radiusd/radiusd.sock

The problem lies with the ownership of the `radiusd` directory, since the `radiusd.sock` file does not even exist. Fix it by changing the `/var/run/radiusd` directory's ownership to that of the user specified in the `radiusd.conf` file. On SUSE the following command will fix the problem:`chown root. /var/run/radius`

CentOS

CentOS does not have a group called `shadow` and the `/etc/shadow` file is owned by user and `group root`. To allow the group that runs the FreeRADIUS server (`radiusd`) to read the `/etc/shadow` file, we will change the group ownership of `/etc/shadow` to radius. We then give read access on the `shadow` file to the group that owns it, by using the following commands:

```
chgrp radiusd /etc/shadow
chmod g+r /etc/shadow
```

This brings us to the end of environment preparation; now we can activate system users.

Activating system users

To include the system users as a user store in FreeRADIUS is a short and sweet process. Follow these steps:

1. Edit the `sites-enabled/default` file and uncomment `unix` under the `authorize` section.

2. Restart FreeRADIUS in debug mode.

3. Perform an authentication test using an existing system user on the Linux server. We assume `bob` is a system user, and his password is `passbob`.

   ```
   radtest bob passbob 127.0.0.1 100 testing123
   ```

4. Observe the debug output to see if the test was successful.

What just happened?

We have included the `unix` module in the `authorize` section of the `default` virtual server. This enables FreeRADIUS to check an incoming `Access-Request` against the system users defined on the server.

Let's investigate the debug output of FreeRADIUS to see how an `Access-Accept` could be returned.

Authorize using the unix module

In the debug output of FreeRADIUS the following line indicates that the `unix` module found a user called `bob` and updated some internal values in FreeRADIUS:

`++[unix] returns updated`

You can compare this with the output when `alice` who is defined in the `users` file authenticates:

`++[unix] returns notfound`

The `unix` module returned a known good password (in Crypt format), which can be used by the `pap` module to authenticate the user.

> If the `unix` module returns `notfound` even when the user is defined, confirm that the rights on the `/etc/shadow` file are correct. If it still fails, change the `user` and `group` lines in the `radius.conf` file to user `root`, restart FreeRADIUS, and try again.
>
> Also remember that Linux/Unix is case sensitive. This applies to usernames and passwords!

Authenticating using pap

The `authenticate` section of the debug output indicates that `pap` does the authentication with the known good password given by the `unix` module.

```
# Executing group from file /etc/freeradius/sites-enabled/default
+- entering group PAP {...}
[pap] login attempt with password "passbob"
[pap] Using CRYPT password "$6$SI3ZfzEr$M0ujsOhTAXT7LP5KzzYhHdFL4/
iJtfEdX31OeGJLbDDc.SQsTnl8yuOqB948DDvdKBScb7Mp8Myro5FeekgLw."
[pap] User authenticated successfully
++[pap] returns ok
```

Tips for including system users

There are a few important points to remember when including the system users as a user store:

◆ Only the PAP authentication protocol can be used. CHAP and MS-CHAP will not work.

◆ Linux systems use the /etc/shadow file to store the passwords. This file is not accessible to non-privileged users. When you run FreeRADIUS as a user other than root (as recommended) ensure this user can access the shadow file.

◆ SUSE is different and requires that FreeRADIUS be run as user and group root. This is specified in the radiusd.conf file.

◆ If you create system users that will exclusively be used by FreeRADIUS, it is good practice to change their default home directory and shell to be the same as the user nobody for security reasons.

Older Linux/Unix systems may use only the /etc/passwd file and not implement the shadow password database mechanism. The user passwords will then be stored with the user's details in the /etc/passwd file.

On those systems the second field of the /etc/passwd file will contain an encrypted password instead of an x.

In the /etc/shadow file's second field the following special characters may be found:

◆ NP or ! or null (No password)

◆ LK or * (Account is locked)

◆ !! (Password expired)

In the next section we will connect to a MySQL database using FreeRADIUS.

MySQL as a user store

FreeRADIUS can connect to an SQL database to retrieve a user's details. The FreeRADIUS SQL modules work in pairs. A *generic* SQL module makes use of a *specific* database module to interact with the database. This allows easy support for different databases.

Just as the files module uses the users file to retrieve information for authorization and authentication, so does the generic SQL module use the specific database module to retrieve the same type of information from a database.

MySQL is a very popular open source database. Despite speculation about its future under Oracle, it still remains a trustworthy database on which millions of people depend.

MySQL is easy to configure and most people are familiar with it. FreeRADIUS deployments with MySQL outnumber FreeRADIUS deployments with any other database. We are following this trend and will show you how to include a MySQL database as a user store.

Time for action – incorporating a MySQL database in FreeRADIUS

We assume that MySQL is not yet installed on the system where you have FreeRADIUS deployed. We will first install and then configure MySQL in order for it to be usable to FreeRADIUS.

Installing MySQL

Ensure that MySQL server is installed on your Linux machine. The following table can be used as a guideline to install MySQL on each of the three distributions discussed in this book:

Distribution	Command to install MySQL server
CentOS	`yum install mysql-server`
SUSE	`zypper install mysql`
Ubuntu	`sudo apt-get install mysql-server`

 MySQL server has a user called `root`, which by default does not have any password on the local machine. You are strongly encouraged to supply a password for this user.

Take note of the following points on each distribution:

- CentOS:
    - The `mysql-client` package may already be installed.
    - After MySQL server installs it needs to be started for the first time. Use the command `/etc/init.d/mysqld start`. The feedback message has instructions on how to add a password for the `root` user.
    - Ensure the MySQL server starts up after a reboot by using `/sbin/chkconfig mysqld on`.

- SUSE:
    - After MySQL server installs it needs to be started for the first time. Use the `rcmysql start` command. The feedback message has instructions on how to add a password for the `root` user.

- ❑ Ensure the MySQL server starts up after a reboot by using the `/sbin/chkconfig -a mysql` command.

- ◆ Ubuntu:

  - ❑ The `mysql-server` package is a meta-package, which will install the latest version of the MySQL server (MySQL 5.1 on Ubuntu 10.4).

  - ❑ The `mysql-server` package uses the `debconf` utility for user input. You will be asked to supply a password for the `root` user on the MySQL server during installation.

  - ❑ If you need to supply or change the `root` MySQL user's password later, then you can do so using the `dpkg-reconfigure mysql-server-5.1` command.

  - ❑ Ubuntu uses `Upstart` to start and stop MySQL. You can use the `sudo service mysql start` command to start and `sudo service mysql stop` command to stop the MySQL server. The startup configuration file for MySQL is in `/etc/init/mysql.conf`.

We can now continue to install the MySQL modules for FreeRADIUS (if required) and to prepare a database for FreeRADIUS to use.

Installing FreeRADIUS's MySQL package

CentOS and Ubuntu have separate FreeRADIUS packages that contain the specific `sql` module for MySQL (`rlm_sql_mysql`). Use the following table as a guideline to install them:

Distribution	Command to install FreeRADIUS's MySQL package
CentOS	`yum install freeradius2-mysql`
	Or
	`yum --nogpgcheck install freeradius-mysql-2.1.10-1.i386.rpm`
	(if built from source)
Ubuntu	`sudo apt-get install freeradius-mysql`
	Or
	`sudo dpkg -i freeradius-mysql_2.x.y+git_i386.deb`
	(if built from source)

Remember that you have to install FreeRADIUS's MySQL package, which is part of the FreeRADIUS build already installed. You cannot build and install the latest FreeRADIUS from source and then expect that the older package referenced by the package manager will install. For this reason we distinguish between the two in the previous table.

SUSE already includes the `rlm_sql_mysql` module as part of the `freeradius-server` package.

Preparing the database

FreeRADIUS supplies all the required files to prepare a database for its use.

The FreeRADIUS configuration directory contains a subdirectory called `sql`. Under the `sql` subdirectory are subdirectories for the various databases that FreeRADIUS supports. If there is only a directory for MySQL, it is because the FreeRADIUS packages supporting other databases are not installed.

1. To create the database named `radius`, issue the following command:

   ```
   mysqladmin -u root -p create radius
   ```

2. To create an admin user with the correct permissions for the radius database use the `admin.sql` file as a template and run it against the `radius` database. You are encouraged to change the default values. Use the following command:

   ```
   mysql -u root -p < /etc/raddb/sql/mysql/admin.sql
   ```

3. Create the schema for the database using the `schema.sql` file, by using the following command: *freeradius*

   ```
   mysql -u root -p radius < /etc/raddb/sql/mysql/schema.sql
   ```
   strict permission

4. Add Bob to the database as a test user.

   ```
   mysql -u root -p radius
   INSERT INTO radcheck (username, attribute, op, value) VALUES
   ('bob', 'Cleartext-Password', ':=', 'passbob');
   INSERT INTO radreply (username, attribute, op, value) VALUES
   ('bob', 'Reply-Message', '=', 'Hello Bob!');
   ```

If you are new to MySQL, there is a handy command called `mysqlshow` that you can use to get quick information. To get a list of the databases you can use:

`mysqlshow -u root`

You can then subsequently drill further down a database, table, and column in a table by adding arguments to the `mysqlshow` command (for example. `mysqlshow -u root radius radcheck`). Use this command to confirm the creation of the `radius` database with its tables.

> use radius
> Select * from radcheck
>   vad reply

Configuring FreeRADIUS

The SQL module breaks the FreeRADIUS tradition where a module's configuration is situated under the `modules` subdirectory under the FreeRADIUS configuration directory.

Connection information

The `sql.conf` file located in the FreeRADIUS configuration directory contains all the configuration options to connect to a database. If you have used the default values, you do not have to change anything in this file. You are, however, encouraged to go through the contents of this file in order to better understand the various directives that can be specified. This will also help to double-check and confirm the values used in the previous steps.

Including the SQL configuration

To let FreeRADIUS include the SQL module upon startup, uncomment the following line in `radiusd.conf`:

```
#$INCLUDE sql.conf
```

Virtual server

As stated previously, each virtual server contains main sections. To use the SQL module as a user store, uncomment the `sql` line in the `authorize` section in `sites-enabled/default`.

If you still have the `unix` section uncommented from the previous exercise, disable it again. Failing to do so will cause FreeRADIUS to authenticate `bob` using the system user's detail.

Testing the MySQL user store

Everything is configured and ready for us to test. Follow these steps to test the user store:

1. Restart FreeRADIUS in debug mode. Scan the debug output and check for `rlm_sql` feedback. This indicates that the SQL module is included.

2. Authenticate as `bob` using the `radtest` program:

```
radtest bob passbob 127.0.0.1 100 testing123
```

3. Observe the output from the FreeRADIUS server to see how the request is handled by `rlm_sql`.

What just happened?

We have configured and added a MySQL database to serve as a user store for FreeRADIUS. Let's look at some interesting points.

As stated at the beginning of this chapter, FreeRADIUS has two ways to use data stores. With the MySQL database, it reads the user's information from the database. This data can then be used by authentication modules like the `pap` module for password verification.

FreeRADIUS does not authenticate against the database, but rather uses the database as a store to keep user data. The database serves as a replacement or substitute for the `users` file.

 If it seems that the user's details do not originate from the MySQL database, confirm if you have disabled the `unix` module in the `authorize` section and observe the debug output for more information to locate the problem.

Advantages of SQL over flat files

Storing a user's details inside an SQL database has various advantages compared to storing them inside a flat file. The following are some of the advantages:

◆ **Scalable**: The database can be located on another server and is not required to be on the FreeRADIUS server.

◆ **User friendly**: There is a lot of web-based software available to manage the data in the database.

◆ **Flexible**: Users and attributes can be added or removed on the fly without the need to restart FreeRADIUS.

◆ **Manageable**: A user can be assigned to one or more groups in order to manage common attributes. The use of profiles is also possible.

◆ **Secure**: Sensitive information can be hashed and encrypted using built-in functions that are usually part of the SQL database engine.

Other uses for the SQL database

The SQL database is not only used to store user details in FreeRADIUS. Additional functions include:

◆ **Accounting**: We can write a user's accounting details to the database instead of flat files.

◆ **Usage control**: The `rlm_sqlcounter` module allows defining various counters (time or data based) to keep track of a user's usage.

◆ **NAS devices**: NAS devices defined by default in the `clients.conf` file can alternatively be stored in a database table.

◆ **IP pool management**: Adding extra tables to the database allows us to manage the IP leases with the help of the database.

Accounting and usage control are covered in a dedicated chapter later in the book.

Duplicate users

FreeRADIUS allows for different user stores to co-exist, but what happens when the same user is defined in different user stores?

This depends on the order in which the modules are listed in the `authorize` section. The last module's user details will be used by the authenticate section.

Unfortunately this rule does not work with all the modules. The `unix` module always sends its details of the duplicate user to the `authenticate` section no matter what the order is inside the `authorize` section.

With the default order a user defined in the SQL database will 'win' over one defined in the `users` file.

If you instead want the user defined in the `users` file to 'win' over a duplicate in the SQL database, the `files` module should be listed after the `sql` module.

The database schema

The SQL database contains the same type of details as the `users` file that is used by the `files` module. Just as with the `users` file we have `check` and `reply` items. These items are stored in the `radcheck` and `radreply` tables respectively.

Groups

The SQL database also allows us to define check and reply attributes for groups. These are stored in the `radgroupcheck` and `radgroupreply` tables respectively.

A user can now be assigned to zero or more of the defined groups. Groups are assigned through the `radusergroup` table. An entry into this table specifies a priority of a certain group to a user. This allows certain item values in groups with higher priorities (smaller values) to override item values in groups with lower priorities (larger values).

With this in mind, let's look at some practical examples.

Have a go hero – exploring group usage

This section covers more advanced aspects of the SQL database. We will cover the following through practical exercises:

- Group assignment
- Using the `Fall-Through` internal AVP
- Using the `User-Profile` internal AVP for profile assignment

Using SQL Groups

In this exercise we will add `bob` to the `students` group. The `students` group has a `check` attribute to test if `Access-Request` contains the `Framed-Protocol` AVP with a value of `PPP`. If the AVP is present and correct, we return a reply AVP:

1. Log into the radius MySQL database and issue the following SQL commands to create the required entries:

   ```
   delete from radcheck;
   delete from radreply;
   delete from radgroupreply;
   delete from radgroupcheck;
   delete from radusergroup;
   INSERT INTO radcheck (username, attribute, value,op) VALUES
   ('bob', 'Cleartext-Password', 'passbob',':=');
   INSERT INTO radreply (username, attribute, value,op) VALUES
   ('bob', 'Reply-Message', 'Hello Bob!','=');
   INSERT INTO radgroupreply (groupname, attribute, value,op) VALUES
   ('students', 'Reply-Message', 'Hello PPP protocol!',':=');
   INSERT INTO radgroupreply (groupname, attribute, value,op) VALUES
   ('students', 'Session-Timeout', '900',':=');
   ```

```
INSERT INTO radgroupcheck (groupname, attribute, value,op) VALUES
('students', 'Framed-Protocol', 'PPP','==');

INSERT INTO radusergroup (username, groupname, priority) VALUES
('bob', 'students', 10);
```

2. Authenticate as bob using the radtest program but add a 1 at the end. This will cause the Access-Request packet to include the AVP of Framed-Protocol = PPP:

```
radtest bob passbob 127.0.0.1 100 testing123 1
```

3. You should get an Access-Accept packet with a Reply-Message of Reply-Message = "Hello PPP protocol!".

4. Authenticate again as bob, but this time exclude the 1. You should still get an Access-Accept packet with a Reply-Message of Reply-Message = "Hello Bob!".

You may have expected the request to be rejected when the Framed-Protocol AVP is missing or of a different value. Radgroupcheck works differently from radcheck, in the following way:

◆ When a check attribute is defined in radcheck, and it does not match, or is missing, the request fails and an Access-Reject is returned.

◆ When a check attribute is defined in radgroupcheck and it does not match, or is missing, the request passes, but the reply attributes in radgroupreply is not returned.

This behavior makes it possible for one user to belong to many groups and depending on which radgroupcheck attributes pass, that group's reply attributes will be returned with the reply.

As a reminder on the values of the op field, you can stick to the following rules until we get to the chapter on Authorization.

Reply items contain = and check items that need to match incoming AVPs use == while others use :=. If you want a reply item to override an existing one, use :=.

Radgroupcheck items are logically ANDed. The first one to fail will cause the group not to return any reply attributes.

Controlling the use of groups

By default the SQL module checks if there are groups assigned to a user if the user is present in the `radcheck` table. This behavior can be controlled in two ways:

1. To turn this off globally, set the value of the `read_groups` directive to `no` in the `sql.conf` file.

2. To activate the checking for assigned groups again for an individual user, specify `Fall-Through = Yes` in the `radreply` table.

Try this by first setting `read_groups` to `no`. Restart FreeRADIUS and authenticate as Bob. Even after adding the `1` to the `radtest` command you should still get "`Hello Bob!`".

Add the following SQL query:

```
INSERT INTO radreply (username, attribute, value,op)
VALUES ('bob', 'Fall-Through', 'Yes','=');
```

This will cause the SQL module to check for groups assigned to Bob. When you add the `1` at the end of the `radtest` command you should now get "`Hello PPP protocol!`".

The preceding scenarios happen with normal authentication when a user is defined with a password in the `radcheck` table and all the checks pass.

When things go wrong, for instance if the password is not correct, or there are checks defined in `radcheck` that do not pass, or the user is not even listed in the `radcheck` table, the SQL module will then check for groups assigned to the user.

Remember the following two points when a user is not in the `radcheck` table or when required AVPs specified in `radcheck` do not match. These points are not affected by the value of `read_groups` in the `sql.conf` file. This means it happens whether you like it or not.

- The SQL module checks if there are groups assigned to a user when it cannot find the user in the `radcheck` table.

- The SQL module checks if there are groups assigned to a user when the `radcheck` items defined for the user did not match.

Reply-Message AVP

When you specify a `Reply-Message` AVP in the `radgroupreply` it will be returned even when a user supplies the wrong password but when a `radgroupcheck` 'sub test' passes. The `Reply-Message` AVP is special since it is the only AVP that can accompany the `Access-Reject` packet in RADIUS. Other AVPs specified in the `groupreply` will not be returned with the `Access-Reject` packet even when a `radgroupcheck` 'sub test' passes.

Profiles

Profiles can be created in SQL and then be assigned to a user in two ways:

- By specifying a default profile for all users in the `sql/mysql/dialup.conf` file through the `default_user_profile` directive

- By specifying a profile explicitly for a user in the form of the `User-Profile` check attribute

A profile is a user that is a member of at least one group. This user does not require any entries in the `radcheck` and `radreply` tables. Let's modify the database so that bob will make use of a profile:

1. Log into the RADIUS MySQL database and issue the following SQL commands to create the required entries:

   ```
   delete from radcheck;
   delete from radreply;
   delete from radgroupreply;
   delete from radgroupcheck;
   delete from radusergroup;
   INSERT INTO radcheck (username, attribute, value,op) VALUES
   ('bob', 'Cleartext-Password', 'passbob',':=');
   INSERT INTO radcheck (username, attribute, value,op) VALUES
   ('bob', 'User-Profile', 'student_profile',':=');
   INSERT INTO radgroupreply (groupname, attribute, value,op)
   VALUES ('students', 'Reply-Message', 'Hello Student!','=');
   INSERT INTO radusergroup (username, groupname, priority) VALUES
   ('student_profile', 'students', 10);
   ```

2. Re-activate the reading of the groups by changing the `read_groups` back to the default of `yes` in `sql.conf`.

3. Restart FreeRADIUS in debug mode.

4. Authenticate as bob using the `radtest` program:

   radtest bob passbob 127.0.0.1 100 testing123

A reply message intended for the user `student_profile` should be returned.

The value of the `User-Profile` AVP is that of a user who is a member of at least one group. In our example the profile user is called `student_profile` and it is a member of the `students` group.

The `radgroupcheck` and `radgroupreply` attributes assigned to the students will then be applied to any user who has check attribute `User-Profile := student_profile`. The user `student_profile` is used here as a profile rather than a normal user.

This section touched on important points on the use of the SQL modules in FreeRADIUS. In the next section we will use an LDAP directory as a user store.

LDAP as a user store

Directories are designed for fast reading. They are stricter compared to databases when it comes to the data types they can contain. Directories are organized according to a hierarchical structure. Directories can store user details, which can be queried and authenticated against. Directories are also designed to replicate easily. This makes directories the ideal user store.

LDAP is a protocol for accessing a directory over a TCP/IP network. It can be used to store public e-mail addresses, authenticate users, manage digital certificates, and supply information about the nodes or devices on a network. Novell's eDirectory and Microsoft Active Directory both contain an LDAP server component. An alternative to this is the open source OpenLDAP project. OpenLDAP is a very mature project with reliable LDAP software used in many places and by many projects. The server component is called `slapd`. This section will use a very basic `slapd` server to demonstrate the use of LDAP as a user store in FreeRADIUS.

 LDAP is a loose term and can be used for the protocol to access a directory or the directory itself, depending on the context. This is similar to RADIUS.

Time for action – connecting FreeRADIUS to LDAP

The following sections will show you how to connect FreeRADIUS to LDAP.

Installing slapd

Ensure `slapd` is installed on your Linux server. The following table can be used as a guideline to install `slapd` on each of the three distributions discussed in this book:

Distribution	Command to install slapd LDAP server
CentOS	`yum install openldap-servers openldap-clients`
SUSE	`zypper install openldap2 openldap2-client`
Ubuntu	`sudo apt-get install slapd ldap-utils`

After `slapd` is installed we need to configure it.

Configuring slapd

To get `slapd` up and running we will use a bare minimum `slapd.conf` file. This is only for demonstration purposes; do not use it in a production environment.

 The proper configuration of `slapd` is beyond the scope of this book. This chapter will only help to configure a very basic `slapd` LDAP server.

CentOS

Follow these steps to configure slapd on CentOS:

1. Make a backup of the original `slapd.conf` file:

   `cp /etc/openldap/slapd.conf /etc/openldap/slapd.conf.orig`

2. Edit the contents of `slapd.conf` so that it contains the following:

   ```
   include        /etc/openldap/schema/core.schema
   include        /etc/openldap/schema/cosine.schema
   include        /etc/openldap/schema/inetorgperson.schema
   include        /etc/openldap/schema/nis.schema

   pidfile        /var/run/openldap/slapd.pid
   argsfile       /var/run/openldap/slapd.args
   database       bdb
   suffix         "dc=my-domain,dc=com"checkpoint   1024    5
   cachesize      10000
   rootdn         "cn=Manager,dc=my-domain,dc=com"
   rootpw         secret
   directory      /var/lib/ldap
   ```

3. Start `slapd` by using the following command:

   `/etc/init.d/ldap start`

4. Ensure `slapd` is running by observing the output of this command:

   `ps aux | grep slapd`

5. Ensure `slapd` starts up after a reboot by using the following command:

   `/sbin/chkconfig ldap on`

SUSE

Follow these steps to configure slapd on SUSE:

1. Make a backup of the original `slapd.conf` file:

`cp /etc/openldap/slapd.conf /etc/openldap/slapd.conf.orig`

2. Edit the contents of `slapd.conf` to contain the following:

```
include     /etc/openldap/schema/core.schema
include     /etc/openldap/schema/cosine.schema
include     /etc/openldap/schema/inetorgperson.schema
include     /etc/openldap/schema/nis.schema

pidfile     /var/run/slapd/slapd.pid
argsfile    /var/run/slapd/slapd.args

database    bdb
suffix      "dc=my-domain,dc=com"
checkpoint  1024    5
cachesize   10000
rootdn      "cn=Manager,dc=my-domain,dc=com"
rootpw      secret
directory   /var/lib/ldap
```

3. Start `slapd` by using the following command:

`/etc/init.d/ldap start`

4. Ensure `slapd` is running by observing the output of the following command:

`ps aux | grep slapd`

5. Ensure `slapd` starts up after a reboot by using the following command:

`/sbin/chkconfig -a ldap`

Ubuntu

Version 2.3 and higher of `slapd` have introduced a new way to handle configuration. The old way that used a configuration file (`slapd.conf`) is now replaced with an alternative that allows you to adjust and configure the server while it is running. These settings then become part of the server without requiring a restart.

Ubuntu took the plunge and was one of the first distributions to adopt this new way of configuring `slapd`. Fortunately we can still use the simpler `slapd.conf` file. To keep things uniform across the three distributions we will revert Ubuntu's `slapd` configuration back to using `slapd.conf`.

1. To revert back to `slapd.conf`, edit the `/etc/default/slapd` file and change the `SLAPD_CONF=` entry to `SLAPD_CONF=/etc/ldap/slapd.conf`.

2. Create a file called `slapd.conf` in the `/etc/ldap` directory with the following contents:

   ```
   include         /etc/ldap/schema/core.schema
   include         /etc/ldap/schema/cosine.schema
   include         /etc/ldap/schema/inetorgperson.schema
   include         /etc/ldap/schema/nis.schema

   pidfile         /var/run/slapd/slapd.pid
   argsfile        /var/run/slapd/slapd.args
   modulepath      /usr/lib/ldap
   moduleload      back_bdb.la

   database        bdb
   suffix          "dc=my-domain,dc=com"
   checkpoint      1024    5
   cachesize       10000
   rootdn          "cn=Manager,dc=my-domain,dc=com"
   rootpw          secret
   directory       /var/lib/ldap
   ```

3. Ensure this file is owned by the `openldap` user and group:

   ```
   sudo chown openldap. /etc/ldap/slapd.conf
   ```

4. Start `slapd` by using the following command:

   ```
   sudo /etc/init.d/slapd start
   ```

5. Ensure `slapd` is running by observing the output of the following command:

   ```
   ps aux | grep slapd
   ```

6. Ensure `slapd` starts up after a reboot with the following command:

   ```
   sudo update-rc.d slapd enable
   ```

Let's look at a few of the important configuration items in `slapd.conf`:

- The `include` lines are used to source schema definitions. (We will cover schemas in the next section.)

- We also specify a `pidfile`. This file contains the process ID of `slapd`.

- `argsfile` specifies the file containing the arguments of `slapd`.

- `database` specifies which backend we will use for `slapd`. We use the Berkeley DB (**bdb**). There are also others available but we will use the most common one.

- The `cachesize` and `checkpoint` entries are applied to the database. `cachesize` specifies the size of the in-memory cache (we specified `1000` entries, which is the default). `checkpoint` specifies two values. The `1024` is a kilobyte value and `5` is a minute value. Whichever comes first will cause the database to flush its cache buffers and write to disk.

- `suffix` specifies a common root that all entries in the database will contain. Queries with a DN ending in "dc=my-domain,dc=com" will be passed to this backend.

- `rootdn` and `rootpw` is like an administrator user with its password. This user will not be subjected to any access control or restrictions specified in the configuration.

We should now have a basic `slapd` server configured and running. The rest of this section will be common across the distributions.

Adding the radiusProfile schema

Object classes used in LDAP must be defined in order for LDAP to know the structure and attributes that an object class can contain. The object classes mentioned in LDAP are not related to those used with Object Oriented Programming (OOP). Each entry inside the LDAP directory should belong to at least one object class. The object class of an entry will dictate what attributes the entry should have and also those attributes that the entry can have. One entry can belong to many object classes.

Object classes are defined in `.schema` text files and located under the `schema` directory. They are in a way similar to the `dictionary` files used by FreeRADIUS. You can also define and include your own object classes.

Schema files also need to be included in the `slapd.conf` file in order for `slapd` to know about them. Consult the sample `slapd.conf` file to locate the schema directory on your distribution.

FreeRADIUS includes a schema file for the `radiusProfile` object class. This has to be included in the `slapd.conf` file and `slapd` has to be restarted. When you include this file, take care over two important points:

- The location of this file is different on each distribution.

- The file is named `openldap.schema` but there is already a schema file called `openldap.schema` in OpenLDAP. Rename the `openldap.schema` file of FreeRADIUS to `freeradius.schema` when you copy it to the `slapd` schema directory.

The following table can be used to locate the `openldap.schema` file on each distribution:

Distribution	Location of openldap.schema
CentOS	`/usr/share/doc/freeradius-<version>/examples/openldap.schema`
SUSE	`/usr/share/doc/packages/freeradius-server-doc/examples/openldap.schema`
Ubuntu	`/usr/share/doc/freeradius/examples/openldap.schema`

Let's take Ubuntu as an example:

1. Copy the `openldap.schema` file as `freeradius.schema` to `/etc/ldap`:

   ```
   sudo cp /usr/share/doc/freeradius/examples/openldap.schema /
   etc/ldap/schema/freeradius.schema
   ```

2. Edit the `slapd.conf` file to include the `freeradius.schama` file:

   ```
   include /etc/ldap/schema/freeradius.schema
   ```

3. Restart `slapd` by using the following command:

   ```
   sudo /etc/init.d/slapd restart
   ```

Including the `freeradius.schema` file in `slapd.conf` allows us to also store RADIUS attributes in the LDAP directory. These attributes can then be used by FreeRADIUS.

 In is not compulsory for an LDAP directory to have the `radiusProfile` schema extension. It allows for powerful configurations especially in the authorization section of FreeRADIUS.

Populating the LDAP directory

LDAP has a standard format called LDAP Data Interchange Format (LDIF) that is used to add or modify the directory's data. Wikipedia describes LDIF as the following:

`http://en.wikipedia.org/wiki/LDAP_Data_Interchange_Format`

LDIF is a standard plain text data interchange format for representing LDAP directory content and update requests. LDIF conveys directory content as a set of records, one record for each object (or entry). It represents update requests, such as Add, Modify, Delete, and Rename, as a set of records, one record for each update request.

We will use this LDIF format to create the following structure with some users:

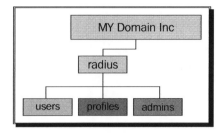

The graphic shows a tree structure with the following:

◆ The root of the tree is the organization called **My Domain Inc**. It belongs to the `dcObject` and `organization` object classes.

◆ Attached to the root of the tree is an organizational unit called **radius** that contains three sub-organizational units: **users**, **profiles**, and **admins**. An organizational unit is like a folder; it belongs to the `organizationalunit` object class.

◆ The **users** organizational unit contains three users: `student1`, `student2`, and `student3`. These users belong to the `person` and `radiusProfile` object classes.

◆ The **profile** organizational unit contains two user templates: `students` and `teachers`. These templates also belong to the `person` and `radiusProfile` object classes but will act as a group to which a user under the `users` organizational unit can belong.

◆ The **admins** organizational unit contains a user that FreeRADIUS will use to bind with to the LDAP directory. The rights of this user can be fine-tuned for maximum security. This user does not require to belong to the `radiusProfile` object class.

Here are the contents of the LDIF file:

```
dn: dc=my-domain,dc=com
dc: my-domain
description: Tutorial for FreeRADIUS
objectClass: dcObject
objectClass: organization
o: My Domain Inc

dn: ou=radius,dc=my-domain,dc=com
objectclass: organizationalunit
ou: radius
dn: ou=profiles,ou=radius,dc=my-domain,dc=com
objectclass: organizationalunit
ou: profiles
```

```
dn: ou=users,ou=radius,dc=my-domain,dc=com
objectclass: organizationalunit
ou: users

dn: ou=admins,ou=radius,dc=my-domain,dc=com
objectclass: organizationalunit
ou: admins

dn: cn=students,ou=profiles,ou=radius,dc=my-domain,dc=com
objectclass: radiusProfile
objectClass: person
cn: students
sn: students
radiusSessionTimeout: 900
radiusReplyItem: ChilliSpot-Bandwidth-Max-Up = "393216"
radiusReplyItem: ChilliSpot-Bandwidth-Max-Down = "393216"
radiusCheckItem: ChilliSpot-Version == "1.0"
radiusReplyMessage: "Good day student"

dn: cn=teachers,ou=profiles,ou=radius,dc=my-domain,dc=com
objectclass: radiusProfile
objectClass: person
cn: teachers
sn: teachers
radiusSessionTimeout: 3600
radiusReplyItem: ChilliSpot-Bandwidth-Max-Up = "1048576"
radiusReplyItem: ChilliSpot-Bandwidth-Max-Down = "1048576"
radiusCheckItem: ChilliSpot-Version == "2.0"
radiusReplyMessage: "Good day teacher"

dn: cn=student1,ou=users,ou=radius,dc=my-domain,dc=com
objectclass: radiusProfile
objectClass: person
cn: student1
sn: student1
userPassword: student1
description: Test user with cleartext password student1
radiusGroupName: students

dn: cn=student2,ou=users,ou=radius,dc=my-domain,dc=com
objectclass: radiusProfile
objectClass: person
cn: student2
sn: student2
userPassword: {CRYPT}saCsqST0rezXE
description: Test user with CRYPT password student2
radiusGroupName: students
radiusGroupName: teachers
```

```
dn: cn=student3,ou=users,ou=radius,dc=my-domain,dc=com
objectclass: radiusProfile
objectClass: person
cn: student3
sn: student3
userPassword: {SHA}Mr5L7b06hTlQOpu75y+dhJVq/6E=
description: Test user with SHA password student3
radiusGroupName: students
radiusGroupName: disabled

dn: cn=binduser,ou=admins,ou=radius,dc=my-domain,dc=com
objectclass: person
sn: freeradius
cn: binduser
userPassword: binduser
```

Do the following in order to populate the directory:

1. Create a file called `4088_05_ldap.ldif` with the LDIF text above as its contents. The best location for this file will probably be your home directory.

2. Add it to the LDAP directory by using the following command:

   ```
   ldapadd -x -D 'cn=Manager,dc=my-domain,dc=com' -w secret -f
   4088_05_ldap.ldif
   ```

All the preparation work for the LDAP server is now complete. The next steps will prepare FreeRADIUS to use this directory as a user store.

Installing FreeRADIUS's LDAP package

CentOS and Ubuntu have separate FreeRADIUS packages that contain the `ldap` module (`rlm_ldap`). Use the following table as a guideline to install them.

Distribution	Command to install FreeRADIUS's LDAP package
CentOS	`yum install freeradius2-ldap`
	`yum --nogpgcheck install freeradius-ldap-2.1.10-1.i386.rpm`
	(if built from source)
Ubuntu	`sudo apt-get install freeradius-ldap`
	`sudo dpkg -i freeradius-ldap_2.x.y+git_i386.deb`
	(if built from source)

SUSE already includes the `rlm_ldap` module as part of the `freeradius-server` package.

Configuring the ldap module

To configure the `ldap` module you have to edit the `ldap` configuration file under the `modules` directory. Change the following directives:

Directive	Value
server	127.0.0.1
identity	cn=binduser,ou=admins,ou=radius,dc=my-domain,dc=com
password	binduser
basedn	ou=users,ou=radius,dc=my-domain,dc=com
filter	(cn=%{%{Stripped-User-Name}:-%{User-Name}})

The values must be in quotes, for example:

```
server = "127.0.0.1"
```

Do not change the rest of the file, the default values will work correctly.

Testing the LDAP user store

The moment of truth is very close, we just need to include LDAP in the `authorize` and `authenticate` sections of the virtual server and test it:

1. Edit the `sites-enabled/default` file in the FreeRADIUS configuration directory. Under the `authorize` section, uncomment `ldap`.

2. Under the `authenticate` section uncomment:
   ```
   Auth-Type LDAP {
           ldap
   }
   ```

3. Restart FreeRADIUS in debug mode.

4. Try to authenticate as `student1` using the `radtest` program:
   ```
   radtest student1 student1 127.0.0.1 100 testing123
   ```

5. Observe the debug output of the FreeRADIUS server.

Although it took some preparation we finally utilized the LDAP user store in FreeRADIUS.

What just happened?

The `ldap` module of FreeRADIUS has been connected to `slapd` to authorize and authenticate `student1`.

Let's take a look at some interesting points while revisiting the debug output of the FreeRADIUS server.

Binding as a user

The configuration of the `ldap` module caused the following to happen:

- LDAP was included in the `authorize` section of the virtual server. This caused the `ldap` module to bind to `slapd` using the identity we specified in the `ldap` configuration file.

- `slapd` was queried to check if `student1` exists. This query was formulated by using the `basedn` value and the `filter` value specified in the `ldap` configuration file.

- The query was successful. This caused the `ldap` module to:
    - Add the `Ldap-UserDn` internal attribute in the check items list
    - Set `Auth-Type = LDAP`
    - Return `ok`

- When FreeRADIUS entered the `authenticate` section, it used `LDAP` to perform the authentication. Authentication is done by trying to bind with the `Ldap-UserDn` attribute and the password supplied in the `Access-Request`.

- If the bind was successful it returns an `Access-Accept` packet.

- If the bind was not successful it returns an `Access-Reject` packet.

 To summarize the process: The `authorize` section searches for the user, finds it, adds `Ldap-UserDn` check attribute, and changes `Auth-Type = LDAP`. The `authenticate` section binds to the LDAP server with `Ldap-UserDn` and password supplied in the `Access-Request` packet.

The above process seems simple but it can break easily if you do not stick to the basics. A golden rule in FreeRADIUS configuration is to change as little possible.

Beware of old documentation! Do not use old or unreliable sources to configure FreeRADIUS and LDAP. If a document instructs you to change or add the Non-Protocol Integer Translations to a dictionary file, you are on dangerous ground!

As with the system user store only the PAP authentication protocol will work. CHAP and MS-CHAP will not work.

Advanced use of LDAP

The ldap module's configuration causes it to bind as the user to verify credentials. To bind as a user will be sufficient for a typical authenticate scenario and should work with most LDAP servers.

There is, however, more we can do, especially when the LDAP server has the radiusProfile schema extension. If a user belongs to the radiusProfile object class we can specify AVP check or reply attributes for a specified user inside the LDAP directory. This is similar to storing it in the users file or in an SQL database.

Also if the LDAP server stores the userPassword attribute in cleartext we can even use the LDAP server in much the same way as the users file or the SQL database. This does not necessarily require that the user belong to the radiusProfile object and is configurable to specify which LDAP attribute should be mapped to the userPassword AVP.

Have a go hero – explore advanced use of LDAP

During the preparation of slapd, we included the schema file for the radiusProfile object class. This extended the server's schema. The radiusProfile object class allows for the inclusion of check and reply AVPs in LDAP objects.

This is unfortunately not straightforward. The names of RADIUS AVPs do not match the names of LDAP attributes. To map the one to the other, FreeRADIUS uses the ldap. attrmap file. In this file you can see RADIUS AVPs with their corresponding LDAP attribute name. Let's look at a line from the file:

```
checkItem        Auth-Type                        radiusAuthType
```

This specifies that the RADIUS Auth-Type AVP (used as a check item) maps to the LDAP radiusAuthType attribute.

Not all RADIUS AVPs are listed in this file. The file, however, also lists the special `radiusProfile` attributes `radiusCheckItem` and `radiusReplyItem`. These two LDAP attributes allow you to specify any other RADIUS AVP not specified in the attribute map. In our LDIF file we used these attributes to specify some AVPs. Here's how we specified the `ChilliSpot-Version` AVP with a value of 2.0:

```
radiusCheckItem: ChilliSpot-Version == "2.0"
```

Ldap-Group and User-Profile AVP

The `Ldap-Group` internal AVP is used to specify a group check. We will specify it in the users file although it can also be specified in other modules.

The `User-Profile` internal AVP can contain a DN instead of a normal text string for its value. When this happens it causes the `ldap` module to query the LDAP directory for the DN during authorization. The `radiusCheckItems` and `radiusReplyItems` of the query's return will be used to create the user's profile.

`Ldap-Group` and `User-Profile` are usually paired together. First an LDAP search is done to check if a user is part of an `Ldap-Group`. If true, the specified `User-Profile` is assigned. If not true, the specified `User-Profile` is not assigned.

Let's make use of it:

1. Edit the `users` file and add the following to the bottom:

    ```
    DEFAULT Ldap-Group == disabled, Auth-Type := Reject
        Reply-Message = "Account disabled"

    DEFAULT Ldap-Group == teachers, User-Profile := "cn=teachers,ou
    =profiles,ou=radius,dc=my-domain,dc=com"
        Fall-Through = no

    DEFAULT Ldap-Group == students, User-Profile := "cn=students,ou
    =profiles,ou=radius,dc=my-domain,dc=com"
        Fall-Through = no
    ```

2. Edit the `ldap` module's configuration file and change the following part from:

    ```
    # groupname_attribute = cn
    # groupmembership_filter = "(|(&(objectClass=Gro.....
    # groupmembership_attribute = radiusGroupName
    ```

    to:

    ```
    groupname_attribute = radiusGroupName
    groupmembership_filter = "(cn=%{%{Stripped-User-Name}:-%{User-
    Name}})"
    groupmembership_attribute = radiusGroupName
    ```

3. Restart FreeRADIUS in debug mode and authenticate `student1`, `student2`, and `student3` observing the feedback each time.

Let's look at some important points:

◆ When you add the `DEFAULT` entries to the `users` file, add the one that sets `Auth-Type := Reject` at the top.

◆ More privileged groups should follow next, ending with the least privileged groups.

◆ This arrangement makes it possible to assign `student2` (Martin Prince) to the `teachers` as well as the `students` group.

◆ When `Ldap-Group` is specified it causes the `file` module to use the `ldap` module to determine if a user is part of the group by checking the LDAP user's `radiusGroupName` attribute.

◆ If the user is part of the `Ldap-Group`, the `User-Profile` will be assigned to the user. A `User-Profile` specified as a DN causes the `ldap` module to search for the DN during authorization:

```
[ldap] performing search in cn=teachers,ou=profiles,ou=radius,d
c=my-domain,dc=com, with filter (objectclass=radiusprofile)
```

◆ The return values of the search are then used to build the user's profile with check and reply AVPs.

The next part will look at ways to retrieve passwords from an LDAP directory.

Reading passwords from LDAP

The `ldap` module can be configured to read a user's password directly from the LDAP server and then pass this value on to other modules in the authentication section as a 'known good password'. This enables us to bypass the process where the `ldap` module tries to bind with the `Ldap-UserDn` attribute to verify credentials.

To do this we need to do the following:

1. Edit the `ldap` module's configuration file and add the `auto_header = yes` directive. This will allow the `pap` module to figure out the password's hash if present.

2. Edit the `ldap` module's configuration file and uncomment the following line:

```
#password_attribute = userPassword
```

This specifies which LDAP attribute contains the user's password.

3. Edit the `ldap` module's configuration file and ensure the following is set:

```
set_auth_type = no
```

This prevents the `ldap` module from setting `Auth-Type := LDAP`.

4. Add the following line to the `ldap.attrmap` file:

```
checkItem          Cleartext-Password                 userPassword
```

This will return the `userPassword` LDAP attribute as `Cleartext-Password` AVP.

5. Restart FreeRADIUS in debug mode and try to authenticate with `student1`, `student2`, and `student3`, observing the feedback of the different password hashes each time.

6. If the `radtest` program you use supports the `-t` switch (FreeRADIUS version 2.1.10 and higher) you can also test the results of CHAP and MS-CHAP authentication on the different password hashes. CHAP and MS-CHAP should only work on `student1` and not on `student2` and `student3`.

Reading the password from LDAP instead of binding to authenticate has some advantages:

◆ If the password is stored as cleartext in LDAP, it allows us to also use the CHAP and MS-CHAP authentication protocols.

◆ It is faster because binding as a user to LDAP is not required.

◆ If the user on the LDAP server's `userPassword` is encrypted but the `sambaLmPassword` and `sambaNtPassword` attributes are present and have the same value, we should be able to use MS-CHAP. This is found in a typical `Samba` server with `slapd` as the backend.

There are, however, things to watch out for. Some of them are:

◆ Security; use a secure LDAP connection when transmitting the passwords over the network, especially cleartext passwords.

◆ Not all LDAP servers support the reading of the `userPassword` attribute since it is a security risk. If you do decide to go this route, fine-tune the security on the LDAP server to make it very strict in order to avoid that horrible surprise when a hacker steals all your passwords. Beware also of the use of web management software that may be vulnerable to LDAP injections.

You will typically use the bind as a user method to Novell's eDirectory and Microsoft's Active Directory. The `userPassword` attribute will be read if you can get a cleartext password from LDAP and would like to use the CHAP and MSCHAP protocols.

Novell's eDirectory includes the **Universal Password** (**UP**) feature that allows FreeRADIUS to extract a user's cleartext password from the directory. This, however, requires some specific configuration tweaks on the eDirectory.

This section on LDAP has covered a lot. There are some topics not discussed here but the comments in the `ldap` configuration file and the Wiki pages should be more than sufficient to help.

The next section will help you to use Active Directory as a user store in FreeRADIUS.

Active Directory as a user store

Although Microsoft Active Directory includes an LDAP server, using LDAP excludes MS-CHAP authentication. The use of Active Directory as a user store enables the use of PAP and MS-CHAP authentication.

Configuring FreeRADIUS to use Active Directory as a user store consists of two main activities:

◆ Configure a Samba server and join it to an Active Directory domain.
◆ Configure FreeRADIUS to call the `ntlm_auth` binary to authenticate a user.

Samba is the standard Windows interoperability suite of programs for Linux and UNIX. It is a very mature project, which is in active development (`http://www.samba.org/`).

In this exercise we will join a Samba server to an Active Directory domain. This Samba server will appear as another Windows server to the Active Directory. The Samba server contains a component called Winbind that solves the unified logon problem (`http://www.samba.org/samba/docs/man/Samba-HOWTO-Collection/winbind.html`).

We will make use of Winbind to allow users defined in the Active Directory to authenticate on the Linux server.

Time for action – connecting FreeRADIUS to Active Directory

The following sections will demonstrate how to connect FreeRADIUS to Microsoft Active Directory.

Installing Samba

Ensure Samba and Winbind are installed on your Linux server. The following table can be used as a guideline for installing Samba and Winbind on each of the three distributions discussed in this book:

Distribution	Command to install Samba server
CentOS	`yum install samba`
SUSE	`zypper install samba samba-winbind`
Ubuntu	`sudo apt-get install samba winbind`

After Samba and Winbind are installed we need to configure them.

Configuring Samba

This section should be used as a guideline. It assumes a working Active Directory domain called `fr.com`, which we will join. The following table lists some detail of the setup:

Setting/item	Comment
Active Directory Domain	Name: fr.com
	Domain Controller: dc.fr.com
	Domain Controller IP: 192.168.1.250
	DNS server for domain: 192.168.1.250
Linux `/etc/resolv.conf` file	This file is used to define the DNS servers on Linux. It is important to use the Active Directory as `nameserver` and also specify the `domain` and `search` components.
	nameserver 192.168.1.250
	domain fr.com
	search fr.com

Samba and Winbind are configured through the `/etc/samba/smb.conf` file. The following can be used as an example:

```
[global]
    workgroup = FR
    realm = FR.COM
    preferred master = no
    server string = Ubuntu FreeRADIUS Test Machine
    security = ADS
    encrypt passwords = yes
    log level = 3
    log file = /var/log/samba/%m
    max log size = 50
    printcap name = cups
    printing = cups
    winbind enum users = Yes
    winbind enum groups = Yes
```

```
winbind use default domain = Yes
winbind nested groups = Yes
winbind separator = +
idmap uid = 600-20000
idmap gid = 600-20000
template shell = /bin/bash
```

Restart the `smbd`, `nmbd`, and `winbind` services after you have completed the changes to `smb.conf`. Also ensure that these services will start up after a reboot. You can use services like `slapd` and FreeRADIUS, which were discussed already, as a pattern to make sure the start-up scripts are activated.

Joining the domain

To join the Samba server to the Active Directory domain, follow these steps:

1. You need the domain administrator's password to join the domain:

   `net ads join -U Administrator`

2. Confirm whether domain users are now available to the Samba server. The following command should list them:

   `wbinfo -u`

3. Test authentication to the domain with the `wbinfo` command test. `Billy` is a domain user with password `passbilly`:

   `wbinfo -a billy%passbilly`

4. FreeRADIUS will use the `ntlm_auth` binary to test authentication against the domain. Authenticate `billy` by using the following command:

   `ntlm_auth --request-lm-key --domain=FR.COM --username=billy --password=passbilly`

Sometimes joining the Active Directory can be troublesome. Here are a few things to check:

◆ Is the time the same on both systems? Kerberos does not like large time differences. Try to fix this by either synchronizing the system times to an external NTP server, or using `net time set` on the Linux machine.

◆ Is the DNS working correct and can both systems ping each other by hostname and FQDN?

◆ Some available tutorials included configuration for Kerberos but on my servers it just worked without any extra configuration. YMMV.

◆ Ensure the `smbd`, `nmbd`, and `winbind` services are running, especially after a reboot. This will require you to confirm that the start-up scripts are activated.

As a final activity we need to set the permissions for the user who runs the FreeRADIUS server. Unfortunately the way to do this is different on each distribution. Let's look at each one.

CentOS

The directory is `/var/cache/samba/winbindd_privileged`. Give group ownership to the `radiusd` group by using the following command:

```
chgrp radiusd /var/cache/samba/winbindd_privileged
```

SUSE

The directory is `/var/lib/samba/winbindd_privileged`. Give group ownership to the `radiusd` group by using the following command:

```
chgrp radiusd /var/lib/samba/winbindd_privileged
```

Ubuntu

The directory is `/var/run/samba/winbindd_privileged`. This directory is owned by a group called `winbind_priv`. Make the `freerad` user a member of this group by using the following command:

```
sudo adduser freerad winbindd_priv
```

This completes the first main activity. Now we can configure FreeRADIUS.

> Remember that this section was a textbook example. In the real world it may not always be that simple to join a domain. This is because not all Active Directories are configured the same and not all networks look the same. The Samba website contains a lot of documentation to help when things do not work as intended. It is essential that you are able to use the `ntlm_auth` command to test authentication before continuing further.

FreeRADIUS and ntlm_auth

FreeRADIUS can use the `ntlm_auth` binary in two ways:

- ◆ For PAP authentication, include an `exec` section that calls the `ntlm_auth` binary.
- ◆ For MS-CHAP authentication, modify the MS-CHAP module's configuration file to specify `ntlm_auth` for authentication.

PAP Authentication

FreeRADIUS includes a text file called `ntlm_auth` under the `modules` directory. This file contains an `exec` section called `ntlm_auth`:

```
exec ntlm_auth {
    wait = yes
    program = "/path/to/ntlm_auth --request-nt-key --domain=MYDOMAIN
--username=%{mschap:User-Name} --password=%{User-Password}"
}
```

The name of the `exec` section can be anything, but naming it `ntlm_auth` helps to identify the program that will be called by the `exec` module. Modify the program directive to reflect your set up:

```
"/usr/bin/ntlm_auth --request-nt-key --domain=FR.COM
--username=%{mschap:User-Name} --password=%{User-Password}"
```

To configure FreeRADIUS to utilize the Active Directory user store with PAP, do the following:

1. Edit the `sites-enabled/default` file and add this section beneath the `authorize → pap` line:

    ```
    if(!control:Auth-Type) {
        update control {
            Auth-Type = "ntlm_auth"
        }
    }
    ```

    This entry uses `unlang` which is covered extensively in the chapter on authorization. The expression indicates that if none of the above modules have already set the value of `Auth-Type`, it should be set to `ntlm_auth`.

2. We also need to add an `Auth-Type`, called `NTLM_AUTH` to the authenticate section of the `sites-enabled/default` file:

    ```
    Auth-Type NTLM_AUTH {
        ntlm_auth
    }
    ```

    This creates an `Auth-Type` called `NTLM_AUTH` which uses the `ntlm_auth` exec section to perform the authentication.

    The value of `Auth-Type` is not case sensitive, which allows us to follow the convention to have it in uppercase although the `unlang` entry in the `authorize` section is lowercase.

3. Restart FreeRADIUS in debug mode and try to authenticate with an Active Directory user.

The feedback will indicate how the `Auth-Type` is set and the `ntlm_auth exec` section is called to do the authentication:

```
++? if (!control:Auth-Type)
? Evaluating !(control:Auth-Type) -> TRUE
++? if (!control:Auth-Type) -> TRUE
++- entering if (!control:Auth-Type) {...}
+++[control] returns noop
++- if (!control:Auth-Type) returns noop
Found Auth-Type = NTLM_AUTH
# Executing group from file /etc/raddb/sites-enabled/default
+- entering group NTLM_AUTH {...}
[ntlm_auth]    expand: --username=%{mschap:User-Name} ->
--username=billy
[ntlm_auth]    expand: --password=%{User-Password} ->
--password=passbilly
Exec-Program output: NT_STATUS_OK: Success (0x0)
Exec-Program-Wait: plaintext: NT_STATUS_OK: Success (0x0)
Exec-Program: returned: 0
++[ntlm_auth] returns ok
```

MS-CHAP Authentication

During MS-CHAP authentication the `mschap` module extracts an `NT-Password` hash supplied by the user. To verify that it is correct the module can do one of three things:

- Take a user's `Cleartext-Password` and make an `NT-Password` hash from it, then compare this with the one from MS-CHAP.

- If the user's password is already stored as an `NT-Password` AVP, compare this to the one from MS-CHAP.

- Configure the `ntlm_auth` directive of the `mschap` module. This will use the `ntlm_auth` binary to authenticate against the Active Directory domain.

The first two methods have already been discussed in previous chapters. Configuring the `ntlm_auth` directive is easy. Just follow these steps:

1. Edit the `modules/mschap` file and uncomment the following line:

```
ntlm_auth = "/path/to/ntlm_auth --request-nt-key
--username=%{mschap:User-Name} --challenge=%{mschap:Challen
ge:-00} -nt-response=%{mschap:NT-Response:-00}"
```

2. Replace `/path/to/ntlm_auth` with the actual path to `ntlm_auth` on your server (`/usr/bin/ntlm_auth`).

3. This will tell the `mschap` module to use `ntlm_auth` instead of the other two methods for credential verification.

4. If there are still users elsewhere whom you want to authenticate using the `mschap` module, you must ensure that they have the check attribute `MS-CHAP-Use-NTLM-Auth := No`. The entry for `alice` will now look like this:

   ```
   "alice" Cleartext-Password := "passme", MS-CHAP-Use-NTLM-Auth
   := No
   ```

5. `MS-CHAP-Use-NTLM-Auth` is an internal AVP used to control the behavior of the `mschap` module.

6. Restart FreeRADIUS in debug mode.

7. Try to authenticate with an Active Directory user using the MS-CHAP protocol.

 Version 2.1.10 and upward of FreeRADIUS allows you to specify MS-CHAP authentication with `radtest` (`-t mschap`). Should the running FreeRADIUS server be an earlier version, do a latest install elsewhere and use the newer `radtest` to authenticate remotely. Another alternative is to use the **JRadius Simulator** program (`http://coova.org/JRadius/Simulator`).

Summary

This chapter is large and has covered a lot of matter. With a typical deployment you would probably use one or two user stores. As a summary let's revisit important points on each user store discussed here.

Linux system users

The `unix` module (`rlm_unix`) needs access to the `/etc/shadow` file to be able to read the user's encrypted password. This encrypted password is used by the `pap` module to authenticate the user. CHAP and MS-CHAP authentication will not work; only PAP authentication works with system users.

SQL database

FreeRADIUS supports various SQL databases. It does this through a combination of a generic SQL module and a database-specific SQL module. The database is used purely as a data store and keeps the same type of data as the `users` file. A user can belong to one or more groups. This eases management. The `User-Profile` attribute of a user allows us to assign a profile to a user. Profiles are more flexible than adding a user to a group.

LDAP directory

LDAP can be used in two ways:

◆ The first method is to use 'bind as user' for authentication. This way is supported by all LDAP servers but limits us to PAP authentication.

◆ The second method is by reading attributes like the `userPassword` attribute and allowing other modules to use it as a 'known good password'. If the required attributes are readable and in the correct format it allows the use of other authentication protocols like CHAP and MS-CHAP. Unfortunately this is a security risk and also not supported by all LDAP servers.

Active Directory

Active Directory integration depends on the Winbind component of Samba. When Winbind runs correctly it enables us to use the `ntlm_auth` binary to authenticate against the domain. The `ntlm_auth` binary is used by the `exec` module (`rlm_exec`) for PAP authentication and by the `mschap` module (`rlm_mschap`) for MS-CHAP authentication.

All the chapters up to now have covered the various aspects of authentication and a bit on authorization. In the next chapter we will learn all about accounting.

Pop quiz – user stores

1. You have inherited a FreeRADIUS server with an existing MySQL user store. The previous owner did not make use of the `radgroucheck` and `radgroupreply` tables. You want to use them and do a test run but it seems that nothing has changed. What could the problem be?

2. On an Ubuntu server you would rather run PostgreSQL instead of MySQL. You try to see if there are any sample database structures available for PostgresSQL but only `mysql` is listed under the `/etc/freeradius/sql` directory. Why is this?

3. Your manager asks if it is possible for you to use a database instead of text files to authenticate against. Is his question technically correct?

4. You have a `slapd` server, which stores the `userPassword` attribute in cleartext. How can you make it more secure while keeping the cleartext passwords?

5. Someone has told you that you need to enable **Universal Password** on **Novell eDirectory** before you can use **Novell eDirectory** as a user store. Can this be true?

6. You have configured the FreeRADIUS server to use `ntlm_auth` for both PAP and MS-CHAP. PAP works fine, but MS-CHAP fails with a message about `'Ensure permissions on /var/run/samba/winbindd_privileged are set correctly'`. How can we fix this?

7. You have just completed the section in this chapter on how to include Active Directory as a user store. It works like a charm. During the night there is a major power failure; now after a restart nothing works. Where should you start to troubleshoot?

6
Accounting

The previous chapters have covered much ground on authentication as well as some aspects of authorization. This chapter is all about accounting.

In this chapter we shall:

- ◆ See how basic accounting works in FreeRADIUS
- ◆ See how to limit a user's sessions
- ◆ Discover ways to limit a user's usage
- ◆ Look at the housekeeping of accounting data

So let's get on with it...

Requirements for this chapter

You need a working FreeRADIUS server to do the practical exercises on; a clean installation is preferred.

Basic accounting

Accounting refers to tracking of the consumption of NAS resources by users. Accounting does not only include cost recovery in the form of billing. It can also be used for capacity planning, to generate trend graphs, and to know more about the resource usage at a given point in time. In this chapter, we will see how accounting is done in FreeRADIUS.

FreeRADIUS is a AAA server. AAA in RADIUS can be grouped into two components. One component consists of authorization and authentication, which uses UDP port 1812. The second component is accounting and uses UDP port 1813. These two components function independently of each other. The different `listen` sections in the `radiusd.conf` file confirm this. The following is the `listen` section for accounting:

```
#  This second "listen" section is for listening on the accounting
#  port, too.
#
listen {
        ipaddr = *
#       ipv6addr = ::
          port = 0
          type = acct
#       interface = eth0
#       clients = per_socket_clients
}
```

This `listen` section causes FreeRADIUS to listen for accounting requests. For more information about `listen` sections in general, refer to the comments inside `radiusd.conf`.

Notice `port = 0` in the `listen` code. When `port` is specified as 0, FreeRADIUS will read the value of the port from the `/etc/services` file. You can, however, override this value during start-up by passing the `–p <port number>` argument, which will force the FreeRADIUS server to only listen on the specified port.

The `/etc/services` file is used to map port numbers and protocols to service names.

radius	1812/tcp	
radius	1812/udp	
radius-acct	1813/tcp	radacct # Radius Accounting
radius-acct	1813/udp	radacct

The `/etc/services` file refers to port 1645 and 1646 as `old-radius` and `old-radacct` respectively. These ports are still used sometimes by other RADIUS servers.

The extract above indicates that FreeRADIUS is by default able to handle accounting requests. Let's see how accounting is done.

Time for action – simulate accounting from an NAS

In *Chapter 3, Getting Started with FreeRADIUS* we covered the `radclient` command. This section creates three files that can be used with `radclient` in order to simulate the accounting packets an NAS typically sends to a RADIUS server.

Files for simulation

The AVPs inside the three files are similar to the AVPs sent from the `hostapd` program.

 `hostapd` is a daemon used for controlling authentication on Wi-Fi networks. It can be configured to do accounting along with authentication and is typically installed with **OpenWRT** on **Atheros**-based Wi-Fi access points. You can also use it to turn a Wi-Fi NIC into an access point on Linux.

When a user's session starts, the NAS will inform the RADIUS server. During the session the NAS may send updates on the session to the RADIUS server and then when the session ends the NAS will also inform the RADIUS server.

Inside these accounting packets is the `Acct-Status-Type` AVP, which will reflect the session status of `Start`, `Interim-Update`, and `Stop`. This corresponds to the three files we will create. The following file, named `4088_06_acct_start.txt`, will create a session:

```
Packet-Type=4
Packet-Dst-Port=1813
Acct-Session-Id = "4D2BB8AC-00000098"
Acct-Status-Type = Start
Acct-Authentic = RADIUS
User-Name = "alice"
NAS-Port = 0
Called-Station-Id = "00-02-6F-AA-AA-AA:My Wireless"
Calling-Station-Id = "00-1C-B3-AA-AA-AA"
NAS-Port-Type = Wireless-802.11
Connect-Info = "CONNECT 48Mbps 802.11b"
```

The following file, named `4088_06_acct_interim-update.txt`, will update the session:

```
Packet-Type=4
Packet-Dst-Port=1813
Acct-Session-Id = "4D2BB8AC-00000098"
Acct-Status-Type = Interim-Update
Acct-Authentic = RADIUS
User-Name = "alice"
```

```
NAS-Port = 0
Called-Station-Id = "00-02-6F-AA-AA-AA:My Wireless"
Calling-Station-Id = "00-1C-B3-AA-AA-AA"
NAS-Port-Type = Wireless-802.11
Connect-Info = "CONNECT 48Mbps 802.11b"
Acct-Session-Time = 11
Acct-Input-Packets = 15
Acct-Output-Packets = 3
Acct-Input-Octets = 1407
Acct-Output-Octets = 467
```

And finally, the following file, named `4088_06_acct_stop.txt`, will end the session:

```
Packet-Type=4
Packet-Dst-Port=1813
Acct-Session-Id = "4D2BB8AC-00000098"
Acct-Status-Type = Stop
Acct-Authentic = RADIUS
User-Name = "alice"
NAS-Port = 0
Called-Station-Id = "00-02-6F-AA-AA-AA:My Wireless"
Calling-Station-Id = "00-1C-B3-AA-AA-AA"
NAS-Port-Type = Wireless-802.11
Connect-Info = "CONNECT 48Mbps 802.11b"
Acct-Session-Time = 30
Acct-Input-Packets = 25
Acct-Output-Packets = 7
Acct-Input-Octets = 3407
Acct-Output-Octets = 867
Acct-Terminate-Cause = User-Request
```

By using these three files with the `radclient` program we can now explore various aspects of FreeRADIUS accounting.

Starting a session

When an NAS receives an `Access-Accept` packet from the RADIUS server, the NAS tries to match the `Identifier` field with that of a pending `Access-Request`. If a match is found, and the NAS is configured for accounting, the NAS will send a `Code 4` RADIUS packet (`Accounting-Request`) to the RADIUS server. This marks the start of the session. Let's imitate this action from the NAS by using `radclient`:

1. Start FreeRADIUS in debug mode.

2. Use the `radclient` command and the `4088_06_acct_start.`
`txt` file to send an `Accounting-Request` to FreeRADIUS:

`$>radclient 127.0.0.1 auto testing123 -f 4088_06_acct_start.txt`

3. Observe the output of both FreeRADIUS and the `radclient` command.
Here is the feedback from `radclient` indicating the request was
successful by returning `Code 5 (Accounting-Response)`:

`Received response ID 66, code 5, length = 20`

4. Confirm there is an active session for alice by issuing the `radwho` command.
You have to be the root user to be able to issue this command.

Depending on how FreeRADIUS was compiled and the distribution you are using, the
`radwho` command may return an error. If this is the case follow the next section to
fix it:

5. Despite being root you get the following error:

`radwho: Error reading /var/log/radius/sradutmp: No such file or`
`directory`

6. The `sradutmp` file does not exist because the `sradutmp` module is disabled
inside the `accounting` section of the `sites-enabled/default` virtual
server. Activate `sradutmp` by uncommenting the following line:

`#sradutmp`

7. Restart FreeRADIUS in debug mode again. Issue the `radclient` and `radwho`
commands as before. You should now see something like the following:

`#radwho`

Login	Name	What	TTY	When	From	Location
alice	alice	shell	S0	Sun	16:34	127.0.0.1

The active session of alice is now reflected through `radwho`. Next we will end this active
session with a stop request.

Ending a session

When a user logs out or when their session times out, the NAS will send a stop request to
the RADIUS server in order for the accounting details to reflect the events that happened on
the NAS. Follow these steps to end a request:

1. Ensure the FreeRADIUS server is still running in debug mode.

2. Use the `radclient` command and the `4088_06_acct_stop.txt` file to send a request to FreeRADIUS:

   ```
   $>radclient 127.0.0.1 auto testing123 -f 4088_06_acct_stop.txt
   ```

3. Confirm the session is closed by checking the output from `radwho`:

   ```
   # radwho

   Login     Name     What    TTY    When    From     Location
   ```

Orphan sessions

Sometimes it may happen that an NAS hangs. When the NAS is reset later, the accounting information on FreeRADIUS still reflects the old state. You can use the `radzap` command to close any open accounting records on FreeRADIUS. Let's see `radzap` in action:

1. Use the `radclient` command and the `4088_06_acct_start.txt` file to start a session on FreeRADIUS:

   ```
   $>radclient 127.0.0.1 auto testing123 -f 4088_06_acct_start.txt
   ```

2. Confirm the open session with the `radwho` command:

   ```
   # radwho

   Login     Name     What    TTY    When    From     Location
   alice     alice    shell   S0     Sun     16:58    127.0.0.1
   ```

3. Now you can zap all active sessions from 127.0.0.1 by using the following command:

   ```
   radzap -N 127.0.0.1 127.0.0.1 testing123
   ```

   Radwho will show that there are no active sessions now.

If you look at the feedback of the FreeRADIUS server when `radzap` is issued you will see that it sends the following request:

```
rad_recv: Accounting-Request packet from host 127.0.0.1 port 43629,
id=195, length=38
    Acct-Status-Type = Accounting-Off
    NAS-IP-Address = 127.0.0.1
    Acct-Delay-Time = 0
```

This brings us to the end of the practical exercises on basic accounting. A detailed discussion will follow next.

What just happened?

We sent accounting requests to the FreeRADIUS server using the `radclient` command in a way similar to how an NAS will do. We have also simulated a scenario where an NAS hung, leaving the accounting data on FreeRADIUS out of synchronization with the state of the NAS. Let's look at some interesting points while referring to the exercise we have just completed.

Independence of accounting

Accounting in FreeRADIUS is independent from authorization and authentication. It uses a separate port and consists of `Accounting-Request` packets sent by the client to the server. The server responds with `Accounting-Response` packets to acknowledge the requests.

Accounting data is used to measure usage on a network. An NAS can report on the time a user is connected to the network as well as the data usage of the user.

Accounting records do not reflect details like websites a user has visited during a session. They only indicate time and data usage.

NAS: important AVPs

Although the AVPs sent by an NAS vary, some AVPs are important and should be present in the `Accounting-Request`.

Acct-Status-Type

This attribute indicates whether this `Accounting-Request` marks the beginning of the user service (`Start`) or the end (`Stop`). Each option is represented by a specific number. When a session starts it will be specified as 1 (`Start`). When the session's data is updated it will be specified as 3 (`Interim-Update`) and when the session ends it will be specified as 2 (`Stop`). `Acct-Status-Type` can also contain values like `Accounting-On` (represented by 7) and `Accounting-Off` (represented by 8) to close all open sessions for an NAS. The value of `Acct-Status-Type` determines the way FreeRADIUS will manipulate a user's accounting data.

Acct-Session-Id

`Acct-Session-Id` is used to uniquely identify a user's session. This is used in combination with `Acct-Status-Type` to record the status of a user's session. While the value of `Acct-Status-Type` changes to reflect the status (`Start`, `Interim-Update`, or `Stop`) of the session, the value of `Acct-Session-Id` remains the same throughout the session.

AVPs indicating usage

The following table shows the AVPs inside the `Accounting-Request` packet, which reflect the usage of a user:

AVP	Description
Acct-Session-Time	The duration of the session
Acct-Input-Octets	Bytes send from the user to the NAS
Acct-Output-Octets	Bytes send from the NAS out to the user

These three AVPs indicate the time and data usage of a user. They are only present in packets with `Acct-Status-Type = Interim-Update` or `Acct-Status-Type = Stop`. Packets with `Acct-Status-Type = Start` cannot contain them.

NAS: included AVPs

The AVPs that will be included with an `Accounting-Request` depend on the value of `Acct-Status-Type`. When a session is started there is no need to send AVPs that indicate time and data usage. These AVPs are included only on subsequent requests.

The `Stop` request will typically indicate the termination cause:

```
Acct-Terminate-Cause = User-Request
```

The AVPs that are included also depend on the NAS. Sometimes an NAS does not include required AVPs (**Hostapd**) and sometimes it swaps the input and output around (**Chillispot**). You are never sure what an NAS will bring to the server. Because of this it is always best to first test and see which AVPs are included and if the client may need extra configuration for the accounting to work as intended.

 Sometimes there will be an AVP present called `Acct-Delay-Time`. The value of this AVP can be used by the RADIUS server to adjust the start and stop times when recording a session's detail. It is usually present when an NAS has difficulty sending the `Accounting-Request` to the RADIUS server and it has to resend the request. If the value of `Acct-Delay-Time` is large you should investigate why this is so.

FreeRADIUS: pre-accounting section

When FreeRADIUS receives an `Accounting-Request` it is first passed to the `preacct` section. This section is defined in the virtual server's file. Like most of the FreeRADIUS configuration the default works just fine but if you would like to manipulate AVP values for a user, this is the place to do so. The comments inside the `preacct` section indicate what can be done in this section.

One interesting module is the `preprocess` module (`rlm_preprocess`). This module brings back sanity to a request's AVPs when it is needed. In our example it added the NAS-IP-Address AVP because it was missing. This AVP is required to be in the `Accounting-Request` as per RFC 2866.

> *Either* NAS-IP-Address *or* NAS-Identifier *MUST be present in a RADIUS* Accounting-Request.

The `acct_unique` entry makes sure each request has a semi-unique identifier by determining a value for `Acct-Unique-Session-ID`.

Realms

The `preacct` section is also very important when you are forwarding accounting requests to another RADIUS server. The `suffix` module (instance of the `realm` module) is used to identify and trigger the routing of such traffic. There are also IPASS and `ntdomain` listed, but commented out, which are both instances of the `realm` module. `suffix`, IPASS, and `ntdomain` are each looking for a unique pattern inside the User-Name AVP to determine the realm of the request. The forwarding of traffic to other RADIUS servers will be covered in depth in *Chapter 12, Roaming and Proxying*.

Setting Acct-Type

You can also use the `files` module in the `preacct` section. This module will be used to set the `Acct-Type` internal AVP. The `Acct-Type` AVP is used to separate accounting traffic inside the `accounting` section by forcing it to be handled by different instances of a module. This is the same principle as where the `Auth-Type` internal AVP can be set in the `authorize` section in order to specify which authentication method in the `authenticate` section to use. You can read more about the use of this feature on the following URL:

`http://freeradius.org/radiusd/doc/Acct-Type`

FreeRADIUS: accounting section

After the `Accounting-Request` has been handled by the `preacct` section it will be passed over to the `accounting` section. This is also defined in the virtual server's file. This is the section where we have activated the `sradutmp` module. The `accounting` section does the actual logging of accounting data. There are various ways to do this. By default it will be logged as text files using the `detail` module. We can, however, also specify that it should rather be logged to an SQL database using the `sql` module. This section can also be used to record the usage of a user (the `daily` module). The usage can then be used to determine the authorization outcome.

You are encouraged to read through the comments in the accounting section to see what the included modules do.

Minimising orphan sessions

When an NAS hangs it is unable to send any requests to a RADIUS server. Upon restarting the NAS should send `Acct-Status-Type = Accounting-On`. Upon normal shut-down it should send `Acct-Status-Type = Accounting-Off`. This makes accounting records more robust and reliable. The `radzap` command simulates a normal shutdown of an NAS and is used to close orphan sessions.

radwho

Depending on how FreeRADIUS was compiled, the `radwho` command may expect the presence of a `sradutmp` file in the FreeRADIUS log directory. We have to enable `sradutmp` in the accounting section in order for this file to be present. This is because of sensitive information inside the `radutmp` file and was covered in *Chapter 3, Getting Started with FreeRADIUS*.

radzap

The `radzap` command like `radwho` may also require the presence of a `sradutmp` file in the FreeRADIUS log directory. It has various switches, but not all of them may work. Use `radzap` with care when `zapping` an NAS that is still working, for example, using `radzap` with the `-N <NAS IP Address>` switch. This could result in the NAS requesting FreeRADIUS to update sessions that are already closed. This is especially true when you use `sql` for accounting.

With this we conclude the section on basic accounting. The next section will look at a way to limit a user's sessions.

Limiting a user's simultaneous sessions

Isaac is a **Wireless Internet Service Provider (WISP)** and his income depends on having as many users as possible because he charges a monthly subscription. Alice is his client. She gives her credentials to Bob who lives next door and so they both connect at the same time. Isaac needs to put an end to this or else he will have to close his WISP and code HTML for food!

Time for action – limiting a user's simultaneous sessions

The `default` virtual server defined in the `sites-enabled/default` file has a session section:

```
#   Session database, used for checking Simultaneous-Use.
#   Either the radutmp or rlm_sql module can handle this.
#   The rlm_sql module is *much* faster
session {
        radutmp
        #
        #  See "Simultaneous Use Checking Queries" in sql.conf
        #  sql
}
```

We want a fast system, so we'll use the recommended `sql`. To use SQL as a session database we also need to use `sql` for accounting.

1. Ensure you have a working SQL database configuration as described in *Chapter 5*.

2. Edit the `sites-enabled/default` file, and make the following changes. We will not use SQL as a user store, so comment out `sql` in the `authorize` section.

3. Uncomment `sql` in the `accounting` section. This will result in accounting requests written into the SQL database.

4. Uncomment `sql` in the `session` section and also comment `radutmp` out in the session section. This enables `sql` and disables `radutmp`.

5. We also need to specify the SQL query that will be executed. This is in the `sql/mysql/dialup.conf` file. Uncomment the following part:

```
#simul_count_query = "SELECT COUNT(*) \
#FROM ${acct_table1} \
#WHERE username = '%{SQL-User-Name}' \
#AND acctstoptime IS NULL"
```

6. Modify the `users` file so that alice is limited to one session:

```
"alice" Cleartext-Password := "passme",Simultaneous-Use := 1
```

7. Restart FreeRADIUS. Make sure that FreeRADIUS connects well to the MySQL database.

8. Initialize a session for alice using `radclient` and `4088_06_acct_start.txt`:

```
$>radclient 127.0.0.1 auto testing123 -f 4088_06_acct_start.txt
```

9. Confirm that there is an open session for alice:

```
# radwho
Login      Name      What    TTY  When    From       Location
alice      alice     shell   S0   Sun     22:25      127.0.0.1
```

10. Try to authenticate as alice using `radtest`. You should now receive an `Access-Reject` packet because the session limit has been reached:

```
$>radtest alice passme 127.0.0.1 100 testing123
Sending Access-Request of id 177 to 127.0.0.1 port 1812
User-Name = "alice"
User-Password = "passme"
NAS-IP-Address = 127.0.0.2
NAS-Port = 100
rad_recv: Access-Reject packet from host 127.0.0.1 port 1812,
id=177, length=68
Reply-Message = "\r\nYou are already logged in - access denied\r\
n\n"
```

11. Terminate all active sessions by using the `radzap` command:

```
# radzap -N 127.0.0.1 127.0.0.1 testing123
Received response ID 175, code 5, length = 20
```

12. Try to authenticate now as alice. You should receive an `Access-Accept` packet:

```
$>radtest alice passme 127.0.0.1 100 testing123

Sending Access-Request of id 83 to 127.0.0.1 port 1812

User-Name = "alice"

User-Password = "passme"

NAS-IP-Address = 127.0.0.2

NAS-Port = 100

rad_recv: Access-Accept packet from host 127.0.0.1 port 1812,
id=83, length=34

Reply-Message = "Hello, alice"
```

What just happened?

We have just managed to save Isaac from coding HTML for food. Alice and Bob will also not be able to use the Internet simultaneously any more.

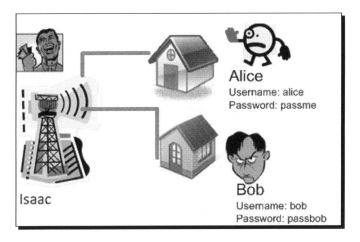

Let's look at some technical aspects.

Session section

The `session` section in FreeRADIUS is defined separately from the `authorize` and `authenticate` sections. Despite this it is functionally part of authorization. FreeRADIUS checks if a user is authorized to have multiple sessions and then compares the user's limit with the current number of active sessions. The outcome of this check then influences the return to an `Access-Request`.

The `session` section makes use of a session database to determine the active sessions a user has. One of the two available session databases has to be used. Radutmp is slower than `sql`. When you use `sql` it is required that `sql` is also included for accounting. Likewise when you use `radutmp` for a session database, you also have to include `radutmp` for accounting.

If you do not use simultaneous usage checking, keep the `session` section empty by commenting out both `radutmp` and `sql`. This will make FreeRADIUS perform faster. Another thing to consider is when you do use a method to check `Simultaneous-Use`, try to use only one method and disable the other.

Problems with orphan sessions

When you are limiting a user's sessions, orphan sessions can now potentially prevent a user from gaining access to the network. If the state on the NAS does not correspond with the state recorded on the FreeRADIUS server, FreeRADIUS may think the user is still logged in while the NAS knows better. Keep this in mind especially if the NAS does not feature the sending of `Acct-Status-Type = Accounting-Off` and `Acct-Status-Type = Accounting-On` when it shuts down and starts up.

checkrad

The `session` section features the calling of a program called `checkrad`. This is a Perl script which, depending on the value of the `nastype` directive of a `client`, may contact the NAS directly to determine if a user is already connected, and how may times.

If a client's `nastype = other`, `checkrad` will do nothing as you can see from this debug output:

```
checkrad: No NAS type, or type "other" not checking
```

The tests on my setup, however, also gave the same message even when `nastype` contains `other` values. YMMV, but take note as this was also reported on the FreeRADIUS mailing list.

Remember also that the execution of the `checkrad` script can potentially be a bottleneck, slowing down authentication times. If you would like to disable it, simply define the `nastype = other` for a `client`.

After we have saved the WISP from bankruptcy it's time to further limit a user's daily usage.

Limiting the usage of a user

As stated at the start of this chapter, we can use accounting data for capacity planning. The rest of this chapter will cover a scenario where we limit the daily usage of a user based on existing accounting data for the specified user.

30 minutes per day in total

Isaac's WISP is flying again and he has been approached by the local pizzeria to provide Internet access for their customers. Each customer will get 30 minutes free Internet with every pizza they purchase. This free Internet must be valid for one day only and should expire at 22:00 hrs the same day when the pizza was bought. Isaac uses a combination of Coova Chilli and Mikrotik captive portals for his WISP.

Each customer get 30 minutes free Internet per pizza per day

How FreeRADIUS can help

During the introduction to the RADIUS protocol we mentioned that a RADIUS server cannot impose limitations on a user. Although a RADIUS server will return AVPs to indicate certain limitations, it is the responsibility of the NAS to impose them.

Common limitations are data or time-based. The `Session-Timeout` return AVP is time-based and understood by many NAS devices. If we only want to allow a user's session to last 30 minutes, simply return `Session-Timeout = 1800` in the `Access-Accept` packet. If the NAS supports `Session-Timeout` it will terminate the user's session after 30 minutes.

 The best place to see which AVPs an NAS supports is to search on the particular vendor or project's website.

This scenario works fine except for one problem. The user can simply log in again after the time-out and get another 30 minutes!

There is, however, a way to handle this problem. FreeRADIUS offers `counter` modules. In this section we will first perform a basic counter set up using the `counter` module (`rlm_counter`) to keep track of time usage across sessions. We will then substitute the `counter` module with the `sqlcounter` module (`rlm_sqlcounter`).

Time for action – limiting a user's usage

The following sections will demonstrate how to limit Internet usage.

Activating a daily counter

The `counter` module has the following counter defined by default:

```
counter daily {
    filename = ${db_dir}/db.daily
    key = User-Name
    count-attribute = Acct-Session-Time
    reset = daily
    counter-name = Daily-Session-Time
    check-name = Max-Daily-Session
    reply-name = Session-Timeout
    allowed-servicetype = Framed-User
    cache-size = 5000
}
```

Modify the counter as follows:

1. Edit the `sites-enabled/default` file in the FreeRADIUS configuration
   directory. Uncomment `daily` in both the `authorize` and `accounting`
   sections. Also, uncomment `daily` in the `instantiate` section of the
   `radius.conf` file to ensure proper instantiation of the counter.

2. The AVPs `Max-Daily-Session` and `Daily-Session-Time` are not listed
   in any dictionary. Edit the `dictionary` file in the FreeRADIUS configuration
   directory and add them:

#ATTRIBUTE	My-Local-String	3000	string
#ATTRIBUTE	My-Local-IPAddr	3001	ipaddr
#ATTRIBUTE	My-Local-Integer	3002	integer
ATTRIBUTE	Daily-Session-Time	3000	integer
ATTRIBUTE	Max-Daily-Session	3001	integer

3. Change the entry for alice in the `users` file to reflect the following:

   ```
   "alice" Cleartext-Password := "passme", Max-Daily-Session :=
   1800
       Reply-Message = "Hello, %{User-Name}"
   ```

4. Edit the `modules/counter` file in the FreeRADIUS configuration
   directory and comment out the `allowed-servicetype` line:

   ```
   #allowed-servicetype = Framed-User
   ```

5. The `rlm_counter` module will create a database file to keep track of the counters for various users. This is located in the FreeRADIUS configuration directory. We need to change the rights of this directory. We assume a normal installation on each of the distributions.

On CentOS and SUSE:

```
#>chmod g+w /etc/raddb
```

On Ubuntu everything works fine and no change is required.

6. Restart the FreeRADIUS server in debug mode.

7. Authenticate as alice. You should receive `Session-Timeout = 1800`:

```
# radtest alice passme 127.0.0.1 100 testing123
Sending Access-Request of id 30 to 127.0.0.1 port 1812
User-Name = "alice"
User-Password = "passme"
NAS-IP-Address = 127.0.0.1
NAS-Port = 100
rad_recv: Access-Accept packet from host 127.0.0.1 port 1812,
id=30, length=40
Reply-Message = "Hello, alice"
Session-Timeout = 1800
```

8. Send an accounting start request using `radclient` and the `4088_06_acct_start.txt` file we created earlier in this chapter. Wait 30 seconds or more. Send the accounting stop request using the `radclient` and the `4088_06_acct_stopt.txt` file. This will record the usage.

9. Authenticate again as alice. This time `Session-Timeout` should now be `1770` or less instead of `1800` (1800 − 30).

This exercise showed how the `counter` module can be used to keep track of time usage across sessions. Depending on the existing usage it will return a specified AVP. If the existing usage has reached a trigger point, authentication will fail.

Terminating the session at a specified time

The second requirement is that Internet access should be only valid until 22:00 of the day when a pizza was bought. For this we will use the `WISPr-Session-Terminate-Time` return AVP. `WISPr-Session-Terminate-Time` is supported by both Coova Chilli and Mikrotik. This AVP's value can specify the precise time (to the second) when a user's connection should be terminated.

Creating Internet vouchers

Although this part is beyond the scope of the book, I would recommend using an SQL database for this. The software that creates Internet vouchers should then determine the value of `WISPr-Session-Terminate-Time` based on the day of the pizza sale.

You might be tempted to use `Login-Time` instead of `WISPr-Session-Terminate-Time` but `Login-Time` will allow a voucher to be used any day.

For this proof of concept we'll simply add a `reply` attribute to `alice` in the `users` file. We imagine that today is Tuesday, January 10, 2012 and the time-zone is UTC/GMT+2 hours.

1. Change the entry of `alice` in the `users` file to reflect the following:

```
"alice" Cleartext-Password := "passme", Max-Daily-Session :=
1800
    Reply-Message = "Hello, %{User-Name}",
    WISPr-Session-Terminate-Time = "2012-01-10T22:00:00+02:00"
```

2. Restart the FreeRADIUS server.

3. Authenticate as alice. The return AVPs should include `Session-Timeout` and `WISPr-Session-Terminate-Time`:

```
rad_recv: Access-Accept packet from host 127.0.0.1 port 1812,
id=19, length=73

Reply-Message = "Hello, alice"

WISPr-Session-Terminate-Time = "2012-01-10T22:00:00+02:00"

Session-Timeout = 1770
```

4. Ensure the timezone on the Coova Chilli and Mikrotik captive portals is correct. If it is not correct you can expect wrong termination times.

What just happened?

This exercise has proved how we are able to limit the total daily time a client can be on the Internet to 30 minutes. We have also ensured they will not be connected anymore after 22:00 on the day when they have bought a pizza. Let's look at what makes the `counter` module tick, or is it count?

rlm_counter

The `counter` module allows you to define various counters. The included counter is time-based and called `daily` because it resets daily. The counter module creates its own database for each counter that is defined. Let's look at the sample `daily` counter's definition:

```
counter daily {
```

```
    filename = ${db_dir}/db.daily
    key = User-Name
    count-attribute = Acct-Session-Time
    reset = daily
    counter-name = Daily-Session-Time
    check-name = Max-Daily-Session
    reply-name = Session-Timeout
    allowed-servicetype = Framed-User
    cache-size = 5000
}
```

Each `counter` section contains various directives, which define the behavior of the counter. There are four directives that form the nucleus of the counter:

Directive	Value	Comment
check-name	Max-Daily-Session	Internal check AVP for a user to indicate the allowance; for example: `Max-Daily-Session := 1800` Remember this AVP is usually an internal AVP, which you define explicitly inside the dictionary file and should be a value between 3000 and 4000.
count-attribute	Acct-Session-Time	The AVP in the accounting packet of which to keep count.
reply-name	Session-Timeout	`Session-Timeout = Max-Daily-Session` minus `Acct-Session-Time`
reset	daily	The timespan to consider. Values can be daily, weekly, monthly, or never.

> In short the `counter` module will calculate the total usage of the `count-attribute` within the specified `reset` period; it will then subtract this value from `check-name`. If it is less than zero it will return a failure; if it is greater than zero it will return the value of `reply-name`.

You can read more about the other directives and their usage inside the `counter` file's comments.

We have removed the `allowed-servicetype` directive since it limits the counter to be only effective when `Access-Request` contains `Service-Type = Framed-User`.

To activate a defined counter it must be specified in both the `accounting` section and the `authorize` section. It should also be specified in the `instantiate` section of the `radius. conf` file. This will ensure proper start up of the counter.

You will note that the `daily` counter is listed after all the modules that can supply the user's information in the `authorize` section. This will give those modules the opportunity to set the `check-name` before `daily` is executed. In our situation this was done by the `files` module when it set the value of `Max-Daily-Session` to `1800`.

The `accounting` section keeps track of usage and lets the `counter` module log usage into a specified database. During authorization, the counter will then consult the specified database to determine the value of the `reply-name` AVP. If the usage exceeds the `check-name` AVP an `Access-Reject` is returned.

Rather than having a database for each defined counter, it will be much more effective if all counters can use one database. In the next section we will use `sqlcounter`. The `sqlcounter` module uses the `sql` accounting database to determine the counter values no matter how many counters are defined.

Have a go hero – using a single database for various counters

We shall now look at running multiple counters from a single database.

Using rlm_sqlcounter

When we configured FreeRADIUS to limit a user's sessions we included `sql` in the `accounting` section. We assume you still have `sql` included in the `accounting` section of the default virtual server.

In this exercise we build on the previous ones where we used the `sql` module for accounting. We make use of MySQL as a database. FreeRADIUS also supports PostgreSQL, Microsoft SQL Server, and Oracle Database as alternatives to MySQL. This `sqlcounter` module should work just as well with the alternatives.

We will substitute the `daily` counter with an equivalent `sqlcounter`:

1. The `sqlcounter` includes a few predefined counters in the `sql/mysql/counter. conf` file, which is located in the FreeRADIUS configuration directory. Open the file and confirm that a counter called `dailycounter` is defined.

2. Change the `sql` directive of `dailycounter` from this:

```
query = "SELECT SUM(acctsessiontime - \
    GREATEST((%b - UNIX_TIMESTAMP(acctstarttime)), 0)) \
    FROM radacct WHERE username = '%{%k}' AND \
    UNIX_TIMESTAMP(acctstarttime) + acctsessiontime > '%b'"
```

to this:

```
query = "SELECT IFNULL(SUM(acctsessiontime - \
    GREATEST((%b - UNIX_TIMESTAMP(acctstarttime)), 0)),0) \
    FROM radacct WHERE username = '%{%k}' AND \
    UNIX_TIMESTAMP(acctstarttime) + acctsessiontime > '%b'"
```

3. Edit the `sites-enabled/default` file in the FreeRADIUS configuration directory. Remove `daily` in both the `authorize` and `accounting` sections by commenting it out.

4. Add `dailycounter` just below the commented out `daily` in the `authorize` section.

5. Confirm `sql` is included in the `accounting` section.

6. Clean the `radacct` table in the MySQL database:

   ```
   mysq -u root -p radius
   delete from radacct;
   ```

7. Restart FreeRADIUS in debug mode.

8. Authenticate as alice. You should receive `Session-Timeout = 1800`:

   ```
   $>radtest alice passme 127.0.0.1 100 testing123
   Sending Access-Request of id 181 to 127.0.0.1 port 1812
       User-Name = "alice"
       User-Password = "passme"
       NAS-IP-Address = 127.0.0.1
       NAS-Port = 100
   rad_recv: Access-Accept packet from host 127.0.0.1 port 1812,
   id=181, length=73
       Reply-Message = "Hello, alice"
       WISPr-Session-Terminate-Time = "2012-01-10T22:00:00+02:00"
       Session-Timeout = 1800
   ```

9. Send an accounting start request using `radclient` and the `4088_06_acct_start.txt` file we created earlier in this chapter. Follow it up with an interim-update using the `4088_06_acct_interim-update.txt` file (with `sql` accounting you do not have to wait between the two).

10. Authenticate again as Alice. The value of `Session-Timeout` should now be something like `1789` (1800-11).

11. Send an accounting stop request using `radclient` and the `4088_06_acct_stop.txt` file we created earlier in this chapter.

12. Authenticate again as alice. This time the value of `Session-Timeout` should be something like `1770` (1800-30).

Now to deplete the user's available time:

1. Edit the `4088_06_acct_stop.txt` file and change the value of `Acct-Session-Time` to `2000`.

2. Send an accounting start and accounting stop request using the `radclient` with `4088_06_acct_start.txt` and `4088_06_acct_stop.txt` respectively.

3. Authenticate again as alice. This time the authentication should fail because the available time is depleted:

   ```
   rad_recv: Access-Reject packet from host 127.0.0.1 port 1812,
   id=143, length=84
       Reply-Message = "Hello, alice"
       Reply-Message = "Your maximum monthly usage time has been
   reached"
   ```

4. The `Reply-Message` can be misleading since it speaks about a monthly usage instead of daily; nevertheless the request has been rejected.

We managed to substitute the `counter` module with the `sqlconter` module. Let's look at some important points to keep in mind.

Resetting the counter

The `reset` directive has five possibilities to choose from. These possibilities are `hourly`, `daily`, `weekly`, `monthly`, and `never`. These values are calendar based. This means that the `monthly` reset will occur on the first of the month. We also have the opportunity to define our own `reset` value in the form of `num [hdwm]` where each letter represents a reset option. If we then specify `reset = 6h`, the counter will reset every six hours, starting at 00:00.

SQL module instance

We can declare various instances of the `sql` module. By default the first instance is called `sql`. We can, however, create additional ones, each connecting to a different database or even a different server. With `sqlmod-inst = sql` we indicated to `sqlcounter` to use the default `sql` module instance. If we have used an additional `sql` instance to do accounting, that `sql` module instance could be specified as the value of `sqlmod-inst`.

Special variables inside the query

You will note that the query has listed a special one-character variable (%k) to represent the attribute of the key. This means that if key = User-Name then we will be substituting the %k with User-Name. There is also %b, which is substituted with the beginning of the reset period and %e, which is substituted with the end of the reset period. These one-character variables are unique to the sqlcounter module and are in addition to those already in existence. Variables will be covered in depth in the next chapter.

Empty account records

We had to modify the SQL query for the counter to handle NULL values. If you do not specify this, the query will return NULL when there are no accounting records in the SQL database for the user who tries to authenticate. This in turn will result in no Session-Timeout reply attribute being returned.

 Remember to include IFNULL with the other predefined counters and also when you define your own counters. If you forget this, it will bite you!

Counters that reset daily

A daily counter resets at midnight. What happens when Alice connects 20 minutes before midnight? Alice will get the remaining 20 minutes of today and will also be limited to 30 minutes into the next day. To prevent the session to last longer than 30 minutes at any time, make use of the Login-Time internal AVP to ensure the user's session expires before midnight:

```
"alice" Cleartext-Password := "passme", Max-Daily-Session :=
1800,Login-Time := 'Al0001-2359'
```

Without the Login-Time AVP we will get something like the following reply back when we authenticate after 23:30:

`Session-Timeout = 3417`

With the Login-Time AVP the user will get something like the following:

`Session-Timeout = 1440`

The fact that the Session-Timeout value is more than 30 minutes can be confusing, but the person is simply getting what is remaining of the 30 minutes for today plus the 30 minutes of tomorrow in one go.

Counting octets

You might be tempted to create a counter for octets with a query like this:

```
query = "SELECT IFNULL(SUM(acctinputoctets - GREATEST((%b -
UNIX_TIMESTAMP(acctstarttime)), 0)),0)+ IFNULL(SUM(acctoutputoctets
-GREATEST((%b - UNIX_TIMESTAMP(acctstarttime)), 0)),0) FROM
radacct WHERE username='%{%k}' AND UNIX_TIMESTAMP(acctstarttime) +
acctsessiontime > '%b'"
```

Don't do it! I repeat do not do it! The `check-name` and `reply-name` directive's AVPs have to be time-based. It may work as intended when the reset directive is defined as `never`, but one day you will change it to `daily` or `monthly` and get burned.

The reason things break is because (as shown in the previous section) the counter returns a remainder for today plus the `Max-Daily-Session` for tomorrow if the seconds remaining for today is less than `Max-Daily-Session` defined for a user. So it assumes these AVPs are time-based AVPs.

Using other AVPs in the counter's definition will not change the `sqlcounter` module's behavior. It assumes these AVPs are time-based.

We will discuss alternative ways to control a user's data based on accumulated usage later in the book.

If you would like to know about the intimate details of this limitation, you can read more on this on the following mailing list:

http://www.mail-archive.com/freeradius-users@
lists.freeradius.org/msg49267.html

Now that the accounting part of FreeRADIUS is configured, it's time to see what we should routinely do to ensure the accounting data is well maintained.

Housekeeping of accounting data

The most common problem with accounting data is when the NAS and the FreeRADIUS server's data do not correspond.

You can then use `radzap` to close orphan sessions as we have done at the start of the chapter.

Web-based tools

If you use MySQL for accounting there are various web-based tools to manage the accounting data. phpMyAdmin is very popular. There are also complete software packages (open source or commercial) focused on giving a central management dashboard for user management, billing, vouchers, and other such applications.

 Should you have opted for PostgreSQL instead of MySQL, you just have to try out phpPgAdmin. This serves as a great help to beginners.

In large deployments it is good practice to archive older accounting records from the MySQL database in order to keep the size of the database manageable.

You may also want to index certain columns that are common to regular queries.

This brings us to the end of the chapter on accounting. Let's go over the important points that we have learned.

Summary

We have learned a lot in this chapter about accounting in FreeRADIUS. Specifically, we have covered:

- **Basic accounting**: We have learned that accounting is separate from authentication and authorization and runs on port 1813. It consists of the client sending `Accounting-Request` packets and the server replying with `Accounting-Response` packets. The `Acct-Status-Type` AVP inside an `Accounting-Request` can have a value of `Start`, `Stop`, `Interim-Update`, `Accounting-Off` or `Accounting-On`.

- **Rogue accounting data**: These are also known as orphan sessions and happen when the FreeRADIUS server's accounting data does not reflect the activities on the NAS. The `radzap` command helps us to control these data.

- **Simultaneous sessions**: There can be a limit to the simultaneous sessions of a user. A session section in FreeRADIUS specifies the session database that should be referenced. The session database obtains session data from the accounting section. To limit simultaneous sessions we use the internal `Simultaneous-Use` AVP as a check for a user.

- **Counters**: FreeRADIUS has counters to keep track of the total usage of a user. This can be used to limit the total time a user has network access. The `rlm_counter` module uses its own private database for each counter that is defined. The `rlm_sqlcounter` module piggybacks onto the `sql` accounting database, which is more effective.

We have also discussed ways to access and manage the MySQL database's accounting data and common problems associated with accounting.

The next chapter is going to crack open authorization's shell to show you just how much power FreeRADIUS can give you.

Pop quiz – accounting

1. A Telco is forwarding RADIUS authentication requests to your RADIUS server. Everything works well. They are now also able to forward accounting requests to your RADIUS server, but somehow not one request reaches your RADIUS server. Where will be a good place to troubleshoot?

2. You have configured simultaneous session limits and it works like a charm. During the night a fierce rainstorm has knocked out one of the Wi-Fi towers. Now some people are complaining they cannot connect although they have signal from another nearby tower. What could be wrong?

3. You generate vouchers with a specific value for `WisPr-Session-Terminate-Time`. Some of your captive portals seem to ignore this reply AVP although the vendor does support this AVP. What could be wrong?

4. Using the `sqlcounter` module you have created a counter to limit the daily data for a user. Somehow this counter is just acting weird. You change the `reset` directive to `never` and it becomes stable. Are you losing your mind?

7
Authorization

Authorization is a process where information in a request is evaluated. This information may be used to validate against information about the user that was obtained from file, database, or LDAP directory. Authorization happens before authentication and does not involve the checking of a password. We can use various logic and comparisons to determine if a user is authorized to connect to a network. We can also determine things like how long they can use a network or the quality of service to offer them. These are all components of authorization and discussed in this chapter.

In this chapter we shall:

- ◆ See how restrictions are applied to users
- ◆ See how FreeRADIUS performs authorization
- ◆ Explore the unlang processing language in FreeRADIUS
- ◆ Use unlang to create a data reset counter

So, let's get on with it...

Implementing restrictions

Authorization, in essence, is about restrictions. Based on certain checks a user may be restricted. Restrictions can be applied in one of two places:

- ◆ At the RADIUS server
- ◆ At the NAS

Restrictions are determined during the authentication process when an `Access-Request` packet is sent to the RADIUS server. `Accounting-Request` packets do not and cannot determine restrictions.

When a restriction is applied at the RADIUS server, the server returns an `Access-Reject` packet, which should include a `Reply-Message` AVP specifying the reason for rejection.

When a restriction is applied at the NAS, the RADIUS server returns an `Access-Accept` packet that includes AVPs that should be applied by the NAS. This means that you have to ensure that the NAS receives the correct AVPs to implement the restriction and that it also supports these AVPs in the first place.

Authorization in FreeRADIUS

This section can be seen as an overview of subjects we have covered up to now and as a refresher before moving on to more hands-on exercises with authorization.

- Requests are sent from an NAS (the client) to FreeRADIUS (the server).
- These requests are handled by virtual servers, which are defined in the FreeRADIUS configuration. The default virtual server is called `default`.
- The manner in which incoming requests are handled depends on the configuration of the various sections inside a virtual server file.
- The request itself is handled by the various sections in a logical order. The `authorize` section always handles `Access-Request` packets before the `authenticate` section does. The `preacct` section likewise always handles `Accounting-Request` packets before the `accounting` section does.
- Although the section order cannot be changed, we have much flexibility inside the section to manipulate the request.

The next part will be a basic introduction to ways to process a request. With the use of comparisons and logic we can control the flow of a request and manipulate attributes.

Introduction to unlang

The unlang language available in FreeRADIUS takes flexibility in authorization to new heights. Unlang is not a full blown programming language, but rather a processing language. The purpose of unlang is to implement policies and not to replace complex scripts like those created with Perl or Python. Unlang sticks to a basic syntax that includes conditional statements and manipulation of variables. The unlang code does not get compiled but is interpreted by the FreeRADIUS server. The interpretation happens when the server reads the configuration files, which typically happens during start-up. The use of unlang is restricted to specified sections inside the configuration files and cannot be used inside the modules.

A key feature of unlang is the ability to use conditional statements to control the process which handles the request.

 FreeRADIUS installs a man page for unlang, which you can consult:
```
$>man unlang
```

We will demonstrate the use of various conditional statements in order to show how a request can be processed.

Using conditional statements

Conditional statements are simple, yet so powerful that they remain a building block in any piece of software. Unlang features two ways to implement conditional checks:

◆ The `if` statement. This includes the `else` and `elsif` options as part of the statement.

◆ The `switch` statement.

This section will look at various uses of the `if` statement.

Time for action – using the if statement in unlang

The `if` statement itself is not very complex. It has the following format:

```
if(condition){
    . . .
}
```

The condition part can become complex due to its many possibilities.

Obtaining a return code using the if statement

We will now look at the return code of a module and use this code to compare against the specified condition. Each module in FreeRADIUS is required to return a code after it is called. The value of this code can subsequently be used as a conditional check in the `if` statement.

Authorizing a user using the if statement

This exercise uses the `if` condition to reject an `Access-Request` if the user is not in the `users` file.

1. Edit the `sites-available/default` virtual server under the FreeRADIUS configuration directory and add the following lines below the `files` entry inside the `authorize` section:

```
if(noop){
    reject
}
```

2. Restart FreeRADIUS in debug mode and try to authenticate with a username and password not present in the `users` file. We assume `ali` is not defined anywhere:

```
radtest ali passme 127.0.0.1 100 testing123
```

You should get an `Access-Reject` packet back.

What just happened?

We have added a conditional check below the `files` module under the `authorize` section. To activate this change FreeRADIUS had to be restarted. This will cause the radius server to read and interpret the unlang code. The unlang code is then tested by sending an `Access-Request` packet to the server.

We'll first look at the `if` condition and then at the action taken when the `if` condition is met.

Module return codes

If you look at the debug output from FreeRADIUS, you will see how each module returns a code. Here is a list of available return codes and what they mean:

Module return code	Description
notfound	Information was not found
noop	The module did nothing
ok	The module succeeded
updated	The module updated the request
	For example, it set the `Auth-Type` internal AVP
fail	The module failed
reject	The module rejected the request
userlock	The user was locked out

Module return code	Description
invalid	The configuration was invalid
handled	The module handled the request itself

We can use unlang's `if` statement to test for a specified return code from a module. To do this we have to give unlang a hint that it must test for a module return code. We do this by specifying the return code to test for as an **unquoted string** in the condition of the `if` statement.

 If the condition is an unquoted string and one of the module return codes listed in the preceding table, unlang will compare this string with the return code of the most recent module.

You may think that we should rather have tested for `notfound` instead of `noop`. The `files` module returns `noop` instead of `notfound` when a user is not in the `users` file. Remember to test or find out what value a module returns in certain situations before creating the conditional test. If you fail to do this, the results may be different from what you expect.

Keywords in unlang

We can take various actions when the `if` condition is met. Unlang uses keywords to process a request. The `if` statement is such a keyword. There is also the `update` keyword, which is used when manipulating attributes and is discussed later in this chapter. Then there is also a list of keywords that can be used inside the `if` statement. We used the `reject` keyword to immediately reject the request if the user is not in the `users` file. The following table lists the keywords that can be used inside the `if` statement and the effect they have on the request.

Keywords	Description
noop	Do nothing.
ok	Instructs the server that the request was processed properly. This keyword can be used to over-ride earlier failures, if the local administrator determines that the failures are not catastrophic.
fail	Causes the request to be treated as if a failure had occurred.
reject	Causes the request to be rejected immediately.

Note that although the names are the same as the return codes of a module, there is a difference between module return codes and these keywords. These keywords are part of unlang and used inside the `if` statement. If there is no keyword defined inside the `if` statement, it will return, by default, `noop`.

Along with these keywords we can also specify the name of any FreeRADIUS module. The module name is treated as a keyword. `if` statements can also be nested.

Have a go hero – other tests using conditional statements

Conditional statements offer us a variety of testing capabilities. These can be used during authorization, for instance, to check if an NAS has supplied a required attribute with the `Access-Request`. We can even combine tests using logical operators to create complex conditions that have to be met before authorizing a user. This section will cover two more conditional tests, which can be used as building blocks to create a flexible authorization policy.

These exercises assume an untouched `sites-available/default` file and can be done independently. We also assume the `users` file contains a user called `alice` with a password of `passme` (this is the same user defined and used in all the previous chapters).

Checking if an attribute exists

We can check if a specified AVP exists. If we specify the name of an attribute as an unquoted string in the condition, unlang will check if this AVP is present in the request.

1. Edit the `sites-available/default` virtual server under the FreeRADIUS configuration directory and add the following below the `files` entry inside the `authorize` section:

    ```
    if(Framed-Protocol){
        reject
    }
    ```

2. Restart FreeRADIUS in debug mode and try to authenticate as alice but also add a `1` to the end of the `radtest` command. This will include the `Framed-Protocol` AVP in the request:

    ```
    radtest alice passme 127.0.0.1 100 testing123 1
    ```

    You should get an `Access-Reject` packet back.

We can see from the debug output how the `if` statement is evaluated. Compare the output when the `Framed-Protocol` is included in the request to when it is missing.

 Although we use the `Framed-Protocol` attribute for convenience during the proof of concept here, in the real world, the `Framed-Protocol` AVP can be present in both the `Access-Accept` and `Access-Reply` packets. It indicates the framing to be used for framed access. The most common value is Point to Point Protocol (PPP).

The following is the output if the Framed-Protocol is present:

```
++? if (Framed-Protocol)
? Evaluating (Framed-Protocol) -> TRUE
++? if (Framed-Protocol) -> TRUE
++- entering if (Framed-Protocol) {...}
+++[reject] returns reject
++- if (Framed-Protocol) returns reject
```

The following is the output if the Framed-Protocol is missing:

```
++? if (Framed-Protocol)
? Evaluating (Framed-Protocol) -> FALSE
++? if (Framed-Protocol) -> FALSE
```

Remember that this conditional test only checks if the AVP is present inside the request. It does not check for a specific value of the AVP. We will test for certain values later in the chapter.

Up to now we have two types of unquoted strings:

- noop was interpreted by unlang as the return code of the last module.
- Framed-Protocol was interpreted by unlang as an attribute.

What happens if the unquoted string is neither? The answer is as follows:

- A word equals true.
- A number of zero equals false, other numbers equal true.

 If you want to check if an attribute does not exist, just add an exclamation mark (!) in front of the attribute. The exclamation mark in unlang is a logical NOT and tests if a condition does not exist.

Using logical expressions to authenticate a user

Unlang also supports logical AND (&&) and logical OR (||) in the condition statement. In this exercise we will reject a user who is not in the users file or when the Framed-Protocol AVP is present in the request.

1. Edit the sites-available/default virtual server under the FreeRADIUS configuration directory and add the following lines below the files entry inside the authorize section:

```
if((noop)||(Framed-Protocol)){
    reject
}
```

2. Restart FreeRADIUS in debug mode and try to authenticate as `alice` but also add a 1 to the end of the `radtest` command. This will include the `Framed-Protocol` AVP in the request:

   ```
   radtest alice passme 127.0.0.1 100 testing123 1
   ```

   You should get an `Acces-Reject` packet back.

3. Try to authenticate with a username and password not present in the `users` file. You should also get an `Access-Reject` packet back.

4. Finally try to authenticate with a username and password not present in the `users` file and also add a 1 to the end of the `radtest` command. You should also get an `Access-Reject` packet back.

The debug feedback from the FreeRADIUS server will indicate how the `if` condition was evaluated during the request.

Attributes and variables

Authorization in RADIUS depends heavily on attributes. We can use the AVPs inside an `Access-Request` to verify if it meets our requirements during authorization. We can also return AVPs inside the `Access-Reply` to instruct the NAS that a user is only authorized to do certain things.

Since the RADIUS protocol is all about attributes, unlang mostly uses attributes as variables. There are also some exceptions where variables are not attributes. This will also be covered in this section.

Attribute lists

FreeRADIUS manages attributes by storing them inside lists. A list is like a namespace, which allows an attribute with the same name to exist in different places independently. Unlang can be used to manipulate or add attributes inside these different lists:

- There is a `request` list, which contains all the AVPs from the request, for example `User-Name`.

- There is a `reply` list, which contains all the AVPs that will eventually be inside the reply, for example `Reply-Message`.

- We have also worked with the `control` list in the previous chapters where we referred to attributes inside this list as internal attributes, for example `Auth-Type`.

- To refer to an attribute inside a specific list, we use the name of the list and a colon followed by the attribute name, for example `request:Framed-Protocol`.

- If the name of the list is omitted it refers to the `request` list. This is why we could get away with not specifying a list name in the previous exercises.

◆ The following attribute lists are available for use: `request`, `reply`, `control`, `proxy-request`, `proxy-reply`, `outer.request`, `outer.reply`, `outer.control`, `outer.proxy-request`, and `outer.proxy-reply`.

◆ Attributes are added or modified through the use of the `update` keyword. The `update` keyword used together with the name of the list that has to be modified creates an `update` section in which attributes can be modified or added.

After this introduction to attributes and attribute lists it is time to use them in a practical exercise.

Time for action – referencing attributes

In this section we shall make use of attributes.

Attributes in the if statement

Unlang can be used in various sections inside a virtual server definition. Previously we have used it in the `authorize` section. You should not use unlang inside the `authenticate` section as per instruction of the FreeRADIUS authors. We will use unlang in the `post-auth` section to determine if `Auth-Type = PAP` was used and give feedback if it was indeed used to authenticate a user.

1. Edit the `sites-available/default` virtual server under the FreeRADIUS configuration directory and add the following inside the `post-auth` section, at the top of the section:

```
if(control:Auth-Type == 'PAP'){
    update reply {
        Reply-Message := "We are using %{control:Auth-Type}
authentication"
    }
}
```

2. Restart FreeRADIUS in debug mode and try to authenticate as alice.

The `Reply-Message` specified should be included inside the reply.

What just happened?

We have used unlang to test the value of the `Auth-Type` AVP inside the `control` attribute list. If it was equal to `PAP` we modified the `Reply-Message` AVP inside the `reply` attribute list. Although the `if` statement consists of a mere five lines, there are important things to discuss. We will discuss the following:

- Ways to reference attributes in a condition
- Comparison operators
- Changing and adding attributes in an attribute list

Referencing attributes in a condition

When referencing an attribute there is an alternative syntax to what we have used in the condition. It is as follows:

```
if("%{control:Auth-Type}" == 'PAP'){
```

Although both can be used, the first is preferred for easy reading. The alternative syntax is normally used inside strings. The attribute's value will then be inserted to become part of the string. This is called string expansion. We have used string expansion to create the value of `Reply-Message`.

```
Reply-Message := "We are using %{control:Auth-Type} authentication"
```

If we omit the reference to the attribute list (`control:`), unlang will use `request:Auth-Type`. If this attribute is not inside the attribute list, unlang returns `false`.

Comparison operators

There are quite a few comparison operators that can be used in the condition test. The data type of the AVP will determine which operators are available for use.

Operator	Data type	Sample
==	Strings and numbers	(control:Auth-Type == 'PAP')
!=		(reply:Idle-Timeout != 60)
<	Numbers	(reply:Idle-Timeout <= 60)
<=		
>		
>=		
=~	Strings to regular expressions	(request:User-Name =~ /^.*\.co\.za/i)
!~		

Attribute manipulation

Unlang can be used to modify AVPs. To modify the value of an AVP we need to use the `update` keyword in unlang. The synopsis for the `update` statement is as follows:

```
update <list> {
    attribute <operator> value
    ...
}
```

The `update` statement can only contain attributes. The value of the operator is very important because it will determine how existing attributes in the list with that name will be treated. We will discuss three commonly used operators here. Note that other operators do exist. Refer to the unlang man page for more information on them.

Operator	Description
=	Add the attribute to the list, if and only if an attribute of the same name is not already present in that list.
:=	Add the attribute to the list. If any attribute of the same name is already present in that list, its value is replaced with the value of the current attribute.
+=	Add the attribute to the tail of the list, even if attributes of the same name are already present in the list.

e.g. get two Reply-Messages

Take care that the value you assign to an attribute is the correct type. When you assign a string value to an attribute that should take an integer value, it will result in an error.

Variables

Variables cannot be declared in unlang like they are in other languages. With unlang all attributes are variables but not all variables are attributes. Before an attribute can be referenced as a variable inside an attribute list it has to be added to the list first. All references to variables must be contained inside a double-quoted or back-quoted string. References to variables inside this quoted string are in the form `%{<variable>}`. In the previous section, we have referred to the `Auth-Type` variable, which is an attribute:

```
Reply-Message := "We are using %{control:Auth-Type} authentication"
```

In this section we will refer to variables that are not attributes.

Time for action – SQL statements as variables

One very powerful function of unlang is that it allows you to execute SQL queries through the `sql` module. The query is actually a variable and the return value of this query is the value of the variable. We will now modify the previous exercise to fetch the time from the database and add this to the `Reply-Message` value.

 To execute SQL queries you need to include and configure FreeRADIUS to use the `sql` module. The `sql` module also needs to be used in at least one section, for instance, the `authorize` or the `accounting` section.

1. Edit the `sites-available/default` virtual server under the FreeRADIUS configuration directory and add the following inside the `post-auth` section, at the top of the section:

```
if(control:Auth-Type == 'PAP'){
    update reply {
        Reply-Message := "We are using %{control:Auth-Type}
authentication and the time in the database is now %{sql:SELECT
curtime();}"
    }
}
```

2. Restart FreeRADIUS in debug mode and try to authenticate as `alice`.

   The `Reply-Message` specified should be included inside the reply and should return the time in the database.

What just happened?

We have used an SQL statement as a variable and returned the result of this statement as the value of this variable.

Here is the debug output from the FreeRADIUS server indicating how the SQL satement was executed:

```
++? if (control:Auth-Type == 'PAP')
? Evaluating (control:Auth-Type == 'PAP') -> TRUE
++? if (control:Auth-Type == 'PAP') -> TRUE
++- entering if (control:Auth-Type == 'PAP') {...}
sql_xlat
    expand: %{User-Name} -> alice
```

```
sql_set_user escaped user --> 'alice'

    expand: SELECT curtime(); -> SELECT curtime();
rlm_sql (sql): Reserving sql socket id: 3
sql_xlat finished
rlm_sql (sql): Released sql socket id: 3
    expand: We are using %{control:Auth-Type} authentication and the
time in the database is now %{sql:SELECT curtime();} -> We are using PAP
authentication and the time in the database is now 17:48:54
+++[reply] returns noop
++- if (control:Auth-Type == 'PAP') returns noop
```

As you can see the SQL query is treated in much the same way as the attribute. The following points about SQL statements as variables are handy to remember:

♦ The SQL query should return a single value. This value is the value assigned to the SQL statement variable.

♦ The SQL query can refer to attributes inside the query itself. If we want to get the total usage for the current user, we can use the following line:

```
"The total octets is: %{sql: SELECT IFNULL(SUM(AcctInputOctets
+ AcctOutputOctets),0) FROM radacct WHERE UserName='%{User-
Name}';}"
```

♦ A quoted or back-quoted string can have a combination of SQL queries and attributes. These will be expanded to return a result.

♦ If the `sql` module is not used in FreeRADIUS, the result of the SQL query expansion will be an empty string and the debug message will show an error:

```
WARNING: Unknown module "sql" in string expansion "%{sql:SELECT
curdate();}"
```

Expanded strings can be up to about 8000 characters long. This leaves enough room for pretty complex SQL statements.

Time for action – setting default values for variables

We are not always sure if a variable exists. Unlang features syntax for us to specify a default value in case a variable does not exist. Again we will demonstrate this by modifying the previous exercise. We will use `radtest` to first include `Framed-Protocol` = PPP in the request and also to leave it out. If the `Framed-Protocol` AVP is not present, we will return a default string.

1. Edit the `sites-available/default` virtual server under the FreeRADIUS configuration directory and add the following code inside the `post-auth` section, at the top of the section:

```
if(control:Auth-Type == 'PAP'){
    update reply {
        Reply-Message := "Framed protocol is:
%{%{request:Framed-Protocol}:-Not in request}"
    }
}
```

2. Restart FreeRADIUS in debug mode and try to authenticate as `alice`. First add a `1` to the end of the `radtest` command, then omit the `1`.

3. The value of `Reply-Message` with `1` added to `radtest` should be:

   Reply-Message = "Framed protocol is: PPP"

4. The value of `Reply-Message` with `1` omitted from `radtest` should be:

   Reply-Message = "Framed protocol is: Not in request"

What just happened?

We have used the ability of unlang to assign default values to variables.

The `:-` character sequence inside a variable reference is an indication for unlang that when the first variable does not exist, it should try to use that what follows the `:-` character sequence. Take note of the following important points:

- If `:-` is followed by an unquoted string, it will return this string.

- If `:-` is followed by a reference to another variable, you can create a chain to eventually test for the existence of several variables, for example:

  ```
  %{%{request:Framed-Protocol}:-%{request: NAS-Name}:- Default
  value}
  ```

- This syntax is called conditional syntax and changes between versions of FreeRADIUS. Some of the modules still use the older syntax, which will result in warnings inside the debug messages. An example of this is in the `ldap` module. You can change the following line in the `ldap` module's configuration file from:

  ```
  filter = "(uid=%{Stripped-User-Name:-%{User-Name}})"
  ```

  to:

  ```
  filter = "(uid=%{%{Stripped-User-Name}:-%{User-Name}})"
  ```

Time for action – using command substitution

Up to now we have used double-quotes to contain a variable that will be referenced. Unlang also features back-quoted strings, which allows for command substitution. The string inside these back-quotes is evaluated similarly to double-quoted strings where string expansion can take place.

Let's modify the previous exercise to show command substitution in action:

1. Edit the `sites-available/default` virtual server under the FreeRADIUS configuration directory and add the following inside the `post-auth` section, at the top of the section:

```
if(control:Auth-Type == 'PAP'){
    update reply {
        Reply-Message := `/bin/echo We are using %{control:Auth-
Type}`
    }
}
```

2. Restart FreeRADIUS in debug mode and try to authenticate as `alice`.

The feedback of the `echo` command will now be assigned to the `Reply-Message` attribute.

What just happened?

We have used back-quotes to perform command substitution. The output of this command has been assigned to an attribute.

Take note of the following points on command substitution in unlang:

- ◆ The command is executed in a sub-shell of the FreeRADIUS server. The content of the string is passed and executed in this sub-shell.
- ◆ The string is split up into command and argument(s). In our example the command will be `/bin/echo` and the argument `We are using PAP`.
- ◆ Use full paths when specifying executables.
- ◆ Executables are run as the user that runs the FreeRADIUS server.
- ◆ You can include other variables inside the command substitution string.
- ◆ If the command fails to execute, it introduces problems. This depends on the exit code of the executable that was called. Unlang tests the exit code of the executable and if it is not zero it returns a reject. Reject, as listed at the start of the chapter, causes the request to be rejected immediately.

- The exit code and the command output are two different things. The command output will be assigned to the variable if the exit code is zero.

- Only the first line in a multiple line output is returned and assigned.

- Use command substitution with care as it impacts performance.

Time for action – using regular expressions

Unlang allows regular expression evaluations in condition checking. These usually are Posix regular expressions. The operators `=~` and `!~` are associated with regular expressions. For a simple proof of concept we will modify the previous exercise:

1. Edit the `sites-available/default` virtual server under the FreeRADIUS configuration directory and add the following inside the `post-auth` section, at the top of the section:

   ```
   if(request:Framed-Protocol =~ /.*PP$/i){
       update reply {
           Reply-Message := "Regexp match for %{0}"
       }
   }
   ```

2. Restart FreeRADIUS in debug mode and try to authenticate as `alice`. First add a `1` to the end of the `radtest` command, then omit the `1`.

   Take note how the regular expression match changes the value of `Reply-Message` when you add the `1` to the `radtest` command.

What just happened?

We have shown the regular expression capabilities of unlang. Take note of the following important points on regular expressions in unlang:

- The operators `=~` and `!~` are used with regular expressions.

- The regular expression is specified between two `/` characters.

- Regular expressions allow you to refer to variables inside them, for example, `/^%{Framed-Protocol}$/i`.

- You can add an optional `i` character at the end of the regular expression to make the search case insensitive.

- If there was a match, the special variable `%{0}` holds the value of the variable that was tested in the regular expression.

This brings us to the end of the unlang introduction. You should now know most of the building blocks that are used in unlang. The next section will make good use of these building blocks to create a real-world application of unlang.

Practical unlang

In the previous chapter, Chapter 6, *Accounting*, we covered the `sql_counter` module. This module is useful to limit the time a user can spend daily, weekly, or monthly on the network, however, `sql_counter` has problems in limiting a user's data usage.

Limiting data usage

To limit a user's daily, weekly, or monthly data usage we have to take a different approach. The ability of unlang to use SQL statements as variables opens up a lot of possibilities. We will use the same scenario previously mentioned of Isaac who runs a WISP. Isaac now wants to restrict the amount of data a person can use over a period of time. He makes use of Mikrotik and Coova Chilli captive portals to control network access and has a FreeRADIUS RADIUS server.

Time for action – using unlang to create a data counter

We first have to ensure that certain things are in place in order for this exercise to be successful. The following items should be completed first as preparation:

- Define custom attributes in the dictionary.
- Create Perl scripts that will be used by the FreeRADIUS `perl` module.
- Update Mikrotik and Chillispot dictionaries.
- Prepare the `users` file.
- Prepare the SQL database.
- Add unlang code to the virtual server to serve as a data counter.
- Identify the `LD_PRELOAD` bug, if present.

There is a lot of work involved in this exercise. Following a divide and conquer approach will prevent us from being overwhelmed. Let's tackle it!

Defining custom attributes

We have seen from the introduction to unlang that the primary use of variables is through attributes. We need to define some attributes to use in the data counter.

Edit the `dictionary` file under the FreeRADIUS configuration directory and add the following attribute definitions:

```
ATTRIBUTE       FRBG-Reset-Type        3050    string
ATTRIBUTE       FRBG-Total-Bytes       3051    string
ATTRIBUTE       FRBG-Start-Time        3052    integer
ATTRIBUTE       FRBG-Used-Bytes        3053    string
ATTRIBUTE       FRBG-Avail-Bytes       3054    string
```

Each attribute starts with "FRBG". This is just to differentiate it from other attributes and stands for **FreeRADIUS Beginner's Guide**.

 The RADIUS protocol can only transmit attributes with numeric values of up to 255 over the wire. Attributes with values larger than 255 are used internally.

The following table lists each attribute and its meaning:

Attribute	Meaning
FRBG-Reset-Type	Specify when the counter should be reset. Values can be `daily`, `weekly`, `monthly`, or `never`.
FRBG-Total-Bytes	The amount of data a user can use in bytes, also known as a data cap.
FRBG-Start-Time	The Unix timestamp specifying the start time of the counter.
FRBG-Used-Bytes	The amount of data used from the start time up to now.
FRBG-Avail-Bytes	The amount of data still available: `FRBG-Avail-Bytes = FRBG-Total-Bytes – FRBG-Used-Bytes`

If you were observant, you would have noticed that the attributes involving bytes are all defined as type `string` instead of type `integer`. We use this as a workaround to the 32-bit limit of type `integer`. The following sub-section explains the 32-bit integer limitation in more detail.

32-bit limitation

Integer values in RADIUS have a limit of 32-bits. This means that an attribute of type integer cannot have a value of more than 4,294,967,295 (2^{31} - 1). To overcome this limitation, RADIUS uses a `Gigaword` attribute, which acts as a carry bit to the 32-bit attribute. `Accounting-Request` packets for instance will contain `Acct-Input-Octets` and `Acct-Input-Gigawords` to represent values larger than 4,294,967,295.

Suppose we have a value of 8.5 GB. This can be defined using the `Gigaword` carry in the following way:

- The integer value of 8.5 GB is 9,126,805,504 bytes (8.5 x 1024 x 1024 x 1024). A byte is equal to an octet in network terms.

- To calculate the value of the `Gigaword` carry, we divide 9,126,805,504 by 4,294,967,296. The result is 2.125. (9126805504 / 4294967296 = 2.125). The value of the `Gigaword` carry is then 2.

- To calculate the remainder, we multiply the `Gigaword` carry value by 4,294,967,296 and subtract this value from the original (9126805504 - (2 x 4294967296) = 536870912).

- This means that 8.5GB can be presented in an `Accounting-Request` packet as follows: `Acct-Input-Gigawords = 2, Acct-Input-Octets = 536870912`.

This 32-bit integer limitation is only on the RADIUS protocol. The database schema already caters for large integer numbers `bigint(20)`.

 FreeRADIUS deployments before the 2.x release will require modifications to incorporate support for `Gigawords`.

With the 32-bit integer limitation it becomes difficult to perform comparisons using unlang when values are larger than 4,294,967,295. For this reason we set the attributes to type string and use the `perl` module to perform comparisons for us. The `perl` module does not have the 32-bit limitation. Defining the attribute type as string allows the following:

- To specify attribute values larger than 4,294,967,295.

- To allow Perl to convert the string value to a numeric value for calculations. This overcomes the 32-bit limitation.

Using the perl module

FreeRADIUS allows for optional naming of a section. This gives us the ability to define various named sections for the `perl` module. Each named section can subsequently be used as a module. The definition is as follows:

```
perl <name> {
    ...
}
```

We will create two named `perl` sections under the `modules` directory:

1. In the `modules` directory under the FreeRADIUS configuration directory, create a file called `reset_time` with the following contents:

```
perl reset_time {
    module = ${confdir}/reset_time.pl
}
```

2. In the `modules` directory under the FreeRADIUS configuration directory, create a file called `check_usage` with the following contents:

```
perl check_usage {
    module = ${confdir}/check_usage.pl
}
```

3. These two `perl` sections each refer to a Perl script, which will be called by the `perl` module. Ensure these Perl scripts are in the FreeRADIUS configuration directory.

The scripts and their contents are listed in the following sections.

reset_time.pl

The `reset_time.pl` script is used to do the following:

♦ If the value of `FRBG-Reset-Type` is `daily`, `weekly`, or `monthly`, it will add the `FRBG-Start-Time` AVP.

♦ The value of `FRBG-Start-Time` is the Unix time when the counter started.

♦ If `FRBG-Start-Time` AVP was added, the script's return code will have a value of `updated`.

♦ If the `FRBG-Start-Time` AVP was not added (`FRBG-Reset-Type = never`), the script's return code will have a value of `noop`.

Here's the contents of `reset_time.pl`:

```
#! /usr/bin/perl -w
use strict;
use POSIX;

# use ...
# This is very important !
use vars qw(%RAD_CHECK);
use constant    RLM_MODULE_OK=>          2;#  /* the module is OK,
continue */
use constant    RLM_MODULE_NOOP=>        7;
use constant    RLM_MODULE_UPDATED=>     8;#  /* OK (pairs modified) */
```

```
sub authorize {
        #Find out when the reset time should be
        if($RAD_CHECK{'FRBG-Reset-Type'} =~ /monthly/i){
                $RAD_CHECK{'FRBG-Start-Time'} = start_of_month()
        }
        if($RAD_CHECK{'FRBG-Reset-Type'} =~ /weekly/i){
                $RAD_CHECK{'FRBG-Start-Time'} = start_of_week()
        }
        if($RAD_CHECK{'FRBG-Reset-Type'} =~ /daily/i){
                $RAD_CHECK{'FRBG-Start-Time'} = start_of_day()
        }
        if(exists($RAD_CHECK{'FRBG-Start-Time'})){
                return RLM_MODULE_UPDATED;
        }else{
                return RLM_MODULE_NOOP;
        }
}
sub start_of_month {
    #Get the current timestamp;
    my $reset_on = 1;    #you decide when the monthly CAP will reset
    my $unixtime;
    my ($sec,$min,$hour,$mday,$mon,$year,$wday,$yday,$isdst)=localtim
e(time);
    if($mday < $reset_on ){
        $unixtime = mktime (0, 0, 0, $reset_on, $mon-1, $year, 0, 0);
#We use the previous month
    }else{
        $unixtime = mktime (0, 0, 0, $reset_on, $mon, $year, 0, 0);
#We use this month
    }
    return $unixtime;
}
sub start_of_week {
    #Get the current timestamp;
    my ($sec,$min,$hour,$mday,$mon,$year,$wday,$yday,$isdst)=localtim
e(time);
    #create a new timestamp:
    my $unixtime = mktime (0, 0, 0, $mday-$wday, $mon, $year, 0, 0);
    return $unixtime;
}
sub start_of_day {
    #Get the current timestamp;
```

```
     my ($sec,$min,$hour,$mday,$mon,$year,$wday,$yday,$isdst)=localtim
e(time);
     #create a new timestamp:
     my $unixtime = mktime (0, 0, 0, $mday, $mon, $year, 0, 0);
     return $unixtime;
}
```

check_usage.pl

The check_usage.pl script is used to do the following:

◆ Add reply attributes to specify the available bytes for a user. This includes the calculation of Gigaword values.

◆ Specify the return code as updated if reply attributes were added.

◆ Reject the request if the data usage exceeds the allotted portion by specifying the return code as reject and adding a Reply-Message.

Here's the contents of check_usage.pl:

```
#! usr/bin/perl -w

use strict;

# use ...
# This is very important!
use vars qw(%RAD_CHECK %RAD_REPLY);
use constant    RLM_MODULE_OK=>          2;#  /* the module is OK,
continue */
use constant    RLM_MODULE_UPDATED=>     8;#  /* OK (pairs modified) */
use constant    RLM_MODULE_REJECT=>      0;#  /* immediately reject the
request */
use constant    RLM_MODULE_NOOP=>        7;

my $int_max = 4294967296;

sub authorize {
        #We will reply, depending on the usage
        #If FRBG-Total-Bytes is larger than the 32-bit limit we have
to set a Gigaword attribute
        if(exists($RAD_CHECK{'FRBG-Total-Bytes'}) && exists($RAD_
CHECK{'FRBG-Used-Bytes'})){
                $RAD_CHECK{'FRBG-Avail-Bytes'} = $RAD_CHECK{'FRBG-
Total-Bytes'} - $RAD_CHECK{'FRBG-Used-Bytes'};
        }else{
                return RLM_MODULE_NOOP;
        }
```

```
            if($RAD_CHECK{'FRBG-Avail-Bytes'} <= $RAD_CHECK{'FRBG-Used-
Bytes'}){
                    if($RAD_CHECK{'FRBG-Reset-Type'} ne 'never'){
                            $RAD_REPLY{'Reply-Message'} = "Maximum $RAD_
CHECK{'FRBG-Reset-Type'} usage exceeded";
                    }else{
                            $RAD_REPLY{'Reply-Message'} = "Maximum usage
exceeded";
                    }
                    return RLM_MODULE_REJECT;
            }
            if($RAD_CHECK{'FRBG-Avail-Bytes'} >= $int_max){
                    #Mikrotik's reply attributes
                    $RAD_REPLY{'Mikrotik-Total-Limit'} = $RAD_CHECK{'FRBG-
Avail-Bytes'} % $int_max;
                    $RAD_REPLY{'Mikrotik-Total-Limit-Gigawords'} =
int($RAD_CHECK{'FRBG-Avail-Bytes'} / $int_max );
                    #Coova Chilli's reply attributes
                    $RAD_REPLY{'ChilliSpot-Max-Total-Octets'} = $RAD_
CHECK{'FRBG-Avail-Bytes'} % $int_max;
                    $RAD_REPLY{'ChilliSpot-Max-Total-Gigawords'} =
int($RAD_CHECK{'FRBG-Avail-Bytes'} / $int_max );
            }else{
                    $RAD_REPLY{'Mikrotik-Total-Limit'} = $RAD_CHECK{'FRBG-
Avail-Bytes'};
                    $RAD_REPLY{'ChilliSpot-Max-Total-Octets'} = $RAD_
CHECK{'FRBG-Avail-Bytes'};
            }
            return RLM_MODULE_UPDATED;
    }
```

Since Isaac uses Mikrotik and Coova Chilli, we include their AVPs used for limiting total data. Consult the documentation of your NAS to determine if it supports data limiting and which AVPs should be used for that.

Installing the perl module on CentOS

The FreeRADIUS `perl` module is packed separately in CentOS. Ensure that this package is installed. SUSE and Ubuntu already include the `perl` module with the standard installation of FreeRADIUS although there is also, added as a bonus, one bug, which we will remove later.

Updating the dictionary files

FreeRADIUS includes dictionary files for the various vendors. The attributes we wish to return are part of later developments from these vendors and are not included inside the dictionary files that come standard with FreeRADIUS. We have to include them by adding them to the existing dictionary files. The dictionary files for vendors are usually under the `/usr/share/freeradius` directory. If you installed FreeRADIUS using the `configure`, `make`, `make install` pattern it will be under `/usr/local/share/freeradius`.

Find the location of the vendor dictionaries and add the following attributes to the respective dictionaries:

- `dictionary.chillispot`

ATTRIBUTE	ChilliSpot-Max-Input-Gigawords	21	integer
ATTRIBUTE	ChilliSpot-Max-Output-Gigawords	22	integer
ATTRIBUTE	ChilliSpot-Max-Total-Gigawords	23	integer

- `dictionary.mikrotik`

ATTRIBUTE	Mikrotik-Total-Limit	17	integer
ATTRIBUTE	Mikrotik-Total-Limit-Gigawords	18	integer

The changes that we have just made are to the attributes of a vendor (VSAs) and can be transmitted inside the RADIUS packets over the wire. VSAs are different from the attributes that we added earlier to the main dictionary file that are used internally by the FreeRADIUS server.

Remember that using the latest version of Mikrotik and Coova Chilli will ensure these attributes are supported. Also see if there are additional attributes introduced with the latest versions that need to be included.

The recommended way of updating dictionaries

This exercise does not follow the recommended way of updating dictionary files. There is a dedicated chapter on dictionaries later in the book, which covers the recommended way to keep dictionaries up-to-date.

The way dictionaries are included during start-up is also covered in more detail in the chapter on dictionaries. In short, the master `dictionary` file under the FreeRADIUS configuration directory includes a file called `/usr/share/freeradius/dictionary`. This file in turn includes the various `.dictionary` files located under `/usr/share/freeradius/`.

Preparing the users file

We will use the `users` file as a user store. In the real world you can use other sources such as an SQL database or an LDAP directory.

Ensure the `users` file contains the following entry for alice:

```
"alice" Cleartext-Password := "passme",FRBG-Total-Bytes
:='9126805504',FRBG-Reset-Type := 'monthly'
Reply-Message = "Hello, %{User-Name}"
```

This will limit data use to 8.5 GB each month.

Preparing the SQL database

Although we define `alice` in the `users` file, we will use SQL for accounting. Follow these steps to prepare the database:

1. Ensure you have a working SQL configuration as specified in *Chapter 5, Sources of Usernames and Passwords*.

2. We will not use SQL as a user store. Confirm that `sql` is disabled (commented out) inside the `authorize` section in the `sites-enabled/default` file under the FreeRADIUS configuration directory.

3. For our data counter to be successful ensure `sql` is enabled (uncommented) inside the `accounting` section in the `sites-enabled/default` file under the FreeRADIUS configuration directory.

4. Use the `mysql` client program and clean-up any previous accounting details that may still exist in the database:

    ```
    $>mysql -u root -p radius
    delete from radacct;
    ```

5. Later in this exercise we will simulate accounting using the `radclient` program. Make sure you create the `4088_06_acct_start.txt` and `4088_06_acct_stop.txt` files specified in *Chapter 6, Accounting*.

You may be concerned that the `sql` module also has the 32-bit integer limitation. Fortunately this has all been taken care of in the newer versions of FreeRADIUS. FreeRADIUS takes care of combining the Gigaword carry bit AVP with the octet AVP before updating the SQL database. The SQL schema for MySQL also uses `bigint(20)` to store octet values, which is more than enough to store large numbers.

Adding unlang code to the virtual server

All the preparation up to now was done in order for us to add the next piece of unlang code to the virtual server definition. Add the following code just below the `daily` entry inside the `authorize` section in the `sites-enabled/default` file under the FreeRADIUS configuration directory.

```
if((control:FRBG-Total-Bytes)&&(control:FRBG-Reset-Type)){
    reset_time
    if(updated){      # Reset Time was updated,
                      # we can now use it in a query
        update control {
            #Get the total usage up to now:
            FRBG-Used-Bytes := "%{sql:SELECT
IFNULL(SUM(acctinputoctets - GREATEST((%{control:FRBG-
Start-Time} - UNIX_TIMESTAMP(acctstarttime)), 0))+
SUM(acctoutputoctets -GREATEST((%{control:FRBG-Start-Time}
- UNIX_TIMESTAMP(acctstarttime)), 0)),0) FROM radacct WHERE
username='%{request:User-Name}' AND UNIX_TIMESTAMP(acctstarttime) +
acctsessiontime > '%{control:FRBG-Start-Time}'}"
        }
    }
    else{
        #Asumes reset type = never
        #Get the total usage of the user
        update control {
            FRBG-Used-Bytes := "%{sql:SELECT IFNULL(SUM(ac
ctinputoctets)+SUM(acctoutputoctets),0) FROM radacct WHERE
username='%{request:User-Name}'}"
        }
    }
    #Now we know how much they are allowed to use and the usage.
    check_usage
}
```

The data counter is now complete.

The SUSE and Ubuntu bug

There is a bug in SUSE and Ubuntu that results in an error if FreeRADIUS is using the `perl` module. Time to squash it!

Restart the FreeRADIUS server in debug mode. Although it may sound strange, if all goes well you should get an error message similar to the following:

```
/usr/sbin/radiusd: symbol lookup error: /usr/lib/perl5/5.10.0/i586-
linux-thread-multi/auto/Fcntl/Fcntl.so: undefined symbol: Perl_Istack_
sp_ptr
```

This is because there is a problem with the dynamic loading of required `perl` modules.

If you do not get an error, it may be because your installation of FreeRADIUS does not have this reported problem. If you have, for instance, compiled FreeRADIUS on your own with the `configure`, `make`, `make install` pattern, this error should not be present.

Pre-loading Perl library

To overcome the dynamic loading problem we first have to set the `LD_PRELOAD` environment variable before starting the FreeRADIUS server. Unfortunately the location and name of the library to specify for pre-loading is different on each distribution.

We have to specify the `libperl.so` library. The following command will help us to locate and determine precisely what this library is called on your distribution. If the results yield more than one, they are usually various symbolic links to a single library.

```
$>find / -name "*libperl.so*"
```

Use the table below as a reference:

Distribution	Location of libperl.so
SLES	`/usr/lib/perl5/5.10.0/i586-linux-thread-multi/CORE/libperl.so`
Ubuntu	`/usr/lib/libperl.so`

Understanding environment variables

Wikipedia defines environment variables as the following:

`http://en.wikipedia.org/wiki/Environment_variable`

Environment variables are a set of dynamic named values that can affect the way running processes will behave on a computer. They can be said in some sense to create the operating environment in which a process runs.

Testing the data counter

The moment of truth has arrived. It is time to test the data counter. If you use SUSE or Ubuntu, remember the `LD_PRELOAD`. CentOS does not have this problem.

1. Restart FreeRADIUS in debug mode; set the `LD_PRELOAD` environment variable if required. We assume Ubuntu here. Please change to suit your distribution:

   ```
   #>LD_PRELOAD=/usr/lib/libperl.so /usr/sbin/freeradius -X
   ```

2. Try to authenticate as alice using the `radtest` command:

```
$>radtest alice passme 127.0.0.1 100 testing123
```

3. You should get the following AVPs in the reply from FreeRADIUS:

```
ChilliSpot-Max-Total-Gigawords = 2
ChilliSpot-Max-Total-Octets = 536870912
Mikrotik-Total-Limit-Gigawords = 2
Mikrotik-Total-Limit = 536870912
Reply-Message = "Hello, alice"
```

4. Simulate some accounting by using `radtest` in combination with the `4088_06_acct_start.txt` and `4088_06_acct_stop.txt` files:

```
$>radclient 127.0.0.1 auto testing123 -f 4088_06_acct_start.txt
$>radclient 127.0.0.1 auto testing123 -f 4088_06_acct_stop.txt
```

5. Try to authenticate again as alice using the `radtest` command. You should now get different values back in the reply showing how the remaining data is depleted:

```
ChilliSpot-Max-Total-Gigawords = 2
ChilliSpot-Max-Total-Octets = 536866638
Mikrotik-Total-Limit-Gigawords = 2
Mikrotik-Total-Limit = 536866638
```

6. Repeat the accounting simulation and authentication testing cycle a couple of times. Note how the available bytes are reduced with each cycle.

Clean-up

To complete this exercise in a proper way you can do the following as a challenge:

- Define a policy in the `policy.conf` file. The contents will be the unlang code that we added to the `default` file. Replace that code with the newly created policy.

- Add the LD_PRELOAD environment variable to the FreeRADIUS start-up scripts on SUSE and Ubuntu.

Summary

Authorization can become the most complex part of FreeRADIUS. By making good use of what unlang offers, we can overcome almost every imaginable problem.

In this chapter, we have covered:

◆ Applications of restrictions: Restrictions can be applied at the RADIUS server or at the NAS device.

◆ Unlang: Unlang is a powerful processing language that allows us to manipulate the way an incoming request is handled by FreeRADIUS. It features conditional checks that can control the flow of a request. It also allows for interaction with certain modules like the `sql` module to obtain results from an SQL database. Unlang enables us to manipulate and add AVPs that will be returned with `Access-Accept` packets. The use of unlang should be mastered by anyone who wants to create flexible and versatile configurations in FreeRADIUS.

With this chapter on Authorization at an end, we have now completed the coverage of the AAA framework. The rest of this book will focus on more advanced topics of RADIUS, as well as subjects specific to FreeRADIUS.

Pop quiz – authorization

1. You are implementing a restriction at the NAS by returning an AVP that is supposed to enforce bandwidth throttling for a user. It somehow does not seem to work correctly. What may be wrong?

2. Like any hardcore IT dude you'd like your FreeRADIUS server to be super fast. Unfortunately you have to make use of external code to get the value for an attribute. This can be done through Bash or Perl. Which option will yield the best performance?

3. Where will you define attributes that will be used internally by unlang?

4. What is the attribute list called where the internal attributes are stored and how will I reference the `Auth-Type` attribute inside this list?

5. You have inherited a FreeRADIUS deployment and while going through the configuration files you come across the following piece of unlang code inside the `policy.conf` file:

```
rewrite_calling_station_id {
    if (request:Calling-Station-Id =~ /([0-9a-f]{2})[-:]?([0-9a-
f]{2})[-:]?([0-9a-f]{2})[-:]?([0-9a-f]{2})[-:]?([0-9a-f]{2})
[-:]?([0-9a-f]{2})/i){
        update request {
            Calling-Station-Id := "%{1}-%{2}-%{3}-%{4}-%{5}-
%{6}"
        }
    }
    else {
        noop
    }
}
```

What does this code do?

8

Virtual Servers

A major new feature in the 2.x branch of FreeRADIUS was the introduction of virtual servers. This concept is not new and was already used by web servers when the 2.x branch came into being. FreeRADIUS, however, was the first to introduce virtual servers to RADIUS. This chapter gives more insight into the world of virtual servers in RADIUS.

In this chapter we shall:

- ◆ See why you would use virtual servers
- ◆ See how virtual servers are defined and enabled
- ◆ Explore the `listen` and `client` sections
- ◆ Discover pre-defined virtual servers

So let's get on with it...

Why use virtual servers?

Virtual servers are the best thing since powdered milk! You may ask just why we make such a statement. The reason is because of the flexibility they introduce. With a virtual server you can create a tailor-made policy and wrap this inside a functional unit.

Virtual RADIUS servers are very different in concept and function from real virtual servers like one that is virtualized with VMware or VirtualBox. Virtual servers in RADIUS makes easy yet powerful configuration possible because they allow a clean separation of policies. This was not possible in earlier versions of FreeRADIUS.

One of a virtual server's policies will, for instance, specify the use of an LDAP directory user store while another virtual server will specify an SQL database. These two servers can then be used independently from each other. The decision of which virtual server to use can be specified in one of the following sections in the FreeRADIUS configuration:

- ◆ `listen`: Depending on a specified IP address, port, and packet type combination, a virtual server will be selected. `Listen` sections are usually found in the `radius.conf` file. The `listen` section is a popular place to specify a virtual server. FreeRADIUS allows multiple `listen` sections and each of these sections can be used to group a certain IP address and UDP port combination together with a virtual server. When used in this way, the server running FreeRADIUS will typically have multiple IP addresses.

- ◆ `client`: Depending on the IP address of a client, a virtual server will be selected. Clients are defined in the `clients.conf` file.

- ◆ `home_server_pool`, `home_server`, or `realm`: Specify a virtual server that will be used to send proxy requests through. Proxying is configured through the `proxy.conf` file and is covered later in the book.

- ◆ `EAP tunnels`: Specify a virtual server to be used by EAP's PEAP or TTLS inner-tunnel methods. EAP is configured through the `eap.conf` file and is covered later in the book.

A virtual server is specified through the `virtual_server = <virtual server>` directive inside these sections. Time to get our hands dirty.

A virtual server policy should not be confused with policies inside the `policy.conf` file. The policy of a virtual server refers to a virtual server's characteristics whereas a policy in the `policy.conf` file is simply a piece of `unlang` code wrapped and named for easy reference and usability.

Defining and enabling virtual servers

FreeRADIUS has two virtual servers enabled by default. They are located under the `sites-enabled` sub-directory of the FreeRADIUS configuration directory. They are:

- ◆ `default`: The name pretty much says what the virtual server does. This virtual server handles all the default requests that are not explicitly specified to be handled by a `virtual_server` directive. We have used this virtual server exclusively up to now.

- ◆ `inner-tunnel`: This virtual server is used for certain tunneled EAP requests like TTLS and PEAP.

These two virtual servers allow FreeRADIUS to handle normal RADIUS authentication requests (`default`) as well as EAP/TTLS and EAP/PEAP requests (`inner-tunnel`) out of the box.

If you look at the `eap.conf` file located under the FreeRADIUS configuration directory you can see the configuration of the two EAP methods specifying the `inner-tunnel` virtual server. The following is an excerpt from the `eap.conf` file:

```
eap {
    ...
    ttls {
    {
        ...
        virtual_server = inner-tunnel
    }
}
```

FreeRADIUS follows the same convention as Apache where virtual servers are defined under a `sites-available` directory and activated by creating a symbolic link to a `sites-enabled` directory. The contents of these files are typically a single named `server` section where the name corresponds to the file name.

Time for action – creating two virtual servers

In this exercise we will create two very simple virtual servers. The one will accept all authentication requests while the other will reject all authentication requests.

1. Under the `sites-available` directory inside the FreeRADIUS configuration directory, create a file called `always_accept` with the following content:

```
server always_accept {
    authorize {
        update control {
            Auth-Type := "Accept"
        }
    }
}
```

2. Under the `sites-available` directory inside the FreeRADIUS configuration directory, create a file called `always_reject` with the following content:

```
server always_reject {
    authorize {
        update control {
                    Auth-Type := "Reject"
```

```
                }
            }
        }
```

3. Ensure you are in the FreeRADIUS configuration directory. Enable these virtual servers by creating symbolic links from the `sites-enabled` directory to the files just created in the `sites-available` directory:

```
# ln -s ../sites-available/always_accept sites-enabled/always_
accept
# ln -s ../sites-available/always_reject sites-enabled/always_
reject
```

A **symbolic link** is a special kind of file that contains a reference to another file. Whether you edit the symbolic link or the original file, in the end you edit the same file since the symbolic link simply points to the original file. Symbolic links can span file systems and can even be used to reference directories.

What just happened?

We have defined and enabled two very simple virtual servers. One will always pass authentication requests while the other will always reject authentication requests.

Available sub-sections

To create a virtual server we use a named `server` section:

```
    server <virtual server name> {
        . . .
    }
```

Various sub-sections are then added inside this `server` section. If there is a `server` section without a name, it is used as the default `server` section. This default `server` section will be used when there is no `virtual_server` directive defined in those sections where it could be defined (the `listen`, `client`, `home_server_pool`, `ttls`, and `peap` sections).

You may have observed that the `sites-enabled/default` file does not even contain a `server { . . . }` section. It is not an absolute requirement to wrap the default virtual server in an anonymous `server { . . . }` section. All the other virtual servers are required to be wrapped inside a named server section though.

The sub-sections that will be used by a virtual server depend on the request that is sent to the virtual server. The following table lists common requests and sub-sections that will be involved with the request.

Request	Section
Access-Request	`authorize`, `authenticate`, `session`, `post-auth`
Accounting-Request	`pre-acct`, `accounting`

We can also use `pre-proxy` and `post-proxy` sub-sections. This is part of proxying and covered later in the book. There are also two special sub-sections called `listen` and `client`. They are called special since they can be global to FreeRADIUS or local to a virtual server, depending on where they are defined. These two sub-sections are covered in this chapter.

The two virtual servers we have created take care of the `Access-Request` in the `authorize` section in full. Defining other sections is not required. Beware not to create duplicates when you define virtual servers. There is no direct correlation between a filename and the virtual server defined inside the file. We only use it as a convention to keep the filename and the virtual server's name the same. FreeRADIUS does not care about the filename or how many server sections are declared in a file. It will even load multiple server definitions with the same name without an error. This can lead to unexpected results.

If you define extra `listen` sections also make sure they connect to the correct interface and have the correct IP address, port, and type.

Enabling and disabling virtual servers

Remember that when a virtual server is enabled, all the modules used by that virtual server will be loaded when FreeRADIUS starts. A virtual server can also introduce additional UDP ports that FreeRADIUS will listen on for requests. If you are memory and security conscious it is good practice to disable unused virtual servers.

Our servers are created, willing, and enabled. Let's take them for a test drive.

Using enabled virtual servers

Creating and making a virtual server available does not put it in use yet. We have to explicitly specify it as the value of the `virtual_server` directive.

Time for action – using a virtual server

Follow these steps to make a virtual server available:

1. Edit the `radiusd.conf` file in the FreeRADIUS configuration directory and add the following to the `listen` section that contains `type = auth` (there are two `listen` sections, one has `type = auth`, the other has `type = acct`):

   `virtual_server = always_accept`.

2. Restart FreeRADIUS in debug mode.

3. Try to authenticate any user with any password. Your request should be accepted every time.

4. Observe the debug output when FreeRADIUS accepts the request.

5. Edit the `radiusd.conf` file again, but this time change the `virtual_server` directive from `virtual_server = always_accept` to `virtual_server = always_reject`.

6. Restart FreeRADIUS in debug mode.

7. Try to authenticate specifying any user with any password. Your request should be rejected every time.

8. Observe the debug output when FreeRADIUS rejects the request.

9. On completion of this exercise comment the `virtual_server` directive out again. This will leave the FreeRADIUS server as it was before the exercise.

What just happened?

We have used the two virtual servers created during the first practical exercise of this chapter to override the default virtual server. First all authentication requests were accepted and then all authentication requests were rejected.

Including a virtual server

The use of a virtual server can be specified inside the `listen` or the `client` sections. The `listen` sections are defined in the `radius.conf` file and the `client` sections are contained inside the `clinets.conf` file. It is specified by adding the optional `virtual_server` directive inside either of these sections. When we specify a virtual server in a `listen` section, it is more general since the `listen` section specifies details on how a client connects to FreeRADIUS. This includes the type of requests FreeRADIUS will receive from anyone as well as the IP address and port it listens on for these requests.

When we specify a virtual server in a `client` section it is specific. Unless the client connects with a specified IP address and shared secret, the virtual server will not be used. A `client` section defines a client and adds it into the configuration. You could repeat the previous exercise by specifying the `virtual_server` directive in the `localhost client` definition in the same way we specified it in the `listen` section. This would then only apply to requests from the localhost, for example, when `radtest` is executed from the same machine on which the FreeRADIUS server runs.

Handling Post-Auth-Type correctly

If you look at the debug output when the authentication request is rejected, you will see the following warning:

```
Using Post-Auth-Type Reject
    WARNING: Unknown value specified for Post-Auth-Type.  Cannot perform
requested action.

Delaying reject of request 0 for 1 seconds
```

This is because `Post-Auth-Type` has a value that is not handled in a `post-auth` section of the virtual server. To fix this, update the `always_reject` file to the following and the warning will be gone:

```
server always_reject {
    authorize {
        update control {
            Auth-Type := Reject
        }
    }

    post-auth {
        Post-Auth-Type REJECT {
            noop
        }
    }
}
```

Taking care of Type attributes

Five of the sections that can be contained inside a virtual server have an accompanying special attribute. When this special attribute is set, FreeRADIUS will look for a sub-section inside the section to handle the value of this attribute. The sub-section is in the following format:

```
<special attribute> <value> {
    ...
}
```

If this special attribute is set to some value it will cause FreeRADIUS to look for a sub-section with that value. Only this sub-section will be executed. Everything else inside the section will be ignored. If the sub-section is not defined a warning will be raised as we experienced with `Post-Auth-Type = REJECT`.

The following table lists these special attributes and the section to which they apply. It also lists an application of their use. You will note that they all end with the word "Type".

Special attribute	Apply to section	Practical implementation
`Post-Auth-Type`	`post-auth`	Record failures to a separate database.
`Auth-Type`	`authenticate`	Use `ldap` for authentication if the `ldap` module found the user inside the LDAP directory.
`Authz-Type`	`authorize`	Use different LDAP servers based on the check attribute of a user.
`Acct-Type`	`accounting`	Specify which accounting database should be used based on the check attribute of a user.
`Session-Type`	`session`	Specify how session checking should be done per user.

In our example we have never explicitly set `Post-Auth-Type` to `REJECT`; however, when the value of `Auth-Type` is changed to `Reject`, `rlm_reject` sets the value of `Post-Auth-Type = REJECT` for us. This enables us to differentiate between access rejects and access accepts and also to handle them differently.

You can also refer to the `authenticate` section inside the `default` virtual server. The `authenticate` section makes use of the `Auth-Type` attribute, which is set by modules inside the `authorize` section. The next exercise will be on the practical implementation of virtual servers.

Virtual server for happy hour

Isaac is supplying Wi-Fi hotspots to a small university. He has deployed a fair number of access points. The president of the university has agreed for Isaac to accept unknown users' authentication attempts on the access point in the canteen between 13:00 and 14:00. This promotion is called Hotspot Happy Hour. Today is April Fools' day and Isaac was granted permission to Rickroll everyone using the canteen's Access Point.

Never been Rickrolled? Consider yourself lucky. You can read more about Rickrolling on Wikipedia: `http://en.wikipedia.org/wiki/Rickrolling`.

Time for action – incorporating the Hotspot Happy Hour policy

We will use a virtual server to incorporate the Hotspot Happy Hour policy. This will then be added to the access point in the canteen's client definition. When we apply the virtual server to a client definition it makes it easy to use the same virtual server with other clients also.

Enabling the Happy Hour virtual server

Follow these steps to enable the server:

1. Under the `sites-available` directory inside the FreeRADIUS configuration directory, create a file called `happy_hour` with the following content:

```
server happy_hour {
    authorize {
        files
        # If user not present allow them free access
        # between 13:00 and 14:00
        if(noop){
            update control {
                Login-Time := 'Al1300-1400'
                Auth-Type := "Accept"
            }
        }
        # April Fools' Day prank - Rickroll everyone
        update reply {
            WISPr-Redirection-URL :=
            "http://www.youtube.com/watch?v=oHg5SJYRHA0"
        }
        logintime
        pap
    }
    authenticate {
        Auth-Type PAP {
            pap
        }
    }
}
```

2. Ensure you are in the FreeRADIUS configuration directory. Enable the `happy_hour` virtual server by creating a symbolic link to the `sites-enabled` directory:

   `# ln -s ../sites-available/happy_hour sites-enabled/happy_hour`

Adding the virtual server to a client

For this exercise we will imagine the `localhost` client is the access point in the canteen. We will tie the `happy_hour` virtual server to the `localhost` client:

1. Edit the `clients.conf` file inside the FreeRADIUS configuration and add a virtual server directive at the end of the `localhost` client section:

   `virtual_server = happy_hour`

2. Restart FreeRADIUS in debug mode and use the `radtest` program to test authentication. The reply attributes will change according to the time of day and whether the user is known or unknown. However today everyone will be Rickrolled!

3. You may change the value of login time in the `happy_hour` virtual server to fall in the time that you test to simulate Hotspot Happy Hour.

4. On completion of this exercise comment the `virtual_server` directive out again. This will leave the FreeRADIUS server as it was before the exercise.

What just happened?

We have used the `virtual_server` directive in the client section to force a client to use a virtual server.

There is not much to the virtual server we created. It uses basic `unlang` to meet our requirements. If the file's flow does not make sense you are encouraged to revisit *Chapter 7, Authorization*.

In the real world

You should never just run a promotion like this without restricting the bandwidth of each connection. Most captive portals feature `reply` attributes that are used for this. In Isaac's case he can choose between the generic `WISPr-Bandwidth-Max-Up` and `WISPr-Bandwidth-Max-Down` or attributes specific to Mikrotik (`Mikrotik-Rate-Limit`) and Coova Chilli (`Chillispot-Bandwidth-Max-[Up|Down]`).

The `default` virtual server will still be used by all the other clients. Only the access point in the canteen will use the `happy_hour` virtual server. This functionality makes it very easy for initial test runs on new policies. The testing can be done on limited clients before putting these policies into production.

Defining clients in SQL

If you would rather define clients in the `nas` table of the MySQL database instead of the `clients.conf` file, you may notice that the `nas` table's schema in `sql/mysql/nas.sql` does not include an option to specify a virtual server by default.

The `server` column, which is commented out inside the `nas` table definition, is used for this. If you want to make use of this `server` column to specify the virtual server, uncomment the line when creating the table. Remember to also update the `nas_query` in the `sql/mysql/dialup.conf` file to include the `server` column:

```
nas_query = "SELECT id, nasname, shortname, type, secret, server FROM
${nas_table}"
```

Finally make sure the `readclients = yes` line is uncommented in the `sql.conf` file.

In this chapter's first exercise we tied a virtual server to a `listen` section. In this exercise we tied the virtual server to a `client` section. The next exercise will explore `client` and `listen` sections that are contained inside the virtual server definition.

Consolidating an existing setup using a virtual server

Isaac has been approached by the dean of the Computer Science faculty. The faculty has always had its own FreeRADIUS server but now it would rather do away with it and make use of one central RADIUS server.

Time for action – creating a virtual server for the Computer Science faculty

Isaac discovered that the Computer Science faculty practices security by obscurity. Its RADIUS server uses port 2812 for authentication and 2813 for accounting. It has a `users` file that contains the entire details of the users. The RADIUS clients only send authentication requests to the RADIUS server. The following table lists important information:

Information item	Detail
User store	users file
Authentication port	2812

Information item	Detail
Accounting port (unused)	2813
Computer Science RADIUS server IP Address	10.10.0.100
RADIUS client IP Address (authentication only)	10.10.0.200

Consolidation implementation

From of the information Isaac gathered we can do the following:

- Create a named `files` section to take care of the `users` file
- Create a virtual server with local `listen` and `client` sections
- Incorporate this new virtual server

Let's tackle these!

A named files section

Module-specific configurations are done through files located in the `modules` sub-directory under the FreeRADIUS configuration directory. The default behavior of the `files` module is specified inside the `files` file. By default the `files` module sources the `users` file to determine if a user is defined. The specific file to source is configurable and is specified by the `usersfile` directive.

If we want to incorporate a second `users` file, we simply create an additional named `files` section. The original `files` section is not named because it is typically the only one in the configuration. All subsequent `files` sections have to be named.

- Under the `modules` directory inside the FreeRADIUS configuration directory, create a file called `files_cs` with the following content:

```
files files_cs{
    usersfile = ${confdir}/users_cs
    acctusersfile = ${confdir}/acct_users
    preproxy_usersfile = ${confdir}/preproxy_users
    compat = no
}
```

- Create a file called `users_cs` inside the FreeRADIUS configuration directory with the following content:

```
"bob" Cleartext-Password := "passbob"
    Reply-Message = "Hello, %{User-Name}"
```

A virtual server for the Computer Science faculty

The server section allows us to declare various `listen` and `client` sub-sections as local to the server section. To contain the Computer Science faculty's configuration inside a single server section we will make use of these sub-sections.

Create a file called `faculty_cs` in the `sites-available` sub-directory under the FreeRADIUS configuration directory with the following contents:

```
server faculty_cs {
    listen {
        ipaddr = *
        port = 2812
        type = auth
    }
    client cs_vpn {
        ipaddr = 10.10.0.200
        secret = bigone
        require_message_authenticator = no
        nastype = other
    }
    client cs_troubleshoot {
        ipaddr = 127.0.0.1
        secret = bigone
        require_message_authenticator = no
        nastype = other
    }
    authorize {
        files_cs
        pap
    }
    authenticate {
        Auth-Type PAP {
            pap
        }
    }
}
```

Ensure you are in the FreeRADIUS configuration directory. Enable the `faculty_cs` virtual server by creating a symbolic link to the `sites-enabled` directory:

```
# ln -s ../sites-available/faculty_cs sites-enabled/faculty_cs
```

Incorporating the new virtual server

Everything should now be ready for us to try out the new virtual server:

1. Restart FreeRADIUS in debug mode.

2. Try to authenticate as bob using the `faculty_cs` virtual server using the following command:

    ```
    $> radtest bob passbob 127.0.0.1:2812 100 bigone
    ```

3. Confirm that alice who is defined in the `users` file and used by the `default` virtual server is not authenticated on the `faculty_cs` virtual server:

    ```
    $> radtest alice passme 127.0.0.1:2812 100 bigone
    ```

What just happened?

We have just proved how easy it is to consolidate different RADIUS servers into one by using virtual servers.

What about users stored in SQL?

A question you may ask is: Suppose we store our user data in an SQL database and the Computer Science faculty's users were also stored in an SQL database, how would we consolidate this? This can be done by defining multiple `sql` instances in the `sql.conf` file:

```
sql sql_canteen {
..
}
sql sql_cs {
..
}
```

Then use the name you want in the virtual server instead of `sql`. This is the same principle we've applied with the `files` module.

When IP addresses and ports clash

We were fortunate because the Computer Science faculty is not using the default port of 1812 for authentication. If it were also using port 1812 we would have to differentiate requests to its virtual server by another means. The usual way will be by assigning a second IP address to the FreeRADIUS server's network interface. Here are some general rules to follow when multiple IP addresses are used for virtual server differentiation.

♦   Use the `ifconfig` command to add a second IP Address to the network interface.

    ```
    # ifconfig eth0:0 10.10.0.100 netmask 255.255.255.0 up
    ```

◆ Update all other `listen` sections that specify `listen = *` to `listen = <IP Address>`. You may have to add optional `listen` sections to include both 127.0.0.1 and the first IP address of the network interface to make the default setup work as before.

Local listen and client sections

By specifying `listen` and `client` sections inside a virtual server definition we keep the unity of a virtual server. Since `client` and `listen` sections are already part of the virtual server this allows a virtual server configuration to be transferred with ease from one physical server to another.

Because local `listen` and `client` sections are already inside a virtual server, we cannot use the `virtual_server` directive in them. The `client` definitions are pretty straightforward. The `listen` section however has a `type` directive with some interesting options.

IPv6

FreeRADIUS supports listening on an IPv6 address as an alternative to the IPv4 address. Because this component of the FreeRADIUS server is newer compared to the more established IPv4 code there may still be bug fixes and improvements coming out. You are advised to use the latest available release when using IPv6. The package for version 2.1.8 of FreeRADIUS, for instance, that comes with Ubuntu 8.04 has a bug that prevents it from listening on an IPv6 address.

As more and more admins use IPv6 addressing these initial teething problems will be solved. Unfortunately we have a chicken and egg scenario in IPv6 now with many vendors, since they are first waiting for a mass uptake of IPv6 before adapting the RADIUS client code to support IPv6 addressing.

Listen section → type directive

Up to now we have used the `auth` and `acct` options for the `type` directive inside the `listen` section. There are, however, also other options available for this directive. Some of them are used in more advanced configurations, which will be covered later in this book. For completeness we will tabulate them here:

Option	Where used
proxy	Proxy requests to other RADIUS servers
detail	High-performance deployments or with requests that have to be send to multiple databases
status	To get stats from the FreeRADIUS server
coa	To forward disconnect requests to other RADIUS servers

When you define a client there is no way to restrict the type of requests we can receive from the client inside the `client` definition. Restricting is done with the `listen` sections. `Listen` sections define the type of request we will respond to. We have only specified `auth`. If we wanted to also respond to accounting requests, we would have to add a second `listen` section of `type = acct`.

The next part of this chapter looks at some pre-defined virtual servers. They each contain a local `listen` section to fulfill a special requirement.

Pre-defined virtual servers

FreeRADIUS includes virtual servers under the `sites-available` sub-directory. Some can be used as is, while others are templates to use for special requirements. The following are some virtual servers:

- ♦ `buffered-sql`: This virtual server is used to overcome speed limitations on large SQL databases (`type = detail`).

- ♦ `copy-acct-to-home-server`: This virtual server can be used as a template for recording one accounting request in two places (`type = detail`).

- ♦ `coa`: A template for handling `coa` (Change of Authority) and `pod` (Packet of Disconnect) requests (`type = coa`).

- ♦ `decoupled-accounting`: A template to decouple accounting. Works on the same principles as the `buffered-sql` virtual server (`type = detail`).

- ♦ `status`: A virtual server to get status information from a FreeRADIUS server (`type = status`).

As we mentioned at the start of this chapter, the strength of virtual servers is their flexibility. Since virtual servers are so flexible, there are no fixed rules when creating and implementing virtual servers. The best way is to experiment in order to get more experience. The motto of Perl also applies here. There's more than one way to do it (TIMTOWTDI).

Summary

As an overview here are some key points on virtual servers:

- ♦ FreeRADIUS has two virtual servers enabled by default. They are called `default` and `inner-tunnel`.

- ♦ Virtual servers are defined inside the `sites-available` directory and activated by linking it to the `sites-enabled` directory.

- ♦ The use of a specific virtual server can be specified in the global `listen` and `client` sections.

◆ A virtual server can alternatively contain local `listen` and `client` sections.

◆ There are example virtual servers available in the `sites-available` directory, which can be used as templates for special requirements.

The various sections inside virtual servers make use of modules. In the next chapter we will take a more in-depth look at the use of modules.

Pop quiz – virtual servers

1. Your need to evaluate a new VPN server that supports RADIUS. This server should use a separate SQL database to store user detail. How can you use a virtual server on your current FreeRADIUS deployment to test this VPN server with minimum impact to the other RADIUS clients?

2. Your FreeRADIUS deployment is using an SQL database to store accounting records. The response, however, has been deteriorating over the last two years as the database grew in size. What virtual server setup can you use to remedy the response problem?

3. You have inherited a half working FreeRADIUS server. The previous owner tried to implement a Perl module without success. When you run the server in debug mode you see the following message:

```
ERROR: Failed parsing value "PERL" for attribute Auth-Type:
Unknown value PERL for attribute Auth-Type
```

Why is this showing and how can you fix this?

9
Modules

The use of modules is a standard practice in well-designed programs. The Linux kernel for instance makes use of modules. The kernel itself is very small with basic functionality. This functionality is extended by loading kernel modules. The kernel will, for instance, load a module for the display card or load a module for the Wi-Fi network card. This allows for the exclusion of unnecessary functionality, which in turn results in a faster and more secure system.

FreeRADIUS follows the same philosophy and can be extended with ease. This allows you to run a fast and secure server; however, this server's functionality can be extended easily through the use of modules.

The aim of this chapter is to give you a thorough understanding of modules as a core component of the FreeRADIUS server. This will help you to populate the various sections that can be contained inside a virtual server definition with more wisdom and better understanding.

In this chapter we shall:

- ◆ See how to include and configure modules
- ◆ See which configuration sections can contain modules
- ◆ Use one module with different configurations
- ◆ Discuss the order and return codes of modules
- ◆ Look at some interesting modules

So let's get on with it...

Installed, available, and missing modules

In the previous chapters we were already exposed to various modules that helped with Authorization, Authentication, and Accounting (AAA). As a refresher and introduction to this chapter the following table lists some of them:

Module	Function
`files`	Makes use of the `users` file located in the FreeRADIUS configuration directory to find a user's detail.
`sql`	A module that is configured to make use of a database-specific sub-module to find a user's details. Also used to store accounting records inside an SQL database and to check for simultaneous connections.
`logintime`	A module that looks for the presence of the `Login-Time` check attribute to see if a user is authorized to access the network.
`perl`	A module that causes FreeRADIUS to load the Perl interpreter plus a specified Perl script into memory during start-up. This ensures super-fast execution.
`pap`	Used when `Auth-Type = PAP` to authenticate a user.

Time for action – discovering available modules

The previous table shows only a few modules. There are many other modules that are used but not listed. Since there are so many available modules it is good to know more about them. In this exercise we will look at the following items:

- Locating **installed** modules
- Finding out more about **available** modules
- Installing **missing** modules

Locating installed modules

FreeRADIUS stores modules inside the same directory as its other libraries. It's time to see where this directory is:

1. Open the `radiusd.conf` file located inside the FreeRADIUS configuration directory and find the `libdir` directive. This will indicate where the modules are installed within the file system.

2. Change to the directory specified and execute the following command to list all the installed modules:

   ```
   $> cd /usr/lib/freeradius
   ```

```
$> ls -l rlm_*
```

A list of installed modules will appear. Most of them will have two entries. One is a symbolic link to a specific version of the module.

What just happened?

We have determined the location specified in the FreeRADIUS configuration file where FreeRADIUS stores the modules. We have also viewed a list of the modules that are currently installed.

Finding text inside configuration files and modifying text

The following is a handy command for locating the line numbers where a phrase appears:

```
grep -i "libdir" -n /etc/freeradius/radiusd.conf
```

If you would like to edit one of the lines returned from the previous command, you could use the vi editor and add the +<line number> switch after you have specified the filename:

```
vi /etc/freeradius/radiusd.conf +106
```

This will open /etc/freeradius/radius.conf with the cursor on line 106 ready to edit.

Naming convention

The naming convention for modules in FreeRADIUS is as follows:

```
rlm_<module name>.so
```

Some modules like eap and sql make use of sub-modules. These sub-modules are usually function-specific like the md5 module for eap or the mysql module for sql. This functionality will then be reflected inside the name of the sub-module. This is why we have rlm_eap_md5.so and rlm_sql_mysql.so.

The .so extension is a convention used on Unix and Linux systems to name shared libraries (also referred to as shared objects). This is similar to the .dll extension used in Windows environments to name DLLs. FreeRADIUS treats a module as a shared library and loads it through the dynamic linker.

Adding alternative paths

If you have installed additional FreeRADIUS modules inside a directory different from the default in the configuration file, you can add additional locations. This will indicate to the dynamic linker to also search there for modules. Alternatively you can also make use of the `LD_LIBRARY_PATH` environment variable.

Sometimes FreeRADIUS does not find a particular library (not module), which may be used either by FreeRADIUS or a specific module of FreeRADIUS. You will then typically see an "undefined symbol" message. If the path of this library is already specified in the `libdir` list and it still does not work, try using the `LD_PRELOAD` environment variable. We did this earlier in the book as a work-around for the distribution-specific `perl` module bug.

We now know about the installed modules, but what about the world of modules out there? Surely there must be more available?

Available modules

Your FreeRADIUS deployment may not contain all the available FreeRADIUS modules. There could be many more modules at your disposal. The best place to start a search is the FreeRADIUS Wiki. The following page lists plenty of modules:

`http://wiki.freeradius.org/List_of_modules`

It gives a good overview of the available modules. Each listed module has a link to documentation on that specific module. The amount of documentation depends on how complex and popular a module is. There are a few links that lead to blank Wiki pages.

Most modules can be configured. Inclusion and configuration of modules will be covered after the next section.

Missing modules

So have you noticed this uber-cool module, which is listed on the FreeRADIUS Wiki but not installed on your FreeRADIUS server. Most of the time it will simply be a case of using the package manager to find all the available FreeRADIUS packages and install the one containing the missing module.

Depending on the distribution you are using, some modules are separately packed. If you are using CentOS for instance and would like to use the `perl` module, you have to install the `freeradius2-perl` package. Another common module that can be missing is the `sql_mysql` module (`rlm_sql_mysql.so`), which is often packed separately.

Because FreeRADIUS is actively developed it contains some exciting modules that are not ready yet for prime time. To include these modules you will typically compile and install FreeRADIUS from the latest source, using the `configure`, `make`, `make install` pattern with the `--with-experimental-modules` configuration option. Before compiling the source code in this way, ensure that all the required development libraries are already installed.

You can also write and compile your own modules by using the FreeRADIUS source code from which the installation on your server originates. This is, however, beyond the scope of this book but the FreeRADIUS Wiki has documentation available to get you started. Distributors of custom modules usually also include instructions on how to compile and install their modules.

We now know about the modules that are installed, those available, and those that might be missing. In the next section we shall see how to include and configure a module.

Including and configuring a module

Some modules can only be used for a specific function. The `pap` module is like that and used solely for authentication. The `sql` module in contrast can be used for authorization, session checking, as well as accounting. It all depends on what functionality the author of the module has included.

The `sql` module (`rlm_sql.so`) makes use of sub-modules. This creates an abstraction layer. Depending on how the main `sql` module is configured, it will make use of a specific sub-module to interact with a certain type of database. Sub-modules are available to connect to MySQL (`rml_sql_mysql.so`), PostgreSQL (`rlm_sql_postgresql.so`), Microsoft SQL Server (`rlm_sql_iodbc.so`), and Oracle (`rlm_sql_oracle.so`) databases.

The `sql` sub-modules in turn can also be configured to fine-tune their behavior.

Time for action – incorporating expiration and linelog modules

Isaac suspects that some of the students at the university have tried to gain Wi-Fi access illegally. He would like to log all the failed authentication attempts to a dedicated log file. While he is at it, he would also like to add an expiry date to each student to prevent them from gaining access to the network after the end of the semester. To implement this, he makes use of the `expiration` and `linelog` modules in FreeRADIUS. Let's see how it's done:

1. Edit the `linelog` file inside the `modules` sub-directory under the FreeRADIUS configuration directory. Change the following line:

   ```
   Access-Request = "Requested access: %{User-Name}"
   ```

to:

```
Access-Request = "Request access: %{User-Name}  %{User-
Password} from %{NAS-IP-Address} %{reply:Reply-Message}"
```

2. Edit the `sites-enabled/default` file under the FreeRADIUS configuration directory. Change the following part in the `post-auth` section from:

```
Post-Auth-Type REJECT {
    # log failed authentications in SQL, too.
    # sql
    attr_filter.access_reject
}
```

to:

```
Post-Auth-Type REJECT {
    # log failed authentications in SQL, too.
    # sql
    linelog
    attr_filter.access_reject
}
```

3. Ensure that the `sites-enabled/default` file under the FreeRADIUS configuration directory has the `expiration` module listed under the `authorize` section (it is included by default).

4. Edit the `expiration` file inside the `modules` sub-directory under the FreeRADIUS configuration directory. Change the following line:

```
reply-message = "Password Has Expired\r\n"
```

to:

```
#reply-message = "Password Has Expired\r\n"
reply-message = "Dude, you are like sooooo expired\r\n"
```

5. Edit the `users` file in the FreeRADIUS configuration directory and ensure the following entry is present for alice:

```
"alice" Cleartext-Password := "passme", Expiration := "4 May
2010"
```

6. Restart FreeRADIUS in debug mode and try to authenticate as alice:

```
$> radtest alice passme 127.0.0.1 100 testing123
```

7. The request should be rejected because of the value of the `Expiration` check attribute.

8. This failure should also be recorded inside the `/var/log/freeradius/logread` file (the name and location may be different depending on your installation).

What just happened?

We have configured and made use of the `expiration` and `linelog` modules.

Configuring a module

The convention to configure a module is by editing a configuration file under the `modules` sub-directory inside the FreeRADIUS configuration directory. These files are named the same as the module and contain a single section for the module. The first instance is unnamed. It is similar to an anonymous subroutine in programming languages.

```
expiration {
    reply-message = "Dude, your account is like in sooooo expired\r\n"
}
```

Subsequent use of the same module with different settings can be done by creating a named section for the module in its separate file. The following is the content of the `exp_ professors` file in the `modules` sub-directory:

```
expiration exp_professors {
    reply-message = "Dear professor %{User-Name}, kindly contact
helpdesk about your expired account\r\n"
}
```

This is much the same as having an object and various instances of the one object. Each instance can have different properties and is independent of the others. Each of these module instances can then be used any number of times in any of the virtual servers that were defined. This leaves us with a pool of module instances and a pool of virtual servers, which we can mix and match to create very flexible configurations.

The original configuration file of a module contains a lot of comments that come in handy when configuring a module.

Naming convention

When you create named sections it is wise to include the module's name in the name. For `sql` you could use `sql_primary` and `sql_secondary`. In our example we maintained the `exp` prefix. This helps to know what type of named module is involved when it is included in a section.

Not all modules follow the convention where the configuration resides in a file under the `modules` sub-directory. The `radiusd.conf` file has a `modules` section that lists all the modules to include. You will note that the `sql` and `eap` modules listed there break this rule. The configuration files of these two modules lie directly under the FreeRADIUS configuration directory.

The convention of one module instance per configuration file is also not always followed. The `realm` configuration file under the modules directory for instance declares a few `realm` instances. It is up to you whether you want to keep all instances in one configuration file, or keep them separate so that each can have its own file.

Using modules

After you have configured a module it can be used. How and where a module is used vary greatly between modules. To find out how the `expiration` module should be used we consult the documentation that is installed with FreeRADIUS.

The `rlm_expiration` documentation specifies the following:

> Module to expire user accounts.
>
> This module can be used to expire user accounts. Expired users receive an Access-Reject on every authentication attempt. Expiration is based on the Expiration attribute which should be present in the check item list for the user we wish to perform expiration checks.
>
> Expiration attribute format:
>
> You can use Expiration := "23 Sep 2004" and the user will no longer be able to connect at 00:00 (midnight) on September 23rd, 2004. If you want a certain time (other than midnight) you can do use Expiration := "23 Sep 2004 12:00".
> The nas will receive a Session-Timeout attribute calculated to kick the user off when the Expiration time occurs.
>
> Example entry (users files):
>
> user1 Expiration := "23 Sep 2004"

 Not all modules have instructions on how to use them included as a separate document. Sometimes the module's configuration file will also cover the usage instructions. Alternatively consult the FreeRADIUS Wiki or use Google.

Modules can also be used in two or more pairs. The `unlang` language offers functionality to configure redundancy, load balancing, or a combination of both through the use of the `redundant`, `load-balance`, and `redundant-load-balance` keywords. This is typically used with the `sql` and `ldap` modules and configured in the `authorize` section.

Remember if you use the `ldap` module in this way and you also use it with the `bind-as` functionality to authenticate a user, the `Auth-Type` will be set to `LDAP`. The `Auth-Type` `LDAP` declaration under the `authenticate` section should then also be configured, for example:

```
Auth-Type LDAP {
    #ldap
    redundant-load-balance {
        ldap_this
        ldap_that
    }
}
```

Sections that can contain modules

Modules can only be specified in designated sections. To include a module in a section you add the module name inside the section. If you want to use a named instance of the module simply include this named value instead of the module name. If we consider the use of the professor's instance of the `expiration` module, it will simply be listed as `exp_professors` instead of `expiration`.

Modules can be included in all the usual sections of a virtual server. These are the `authorize`, `authenticate`, `session`, `preacct`, `accounting`, `post-auth`, `pre-proxy`, and `post-proxy` sections. Modules can also be included in the `instantiate` and `eap` sections. `instantiate` is a special section in the `radiusd.conf` file that ensures a module is loaded even before it is called by sections inside the virtual servers. Before you include a module in a section, be sure that the module was written to be used in the specified section.

We know now which sections can contain modules. Let's see a practical implementation on different instances of the `expiration` module.

Using one module with different configurations

FreeRADIUS allows you to use one module with various configurations. As stated earlier this is similar to an object with different instances if you are familiar with programming lingo.

Have a go hero – creating multiple instances of a module

Isaac is in trouble. It completely slipped his mind that the professors' accounts also expire, and he does not want to speak student lingo to the professors in the reply-message. Time to fix this:

1. Edit the `expiration` file inside the `modules` sub-directory under the FreeRADIUS configuration directory. Change the following lines:

```
#reply-message = "Password Has Expired\r\n"
reply-message = "Dude, you are like sooooo expired\r\n"
```

to:

```
reply-message = "Password Has Expired\r\n"
#reply-message = "Dude, you are like sooooo expired\r\n"
```

2. Create a file called `exp_students` in the `modules` sub-directory under the FreeRADIUS configuration directory with the following contents:

```
expiration exp_students {
    reply-message = "Dude, you are like sooooo expired\r\n"
}
```

3. Create a file called `exp_professors` inside the `modules` sub-directory under the FreeRADIUS configuration directory with the following contents:

```
expiration exp_professors {

    reply-message = "Dear professor %{User-Name}, kindly
contact helpdesk concerning your expired account\r\n"

}
```

4. Edit the `sites-available/default` file under the FreeRADIUS configuration directory and modify the expiration part inside the authorize section to the following:

```
if(control:Group == "students"){
    exp_students
}
elsif(control:Group == "professors"){
    exp_professors
}
else{
    expiration
}
```

5. Ensure the `users` file has the following entries to test with:

```
"alice" Cleartext-Password := "passme", Group := "students",
Expiration := "4 May 2010"
"bob" Cleartext-Password := "passbob",  Group := "professors",
Expiration := "4 May 2010"
```

6. Restart FreeRADIUS in debug mode and try to authenticate as both alice and bob to see the difference in reply messages:

```
$> radtest alice passme 127.0.0.1 100 testing123
$> radtest bob passbob 127.0.0.1 100 testing123
```

What just happened?

We have managed to adapt the lingo within the reply message according to the group a user belongs to. Although the exercise was very simple the principles can be applied to any module.

- ◆ The first instance of a module does not need to be named and using it is simply a case of referring to the module inside a section. Examples like ldap, chap, files, and sql come to mind.

- ◆ If you want to use the same module with a different configuration you have to declare a named section for the module, which contains the alternative configuration. To use this inside a section you have to refer to the name of the named section. We used exp_students and exp_professors, which are named sections created for the expiration module.

This functionality in FreeRADIUS allows you to use the sql module to connect to different databases or the ldap module to use different directories or the files module to use different users files.

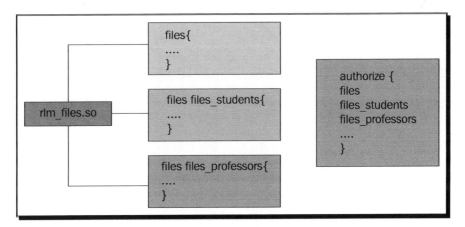

Take note of the structure of conditional statements

The structure of a conditional statement is very important. The if, elsif, and else keywords should each be on a new line. If you fail to do this you will end up with unexpected results.

Wrong:

```
if(condition) {
    ...
}else{
    ...
}
```

Correct:

```
if(condition) {
    ...
}
else{
    ...
}
```

Order of modules and return codes

You cannot just plonk down a module inside a section and hope it will do the work it is supposed to do. The order in which modules are listed inside a section is of the utmost importance.

Time for action – investigating the order of modules

This exercise requires you to take note of the order of modules listed in the various sections inside a virtual server.

> **1.** Open the sites-enabled/default file under the FreeRADIUS configuration directory.
>
> **2.** Read through it and take note of the order in which modules are used inside the various sections. Some of the comments will mention why a module is located at a certain place inside a section.

The following notes regarding the default file should make things clearer.

Access-Request

When an `Access-Request` packet comes in to the FreeRADIUS server it is first handled by the `authorize` section of the virtual server. It may then be handled by the `authenticate` and `session` sections and is finally passed to the `post-auth` section.

The first module listed in the `authorize` section is `preprocess`. It is first for a reason. Here's a general flow of the `authorize` section:

- The `preprocess` module does a sanity check and changes weird attributes to more standard ones.

- Modules like `chap` and `mschap` test if the request is CHAP or MS-CHAP and will change the value of `Auth-Type` accordingly.

- Modules like `sql`, `ldap`, and `files` try to locate the user from their user stores.

- Modules like `expiration` and `logintime` will determine if there are any restrictions imposed on the user. This is based on the information gathered by the `sql`, `ldap`, and `files` modules.

- The `pap` module is listed last because it checks if none of the above modules set the value of `Auth-Type`, if so it will set this to PAP so the `authenticate` section can use the `pap` module for authentication.

As you can see from the listed items the position of a module inside a section has to be logical. If we place the `expiration` and `logintime` modules before the `sql`, `ldap`, and `files` modules they will not have any available data on the user to do their checks.

You can follow `Accounting-Requests` in the same way. An `Accounting-Request` is first handled by the `preacct` and then by the `accounting` section.

Return codes

Each module has to return a code. The various codes available to return were discussed in *Chapter 7, Authorization*. The return code can greatly influence the flow of a request. If a module, for instance, returns `reject` inside the `authorize` section, the request will not be handled by the `authenticate` and `session` sections, but will be passed straight to the `post-auth` section. With the use of `unlang` you can also use logic to test for certain return codes and respond in a specified way if the condition was met.

With this we covered all the important points on the use of modules. The next section covers some interesting modules that are available in FreeRADIUS.

Some interesting modules

Under the `modules` sub-directory are many files. Some are special named sections for modules we already know, but others are totally new. Unfortunately not all installations of FreeRADIUS include the same number by default, but it is good to know what is available. The following table lists some modules:

Filename	Module	Function
detail	detail	Logs activity in detail inside files specific to the NAS and calendar day. Disable this if speed is a concern. The files `detail.log` and `detail.example.com` contains alternative configurations.
mac2ip	passwd	Maps a MAC address to an IP address.
mac2vlan	passwd	Maps a MAC address to a VLAN name.
dynamic-clients	dynamic-clients	Used when the client of the FreeRADIUS server has an IP address that changes.
otp	otp	Used to implement one-time passwords
echo	exec	A template that makes use of the `exec` module to call the `echo` external program.
perl	perl	A template used with the `example.pl` file inside the FreeRADIUS configuration directory.
jradius	jradius	A module that allows you to hook up with Java code. The JRadius project, which is part of the Coova suite, makes use of this module.

Although the table does not contain an exhaustive list, it gives a foretaste of what is available to you. You are encouraged to explore your own installation in order to determine what is included. All that remains now is a brief overview of the chapter and the quiz.

Summary

Let's list some key points to remember on modules:

- Modules help to extend the functionality of FreeRADIUS.
- One module can run different instances through the use of named sections.
- Modules are configured through text files under the `modules` sub-directory in the FreeRADIUS configuration directory.
- The order of modules inside a section is very important.
- A module has return codes that influence the flow of a request.

- We can use `unlang` to test for a specific return code from a module.

- Some modules may be missing because they are packed separately and have to be installed separately before they can be used.

The next chapter covers EAP. Understanding EAP is essential if you want to implement 802.1x security on the LAN or WPA2 Enterprise security on Wi-Fi networks.

Pop quiz – modules

1. You have inherited a FreeRADIUS server from someone who left the company. Although the `files` module is listed in the `authorize` section of the default virtual server, editing the `users` file seems to have no effect. Where will be a good place to troubleshoot?

2. You would like to split the current `users` file in two. One should contain all the students and one should contain all the professors. Can this be done? How would you do it?

3. You are running a CentOS server and want to include a Perl script along with the `perl` module. After you have made the configuration changes to include the `perl` module and have restarted FreeRADIUS it complains that it can not find the `perl` module. Why would this be?

4. The FreeRADIUS server you manage has to connect to a new department's LDAP server. You have created a named `ldap` section and called it `ldap_new_department`. Why would we rather call it `ldap_new_department` instead of `new_department`?

10
EAP

EAP *stands for* **Extensible Authentication Protocol** *and is used by 802.1x and WPA2-Enterprise as an authentication framework. 802.1x and WPA2-Enterprise are industry standards used for end-point security. 802.1x uses EAP over the LAN and WPA2-Enterprise uses EAP over the Wi-Fi network.*

A basic understanding of EAP includes knowing how the **supplicant,** **authenticator,** *and* **backend authentication server** *interact. This chapter covers all of these but will focus primarily on using FreeRADIUS as the backend authentication server.*

In this chapter we shall:

- ◆ Learn the basics of EAP
- ◆ Explore different EAP methods available in FreeRADIUS
- ◆ Discover special considerations when using EAP in production

So let's get on with it...

EAP basics

EAP is used to authenticate a user before he or she is allowed access onto the network. Since EAP is a framework with extensibility in mind, it uses one of many available methods to authenticate a user. This section gives a very basic idea of how EAP works. The gory details of EAP are described in RFC 3748. We will first look at EAP's three core components and continue to see what a typical EAP conversation over the LAN looks like.

EAP components

The following diagram shows the various components of the EAP framework:

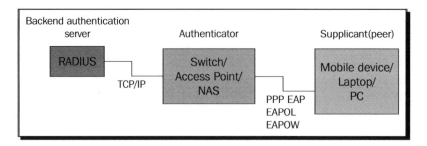

There are three main components involved in the EAP framework.

Authenticator

The authenticator is the gate keeper. It controls who has access to the network and who is blocked. Here are a few examples of authenticators:

◆ A managed switch that supports 802.1x on the LAN.

◆ An access point that incorporates WPA2-Enterprise Wi-Fi security.

◆ A remote access server that supports PPP EAP. Open Source remote access servers available today include OpenVPN, Poptop (PPTP), strongSwan, and Openswan.

The authenticator is the facilitator that will forward and translate the conversation between the supplicant and the backend authentication server. This has the following advantages:

◆ A central server is used for authentication.

◆ EAP becomes an extensible protocol that allows new authentication methods to be introduced into the backend or the supplicant without changing the functionality on the authenticator.

The authenticator does not decide whom to allow or refuse access onto the network but only follows instructions from the backend authentication server. The authenticator uses TCP/IP to communicate with the RADIUS server and EAP to communicate with the supplicant.

Supplicant

The supplicant is a piece of software used by the client machine for authentication. Upon successful authentication the authenticator grants the client access to the network. EAP is merely a framework that supports many authentication methods. A supplicant likewise supports various authentication methods and will use one. Unfortunately the default supplicant on some operating systems may not include support for a particular required EAP method. This is solved by installing a third-party supplicant that includes support for the required EAP method.

The type of network on which the supplicant is used will determine how the supplicant encapsulates the EAP packets in order to communicate with the authenticator. On a LAN it will be encapsulated inside the EAPOL (EAP Over LAN) protocol. On a Wi-Fi network it will be encapsulated inside the EAPOW (EAP Over Wireless) protocol. EAP works on the data link layer (layer2) and does not depend on or use any of the TCP/IP protocols. TCP/IP is the most popular protocol today. However, the use of TCP/IP on the client machine is not a requirement after successful authentication.

Backend authentication server

Although the authenticator controls access to the network, it is the backend authentication server that decides who will be granted or refused access onto the network. This server will typically be a RADIUS server, although the EAP standard does not limit it to only RADIUS. This chapter will show you how to use FreeRADIUS for such a backend authentication server.

Now that we are more familiar with the components of the EAP protocol, it is time to look at a typical authentication request from a client on a LAN.

EAP conversation

The following figure indicates the conversation between the three EAP components before a user is authenticated on a LAN with 802.1x activated. The EAP method that is depicted here is EAP-MD5. Since this method is not very secure it is not recommended in production environments.

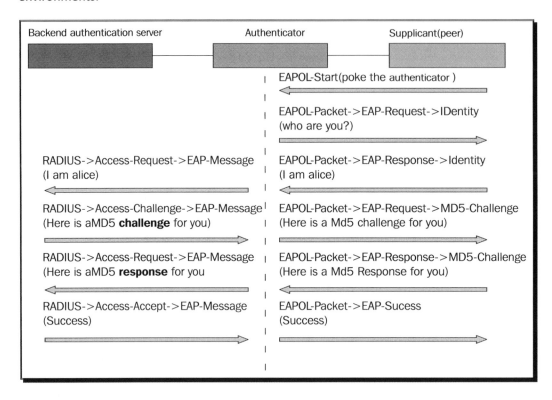

Authentication with the EAP protocol is different from a typical authentication process where the client takes the first step by identifying itself. With EAP the authenticator asks the client to identify itself as the first step.

EAPOL-Start

The EAPOL-Start message is not used that often since the authenticator usually knows when a potential user connects to the switch. The supplicant can, however, let the authenticator know of its presence by sending an EAPOL-Start packet.

Once the authenticator knows that a new client has connected, it will start by asking the client to identify itself by sending an EAPOL-Packet to the client.

EAPOL-Packet

An `EAPOL-Packet` contains a `Code` field, which can be one of four codes, namely:

Name	Value
EAP-Request	1
EAP-Response	2
EAP-Success	3
EAP-Failure	4

An `EAP-Request` should be answered with an `EAP-Response`. If you compare this to RADIUS it is similar to the `Code` field where we have `Access-Request` (1) or `Access-Challenge` (11), and so on.

`EAP-Request` and `EAP-Response` packets also contain a `Type` field. The following table lists some of the types:

Name	Value
Identity	1
Notification	2
Nak	3
MD5-Challenge	4

The first three types have a special use. The remaining types indicate the authentication method that is used. Let us see the `EAPOL-Packet` flow:

1. You can see in the preceding figure that the **Backend authentication server** is not involved in the sending of the **EAPOL-Packet->EAP-Request->Identity** to the **Supplicant**. This is done by the **Authenticator**.

2. When the **Authenticator** receives a response from the **Supplicant** it will forward this response to the **Backend authentication server**. The **Authenticator** does this by converting the **EAPOL-Packet->EAP-Response->Identity** to a RADIUS `Access-Request` packet containing an `EAP-Message` AVP.

3. The RADIUS server responds to the `Access-Request` by sending an `Access-Challenge` packet containing an `EAP-Message` AVP. This `EAP-Message` AVP contains data for sending an MD5 challenge to the **Supplicant**.

4. The **Authenticator** uses the contents of the `EAP-Message` AVP to create an **EAPOL-Packet->EAP-Request->MD5-Challenge** and sends this to the **Supplicant**.

5. The **Supplicant** uses this challenge to send a response back containing the encrypted password of the user inside an **EAPOL-Packet->EAP-Response->MD5->Challenge** packet.

6. This packet is again converted to a RADIUS `Access-Request` packet containing the `EAP-Message` AVP and sent to the **Backend authentication server**.

7. If this password was supplied correctly the RADIUS server will respond with an `Access-Accept` packet containing an `EAP-Message` AVP to the **Authenticator**.

8. The **Authenticator** will now open the port on the switch for other traffic to start flowing.

9. The **Authenticator** will also send an **EAPOL-Packet->EAP-Success** packet to the **Supplicant** to notify it about the success.

One important point to remember is that the responses from the client to the **Backend authentication server**, after the initial packets, are only relayed to it by the **Authenticator**. The **Authenticator** simply reformats the packet from EAP to RADIUS and routes it to the **Backend authentication server**.

This brings us to the end of our crash course on EAP. The next section will transform this objective knowledge into a subjective experience.

Practical EAP

In this section we will test various EAP methods on a FreeRADIUS installation. To do this we make use of **JRadius Simulator**. This program is part of the **JRadius** framework and one of the many projects available from **Coova**. JRadius Simulator is used to simulate an NAS by sending EAP requests to FreeRADIUS. This eliminates the need for a dedicated NAS (authenticator) and client (supplicant) to test EAP methods.

Time for action – testing EAP on FreeRADIUS with JRadius Simulator

We will first prepare the FreeRADIUS environment for JRadius Simulator and then configure JRadius Simulator in order to test EAP authentication.

Preparing FreeRADIUS

The most important thing to do before FreeRADIUS can handle EAP is **nothing**. It is when you do **nothing** that EAP will work at its best. The FreeRADIUS authors made sure that the default configuration supports EAP without any tweaking.

We just need to be sure that there is a valid user in the `users` file and that the NAS that sends the EAP request is registered in the `clients.conf` file.

1. Edit the `users` file located under the FreeRADIUS configuration directory and make sure there is an entry for alice:

```
"alice" Cleartext-Password := "passme"
```

2. The JRadius Simulator needs to run from a machine that has a GUI and Java. Record the IP address of this machine. This machine will act as an NAS (client) to the FreeRADIUS server and has to be defined in the `clients.conf` file located under the FreeRADIUS configuration directory. Here we assume it is 192.168.1.101. Please change to suit your environment. Add this machine as a client:

```
client jradius {
    ipaddr = 192.168.1.101
    require_message_authenticator = no
    secret= testing123
    nastype    = other
}
```

3. Ensure the `inner-tunnel` virtual server is enabled by confirming that it is listed in the `sites-enabled` sub-directory under the FreeRADIUS configuration directory. It is enabled by default but if it is not listed refer to Chapter 8, *Virtual Servers* on how to enable it.

4. Restart FreeRADIUS in debug mode to activate the latest changes.

As you can see the preparation did not include any EAP-specific settings because everything should just work by default.

Configuring JRadius Simulator

As stated before, you need to have a Java runtime on the machine on which you will run JRadius Simulator. JRadius Simulator is a GUI application and also needs a window environment in which to run. If you run Linux it will need a desktop environment like Gnome, KDE, or XFCE. You can download the JRadius Simulator software, unzip, and run it. Alternatively, you can launch it out of the browser if your system has Java Web Start. The following step-by-step procedure was done in Ubuntu:

1. Go to the following URL:

```
http://coova.org/Download
```

2. Click on the **JRadius Minimal (client)** link to start the download.

3. When the download is complete, open a terminal and navigate to the location where the ZIP file downloaded.

4. Unzip the file:

```
$> unzip jradius-client-1.1.4-release.zip
```

5. Change directory to the unzipped `jradius` folder and run the following command:

```
$> sh simulator.sh
```

The following screenshot shows the output from the previous command:

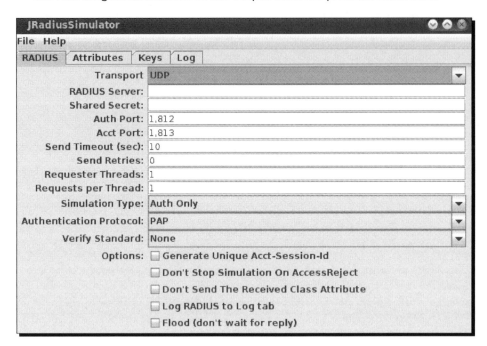

6. Supply values for **RADIUS server** and **Shared Secret**. Click on the **Log RADIUS to Log tab** checkbox to activate logging.

7. Select the **Attributes** tab and add the attributes shown in the screenshot with their values. You may have to change some values to suit your environment. Also ensure they are all selected in the **AccessReq** column:

Attribute Name	AccessReq	TunnelReq	AcctStart	AcctUpd...	AcctStop	Attribute Value
User-Name	✔					alice
User-Password	✔					passme
NAS-Port	✔					100
NAS-IP-Address	✔					192.168.1.101

8. You can now start testing by clicking on the **RADIUS** tab and then on the **Start** button. You will be able to see the feedback in the **Log** tab.

9. Go through the various **Authentication Protocol** options and test each one. All of them except **EAP-TLS** should pass the authentication request.

What just happened?

We have used the JRadius Simulator program to test various authentication protocols on FreeRADIUS. We have particularly tested the following EAP methods: EAP-MD5, EAP-MSCHAPv2, EAP-TLS, PEAP/MSCHAP, and EAP-TTLS/PAP.

For the command-line junkies there is an alternative to JRadius Simulator called eapol_test, which is a utility program included with the wpa_supplicant code. You can read more about eapol_test at this location:

http://hostap.epitest.fi/wpa_supplicant/devel/testing_tools.html

Configuring the eap module

The eap module in FreeRADIUS is a module much like all the other modules. The location of the configuration file for the eap module, however, is different. It is configured in a separate file called eap.conf located directly under the FreeRADIUS configuration directory instead of inside the modules sub-directory.

The eap module includes a few EAP methods by default. These methods are shown as sub-sections inside the eap section. The eap section cannot be empty. It has to include at least one method. If the eap section is empty the server will return an error because it would not know what authentication type to use in the communication channel. The sub-section for a method contains directives that configure the specific EAP method. The following table lists them along with a short comment:

EAP Method	Comment
md5	Method not recommended because of weak security. No configuration required. Not widely supported.
leap	Developed by Cisco, proven to have weaknesses. Neither recommended nor widely supported.
gtc	This method can only be used inside a tunneled method like TTLS and PEAP. Will send a plain-text password to the RADIUS server. Can be useful if supported by a supplicant that does not support TTLS/PAP.

EAP Method	Comment
tls	Can be used on its own where a client will be required to supply a client certificate for authentication. This allows for mutual identification. This method also serves as a base for the encryption element of the TTLS and PEAP methods. Very secure but deployments are difficult because of client certificate management.
ttls	Creates a secure tunnel to transport a second authentication method inside. Typically used with PAP when the user store in FreeRADIUS can only handle cleartext passwords. Very popular and supported by default on most supplicants. Unfortunately not supported on Microsoft products. Very secure. Uses a second virtual server for the inner tunneled request.
peap	Creates a secure tunnel similar to TTLS. Popular inner methods are MSCHAPv2 and GTC. Uses a second virtual server for the inner tunneled request. Unfortunately the GTC inner method is not supported by Microsoft products. Very secure and very popular.
mschapv2	Use the MSCHAP protocol for authentication. This has no secure tunnel although it is secure.

The choice of which EAP method your clients will use is primarily determined by two things:

- The methods supported by the user store
- The methods supported by the clients

The user store

In *Chapter 5, Sources of Usernames and Passwords* we saw that some sources of usernames and passwords will not support authentication methods that involve encryption. If you, for instance, connect to an LDAP server and have to bind as a user in order to determine if the supplied password is correct, you are limited to the authentication protocols that can be used. When you store passwords locally you may severely limit available EAP methods when storing the passwords in encrypted form.

You can use the following URLs to check what encrypted format is supported by which EAP method:

http://deployingradius.com/documents/protocols/compatibility.html

http://deployingradius.com/documents/protocols/oracles.html

As mentioned in the links above, if the password encryption is wrong, there is no way to use an EAP method that requires a password to be stored or accessed in clear text.

If you connect to **Novell's eDirectory** LDAP server FreeRADIUS can use **Universal Password** to get a user's password in clear text from the server. See the comments inside the ldap module's configuration file for more on this.

EAP on the client

The choice of which EAP method to use would be so much simpler if Microsoft included EAP-TTLS/PAP support by default or even the PEAP/GTC from their PEAP partners at Cisco. Unfortunately this is the real world and we have to face reality. Lots of FreeRADIUS EAP deployments cannot support MSCHAP authentication because the user store is typically an LDAP server that one has to bind to for authentication. This is the case with many Eduroam deployments.

To get EAP-TTLS/PAP supported on a machine running Windows you can either install another operating system that supports this standard by default or simply install a supplicant that adds support for it to Windows. Many hardware vendors now supply a dedicated supplicant with their Wi-Fi hardware. This typically includes support for extra EAP methods. Alternatively, you can load a program called **SecureW2**. SecureW2 started out as a GPL-licensed program that added EAP-TTLS/PAP support. Over time the features as well as licensing changed. You now have to buy a license to use the latest version. There are, however, still some of the older GPL based releases floating around on the Internet, especially from universities that are part of Eduroam. Google is your friend who will find it for you.

 Older versions of SecureW2 had pre-configuration problems on 64-bit Windows systems. Another problem that may occur on Windows 7 and Windows Vista machines is that the **SecureW2 TTLS** option is not available as an authentication method. To fix this, run the `services.msc` program and start the **Wired Autoconfig** service. You should also make this permanent by editing the **Properties** and changing **Startup type** to **Automatic**.

As for most of the other operating systems like Apple's iOS, Android, Blackberry OS, Symbian, and the various flavors of Linux, their supplicants usually support a method that allows for FreeRADIUS to use LDAP and bind as someone to the server for authentication.

You should by now be more comfortable with the use of EAP in FreeRADIUS. The next section takes a look at some production-specific tweaks that you can apply to the EAP configuration and implementation.

EAP in production

EAP works out of the box on a default FreeRADIUS installation. There are, however, some points to either take note of or change to suit your environment. In this section we will cover the following points:

- The importance of a proper Public Key Infrastructure (PKI)
- Configuring the `inner-tunnel` virtual server

- ◆ Issues with inner and outer tunnel identities
- ◆ Disabling unused EAP methods

Public Key Infrastructure in brief

Public Key Infrastructure is used primarily for two things:

- ◆ To verify the identity of someone
- ◆ To exchange secure data over an unsecure connection

To ensure that someone is who they claim to be, we make use of a **Certificate Authority (CA)**. A CA will issue and sign digital certificates. We can make use of a trusted third party (TTP) to issue and sign digital certificates or we can be our own CA. These certificates are bound to an identity and should only be used by that identity.

When we transact with the identity, we can verify its validity by checking with the CA if the identity is indeed who it claims to be. This is very important when it comes to WPA2-Enterprise security because anyone can set up an access point and advertise a specific SSID. To verify the validity of an access point we need to have a PKI in place and use it.

Creating a PKI

When FreeRADIUS starts up for the first time it sets up a PKI by using sample configurations. These certificates are fine to use during testing but once you want to move to a production environment you should create a new set that reflects your organization's values in the certificates.

Time for action – creating a RADIUS PKI for you organization

The aim of this book is not to replace existing documentation. There is an excellent README file inside the certs sub-directory under the FreeRADIUS configuration directory. Follow the instructions to create a new set of certificates for your organization.

If you have a secondary FreeRADIUS server you can use the server.cnf file; make a backup of the configuration for the primary FreeRADIUS server and modify it to create a certificate for the secondary RADIUS server. Be careful not to override the primary FreeRADIUS server's files.

What just happened?

We created a PKI specific for our organization. The CA should be used by the EAP supplicant to confirm the validity of the RADIUS server.

Why use a PKI?

Every client that uses EAP-TTLS or PEAP must add the newly created CA certificate to the list of available CAs in the supplicant. If you fail to do this, you are creating a huge security risk. The following diagram should speak for itself:

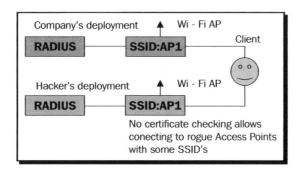

If the client is not checking the validity of the certificate coming from the RADIUS server, anyone can create a rogue setup and reap some passwords from your organization's users.

The README file also advises against using certificates created by root CAs because this can potentially allow a hacker to also obtain a certificate from the same root CA and use this on his deployment while your users think they are in safe hands.

Now that the PKI is production-ready the tls, ttls, and peap methods can use the newly created certificates. Both the ttls and peap methods require that the tls method is configured correctly because they use it as the foundation for their encryption functionality.

Adding a CA to the client

Some supplicants allow us to select from the operating system's list of trusted CAs when we configure EAP-TLS, EAP-TTLS, or PEAP. Unfortunately it is sometimes quite a battle to add our newly created CA to that list. The following table lists some operating systems and notes concerning the inclusion of a new CA in the supplicant:

Operating system	Comment on CA in supplicant
Android	As of version 2.2 there are mixed reports on the success of adding new CAs. On my phone I could add the CA, select it, but the supplicant refused to acknowledge the validity of the RADIUS server's certificate.
Apple	Apple made adding a new Wi-Fi profile really easy with the .mobileconfig file. This file contains a complete Wi-Fi profile including the CA and is added by simply downloading the file using the Safari web browser.

Operating system	Comment on CA in supplicant
Blackberry	On older models you need to add a CA using a Windows application that connects to the phone. Newer models allow you to add the CA using the browser.
Linux	The NetworkManager applet used in most distributions allows you the option to manually select a CA certificate.
Windows	Windows has various places where Root CAs can be added. Some apply a CA only to a user, other places apply the CA to the whole machine. Adding a new CA certificate is very easy. Adding it to the correct location can be more difficult. Windows 7 requires you to import the certificate using the **run as administrator** option on some machines.

Because the operating system market is a fast moving-market with upgrades, improvements, and new players happening in a short time span, it is the best to consult a good search engine in the quest for CA nirvana.

Inside the configuration of the ttls and peap methods in the eap.conf file is a directive called virtual_server. This will be discussed next.

Configuring the inner-tunnel virtual server

If you look at the eap.conf file under the FreeRADIUS configuration directory, the ttls and peap methods both contain a virtual_server directive. This directive points to a virtual server that will handle the authentication requests of the inner EAP tunnel. The inner-tunnel virtual server is used for this by default. This virtual server is independent of the default virtual server. Remember this when you include a module like sql or ldap in the default virtual server. You also have to add it to the inner-tunnel virtual server in order for EAP-TTLS and PEAP to use the same user store.

Having a virtual server to handle the inner-tunnel authentication adds flexibility to FreeRADIUS. This allows us to have two different user stores or even to include unlang logic in the inner-tunnel virtual server that is completely independent from the default virtual server.

Time for action – testing authentication on the inner-tunnel virtual server

The inner-tunnel virtual server has a listen section by default that listens on IP address 127.0.0.1 and port 18120 for authentication requests. This can be used to test how the virtual server will react to authentication requests.

1. Confirm that the `inner-tunnel` virtual server is enabled (listed under the `sites-enabled` directory) and that it contains the following `listen` section. This should be included by default.

```
listen {
     ipaddr = 127.0.0.1
     port = 18120
     type = auth
}
```

2. Restart FreeRADIUS in debug mode.

3. Test the authentication on the `inner-tunnel` virtual server by using the following command:

radtest alice passme 127.0.0.1:18120 100 testing123

4. You should see that the `inner-tunnel` virtual server is used by looking at the feedback in the debug output:

```
server inner-tunnel {
     +- entering group authorize {...}
     ++[chap] returns noop
     ...
```

What just happened?

We have made use of the `listen` section defined inside the `inner-tunnel` virtual server to test how the virtual server reacts to authentication requests.

The difference between inner and outer identities

Tunneled EAP methods like EAP-TTLS and PEAP contain two identities, as follows:

◆ One is called the **outer identity** and is visible to the outside world. This means that when the RADIUS packets are sniffed you can see this value.

◆ The other is called the **inner identity** and cannot be traced when sniffing the RADIUS packets that flow between the authenticator and the RADIUS server.

These identities are specified as the value of a `User-Name` AVP. The outer identity is important in making proxying decisions, which means the realm part of the `User-Name` AVP has to be correct in order for the request to reach the correct destination.

The virtual server functionality available in FreeRADIUS allows us to handle outer and inner identities through two different virtual servers. By default, the outer identity will be handled by the `default` virtual server and the inner identity by the `inner-tunnel` virtual server. This allows us to create and manage two totally independent policies for the inner and outer identities.

Have a go hero – using JRadius Simulator to test with two identities

In this exercise we will use JRadius Simulator to use two different identities in order to differentiate between the inner identity and the outer identity:

1. JRadius Simulator has a column on the **Attributes** tab that allows you to specify attributes for the tunnel (**TunnelReq**). Update the **Attributes** to display the following:

Attribute Name	AccessReq	TunnelReq	AcctStart	AcctUpd...	AcctStop	Attribute Value
User-Name	☐	✔	☐	☐	☐	alice
User-Password	☐	✔	☐	☐	☐	passme
NAS-IP-Address	✔	☐	☐	☐	☐	192.168.1.101
NAS-Port	✔	☐	☐	☐	☐	100
User-Name	✔	☐	☐	☐	☐	bob@fake-realm.com

2. Select the **RADIUS** tab and **EAP-TTLS/PAP** as **Authentication Protocol**. Then click on **Start** to perform an authentication test.

3. Observe the debug output from FreeRADIUS and see the following among the feedback:

```
Sending Access-Accept of id 197 to 192.168.1.101 port 47083
MS-MPPE-Recv-Key = 0x825059e7df2f0dc.....
MS-MPPE-Send-Key = 0x89258e9f9267997ec59a1d5a5.....
EAP-Message = 0x03070004
Message-Authenticator = 0x00000000000......
User-Name = "bob@fake-realm.com"
```

The RFC standard states that the value of the User-Name AVP specified in the Access-Accept packet should be used by the NAS in accounting packets sent to the RADIUS server.

The default of FreeRADIUS is to return the outer identity as the User-Name AVP's value. This leaves us with a potential problem when we want to perform accurate accounting since the user can specify anything as a value for the outer identity as we have just seen.

We can use unlang to correct this:

1. Edit the `sites-enabled/inner-tunnel` file located under the FreeRADIUS configuration directory and add the following portion at the top of the `post-auth` section:

```
if(outer.request:User-Name != "%{request:User-Name}") {
    update reply {
        User-Name := "%{request:User-Name}"
    }
}
```

2. Edit the `eap.conf` file located under the FreeRADIUS configuration directory and change the following directive under the `ttls` and `peap` methods from:

```
use_tunneled_reply = no
```

to:

```
use_tunneled_reply = yes
```

3. Restart FreeRADIUS in debug mode and test the EAP-TTLS/PAP authentication again using JRadius Simulator. The debug feedback should now return `alice` instead of `bob@fake-realm.com` as the return value for the `User-Name` AVP:

```
Sending Access-Accept of id 239 to 192.168.1.101 port 55543
    User-Name = "alice"
    . . .
```

What just happened?

We have managed to improve the truthfulness of our accounting data by returning the inner identity instead of the outer identity as the value of the `User-Name` AVP in the `Access-Accept` reply from FreeRADIUS.

Unlang offers us the opportunity to get hold of the attributes in the outer request from the virtual server used for the inner request. We use the `outer.` prefix to get to the outer request's attribute lists. We can then compare the attribute values in the outer request to those of the inner request.

If we want the `reply` attributes of the `inner-tunnel` virtual server to bleed through to the default virtual server, we have to instruct the `eap` method to do so. We do this by setting the `use_tunneled_reply` directive to `yes`.

Be sure to check that the NAS that receives the `Access-Accept` with the inner identity does support the `User-Name` reply AVP. There have been reports about bad implementations of the RFC. A workaround to this problem may be to compare the inner identity to the outer identity and reject the request if they are not the same. This, however, will require extra user education.

Naming conventions for the outer identity

A good practice is to educate the users to supply their e-mail address as the outer identity. This can, however, be a potential security risk. When your organization becomes part of a hierarchical network of RADIUS servers like Eduroam these requests will pass through third-party servers that can misuse the outer identities. A more generic identity might then be better. So instead of `alice@frbg.com` you would rather use `eduroam@frbg.com`. There is no fixed rule but take note.

 If you are part of a hierarchical network of RADIUS servers only RADIUS proxy requests for EAP-TTLS and PEAP can totally hide user identities and passwords from the third-party RADIUS servers doing the proxying.

If your FreeRADIUS server answers to proxy requests and you are very paranoid about security consider changing the value of the `User-Name` AVP in the `Access-Accept` message returned to third-party RADIUS servers to something generic.

To continue on that paranoid note the next section will show you how to disable unused EAP methods.

Disabling unused EAP methods

The default installation of FreeRADIUS includes support for many EAP methods. When you decide which EAP methods your organization will support the others can be disabled.

Time for action – disabling unused EAP methods

Our organization decided to support the two tunneled EAP methods (PEAP and EAP-TTLS). We will disable the other methods and set the default EAP method to be PEAP:

1. Edit the `eap.conf` file located under the FreeRADIUS configuration directory. Disable the following methods by commenting them out completely: `md5`, `leap`, `gtc`, and `mschapv2`.

2. Change the `default_eap_type` directive from:

```
default_eap_type = md5
```

to:

```
default_eap_type = peap
```

3. Restart FreeRADIUS in debug mode and check that the disabled EAP methods are not available any more. Here is the debug output from FreeRADIUS when we tried EAP-MD5. It confirms that EAP Type 4 (MD5) is not supported anymore:

```
+- entering group authenticate {...}
```

```
[eap] Request found, released from the list
[eap] EAP NAK
[eap] NAK asked for unsupported type 4
[eap] No common EAP types found.
[eap] Failed in EAP select
++[eap] returns invalid
Failed to authenticate the user.
```

What just happened?

We have changed the default EAP method that FreeRADIUS will ask for after identification. We have also disabled unused EAP methods. In the `eap.conf` file we did not comment out the `tls` method because it is used by both the `ttls` and `peap` methods to create a secure tunnel.

Disabling unsupported EAP methods and setting the default EAP method to the most common one in use will reduce the network traffic between the authenticator and the RADIUS server. This in turn should lead to better performance. The use of less secure EAP methods can also be stopped by disabling them.

Message-Authenticator

As a final bit on security we will consider enforcing the presence of a `Message-Authenticator` AVP with every request from an NAS. Each client definition in the `clients.conf` file under the FreeRADIUS configuration directory has a `require_message_authenticator` directive. If you set this to `yes` it will reject requests from the specified device that does not include the `Message-Authenticator` AVP or if the value of `Message-Authenticator` is not correct.

The value of the `Message-Authenticator` is created by generating an HMAC-MD5 checksum on the RADIUS packet. This attribute is intended to thwart attempts by an attacker to set up a "rogue" NAS, and perform online dictionary attacks against the RADIUS server. It does not afford protection against "offline" attacks where the attacker intercepts packets containing (for example) CHAP challenge and response, and performs a dictionary attack against those packets offline. When the server receives a request, it calculates the value of the supposed value of the `Message-Authenticator` and compares it with the one received. If the value does not match, it silently discards the request. This is only done on authentication requests. The `Message-Authenticator` AVP is not included with accounting packets.

Unfortunately, if you store the NAS details inside an SQL database instead of the `clients.conf` file, the SQL table (`nas`) does not provide for setting this directive.

This brings us to the end of our discussion on EAP in FreeRADIUS. Time now to look at some key points to remember.

Summary

The following are some of the key points we touched upon in this chapter:

◆ EAP is a framework with extensibility as a core feature. This allows new EAP methods to be introduced without any changes to the authenticator.

◆ EAP allows us to proxy requests through third-party RADIUS servers without exposing a person's username and password when we use EAP-TTLS or PEAP.

◆ Tunneled EAP methods have two identities, which can be compared with one another.

◆ The use and distribution of a dedicated self-signed CA is recommended for maximum security. Educate the users to install and specify the use of the self-signed CA in the supplicant configuration.

◆ The value of the `User-Name` AVP returned in an `Access-Accept` will be used by the authenticator when sending accounting details to the RADIUS server.

◆ The JRadius Simulator program comes in very handy when testing various EAP methods.

Pop quiz – EAP

1. You have just installed FreeRADIUS and after initial tests using your captive portal as client you want to test EAP by configuring an access point (AP) as a client. Your co-worker sends you some URLs he used to get EAP working on FreeRADIUS. What should you do next?

2. The captive portal allows users from both the users file and the corporate LDAP server but the EAP-TTLS/PAP configured supplicant only allows access to users in the users file. What is wrong?

3. The LDAP configuration you specified binds as a user to verify the username and password. Can you use PEAP/MSCHAPv2 with this?

4. A friend of yours has an LDAP server that is part of Novell's e-Directory. He says they are using it happily with FreeRADIUS to authenticate supplicants using PEAP/MSCHAHv2. Is this a lie?

5. What will be the simplest, most effective way to get a Wi-Fi profile including the CA on the iPhone and iPad users devices?

11
Dictionaries

*At the start of the book we looked at the RADIUS protocol and discovered that each RADIUS packet used by the RADIUS protocol consists of **Attribute Value Pairs (AVPs)** to convey information. Each AVP inside a RADIUS packet contains a type, length, and value field. The type field consists of an integer number representing a specific attribute. FreeRADIUS uses dictionaries to map these type numbers to attribute names.*

This chapter explains how to manage the dictionaries. In this chapter we shall:

- ◆ See why we need dictionaries
- ◆ Update pre-defined dictionaries according to best practices
- ◆ Discuss the format of a dictionary file

So let's get on with it...

Why do we need dictionaries?

Computers work best with numbers while humans work best with names. We created DNS in order to remember host names instead of IP addresses. Dictionaries are used in the same manner so we can remember AVP names instead of type numbers. Dictionaries are consulted when FreeRADIUS parses requests or generates responses.

However, dictionaries differ from DNS as the RADIUS client has no knowledge of these 'friendly' names used by FreeRADIUS. The AVP names are never exchanged between a RADIUS client and a RADIUS server. The AVP names are used solely by the server. The `radclient` and `radtest` programs are special clients that use the same dictionaries as the server because they are part of the FreeRADIUS suite of programs. The dictionaries are solely for the local administrator's convenience and vary depending on the version of FreeRADIUS. The JRadius Simulator in contrast has its own set of dictionaries that is independent from the dictionaries used by FreeRADIUS.

Parsing requests

When FreeRADIUS receives an `Access-Request` packet, the packet includes the type numbers mapped to `User-Name (1)` and `User-Password (2)`. The packet does not contain a string `User-Name` or `User-Password`. Most RADIUS clients seldom need to display the string that represents the type number because the clients are not directly used by humans. This means that they don't need dictionaries. In the case of humans being involved with the use of a RADIUS client (`radclient` or JRadius Simulator), the client will require some dictionaries in order to display meaningful results.

A user's information, on the other hand, is stored in human-readable format on the server. See the following entry for Alice stored in the `users` file:

```
"alice" Cleartext-Password := "passme"
    Mikrotik-Total-Limit =10240
```

In order for the modules involved with authentication and authorization to use the human-readable data, they must consult dictionaries to map the human-readable value to a type number. This allows us to store AVPs as names that we understand instead of type numbers that computers understand. The `Cleartext-Password` AVP for instance is mapped to number 1100, `User-Name` to number 1, and `User-Password` to number 2.

Generating responses

During the process in which FreeRADIUS determines the AVPs to return with the `Access-Reply`, it will again consult dictionaries to map the `reply` attribute names to type numbers before encapsulating the data in a RADIUS packet. This also allows us to store `reply` attributes in human-understandable format instead of the type number that is used inside a RADIUS packet.

We see now that dictionaries are there for our benefit. In the next section, we will see how FreeRADIUS knows which dictionaries to use.

How to include dictionaries

Isaac has a couple of MikroTik RouterBOARDs on which he wants to limit the total bytes (send and received) to 10 MB per session. A friend told him to simply add the `Mikrotik-Total-Limit` AVP in the reply. Let's follow Isaac on his journey to implement this.

> We assume a clean installation of FreeRADIUS in this chapter.
>
> A RouterBOARD is the name of the hardware manufactured by MikroTik. There are various RouterBOARD models available. This hardware is powered by the RouterOS software from MikroTik.

Time for action – including new dictionaries

The following steps will demonstrate how to include new directories:

1. Edit the `users` file located under the FreeRADIUS configuration directory and make sure the following entry for alice exists:

```
"alice" Cleartext-Password := "passme"
    Mikrotik-Total-Limit = 10240
```

2. Restart FreeRADIUS in debug mode. The restart should be unsuccessful and the following error message will display:

```
/etc/raddb/users[11]: Parse error (reply) for entry alice: Invalid
octet string "10240" for attribute name "Mikrotik-Total-Limit"
Errors reading /etc/raddb/users
```

3. The error does not explicitly says the AVP is not in any of the dictionaries but if you do a quick `grep` for this AVP in the `/usr/share/freeradius` directory, it will come back empty indicating we do have a problem:

```
grep -lr 'Mikrotik-Total-Limit' /usr/share/freeradius/*
```

What just happened?

We have discovered that the `Mikrotik-Total-Limit` AVP is not included with the pre-defined dictionaries that come with FreeRADIUS. Before we attempt to fix our broken server there are a few important points which can be discussed here.

How FreeRADIUS includes dictionary files

FreeRADIUS installs many pre-defined dictionary files by default. These dictionary files are stored in the `/usr/share/freeradius` directory (if you installed from source code using the `configure; make; make install` pattern they will be stored in `/usr/local/share/freeradius`). Dictionary files are named according to a convention. The names are in the form `dictionary.<identifier>`. The identifier can be classified into three categories, as follows:

- **Vendor/technology name**: for example `dictionary.mikrotik` or `dictionary.wimax`

- **RFC number**: for example `dictionary.rfc2865`

- **FreeRADIUS's internal dictionaries**: for example `dictionary.freeradius.internal`

If a dictionary file is installed it does NOT automatically imply that this `dictionary` file will be used by FreeRADIUS. FreeRADIUS has to be configured to include that specific dictionary file. We do this in the following way:

1. In the FreeRADIUS configuration directory is a file called dictionary. The content of this file is not very exiting since it contains a single line, which is uncommented:

   ```
   $INCLUDE           /usr/share/freeradius/dictionary
   ```

2. The file (`/usr/share/freeradius/dictionary`) that is sourced is more exciting because this file contains a list of various dictionary files to use:

   ```
   #       For a complete list of the standard attributes and values,
   #       see:
   #               http://www.iana.org/assignments/radius-types
   #
   $INCLUDE dictionary.rfc2865
   $INCLUDE dictionary.rfc2866
   ...
   ```

   The comments inside the two dictionary files warn us not to change any of the pre-defined dictionary files as it will cause problems when FreeRADIUS is updated. The next section will show us what to do according to the best practice.

 The best practice is there for a reason. Editing files located in the `/usr/share/freeradius` directory can be tricky and dangerous. Add attributes and dictionaries by only editing the `dictionary` file located under the FreeRADIUS configuration directory.

Including your own dictionary files

There are three scenarios where you would change the default dictionary configuration in FreeRADIUS.

Including dictionary files already installed

Sometimes a dictionary file is installed under the `/usr/share/freeradius` directory but not listed in the `/usr/share/freeradius/dictionary` file. This dictionary should then be specifically included in the dictionary file under the FreeRADIUS configuration directory. Remember to include the absolute path:

```
$INCLUDE          /usr/share/freeradius/dictionary.chillispot
```

Test for installed AVPs that are not included

If you `grep` for the required attribute in the `/usr/share/freeradius` directory and find the attribute present, check if the dictionary file containing the attribute is indeed listed in `/usr/share/freeradius/dictionary`. When it is not, you have to include it in this way.

Adding private attributes

These private attributes are used internally by FreeRADIUS. In Chapter 7, *Authorization* we used such attributes. They are typically used with more complex `unlang` implementations and are defined in the dictionary file under the FreeRADIUS configuration directory:

```
ATTRIBUTE         FRBG-Reset-Type        3050      string
ATTRIBUTE         FRBG-Total-Bytes       3051      string
```

It is advisable to use a unique prefix for these types of attributes in order to avoid duplicate names. They have numbers between 3000 and 4000 and will never be placed in a RADIUS packet.

Updating an existing dictionary

The IT world is a fast-changing one and it happens that new players enter the scene or existing ones make changes to their software. If changes are made by vendors we need to update the existing dictionary files. The recommended way is not to touch the pre-defined dictionary files but rather to include an updated dictionary in such a way as to override the pre-defined one's information when FreeRADIUS starts up.

In the next exercise we will update the existing MikroTik dictionary to include support for the `Mikrotik-Total-Limit` AVP.

Time for action – updating the MikroTik dictionary

Isaac e-mailed his friend informing him about the broken configuration. His friend then replied and instructed Isaac to visit the following URL, which shows the latest RADIUS attributes that MikroTik supports:

```
http://wiki.mikrotik.com/wiki/Manual:RADIUS_Client
```

Although the content of the web page was a bit confusing initially, Isaac managed to do the following in order to fix everything on his FreeRADIUS server:

1. Copy the pre-defined `dictionary.mikrotik` file to a folder inside the FreeRADIUS configuration directory:

```
mkdir /etc/raddb/dictionary.local
cp /usr/share/freeradius/dictionary.mikrotik /etc/raddb/
dictionary.local
```

2. Update `/etc/raddb/dictionary.local/dictionary.mikrotik` to include the following according to the web page from MikroTik:

```
#Add New Mikrotik Attributes
ATTRIBUTE         Mikrotik-Wireless-PSK              16       string
ATTRIBUTE         Mikrotik-Total-Limit              17       integer
ATTRIBUTE         Mikrotik-Total-Limit-Gigawords    18       integer
ATTRIBUTE         Mikrotik-Address-List             19       string
ATTRIBUTE         Mikrotik-Wireless-MPKEY           20       string
ATTRIBUTE         Mikrotik-Wireless-Comment         21       string
```

3. Edit the dictionary file inside the FreeRADIUS configuration directory to include this updated dictionary:

```
$INCLUDE          /usr/share/freeradius/dictionary
#
#        Place additional attributes or $INCLUDEs here.
#        They will over-ride the definitions in
#        the pre-defined dictionaries
$INCLUDE       /etc/raddb/dictionary.local/dictionary.mikrotik
```

4. Restart FreeRADIUS in debug mode and test the authentication for alice. The following should be returned:

```
rad_recv: Access-Accept packet from host 127.0.0.1 port 1812,
id=10, length=32
    Mikrotik-Total-Limit = 10240
```

What just happened?

We have updated the MikroTik dictionary to include the latest attributes. The pre-defined dictionary file was not deleted but an updated dictionary file was included in such a way as to override the pre-defined dictionary. Although it was not difficult, there are, however, some important points to remember.

Finding the latest supported attributes

To locate the latest RADIUS attributes that a vendor supports is often the most difficult part when updating dictionaries. Good places to start looking are inside release notes of firmware updates or the vendor's website. Do not always take the advice or instructions proposed by the vendor on how to update the dictionaries since this can introduce new problems. It is better to use the instructions proposed by FreeRADIUS.

Location of updated dictionary files

The location of the updated dictionary files is up to you. In this exercise we stored it in a sub-directory inside the FreeRADIUS configuration directory. This helps us to keep all the configuration items in one place.

Order of inclusions

The order in which dictionary files are listed is very important. To ensure the updated dictionary file's content overrides the pre-defined ones we list it in such a way that it is sourced after the original one.

Attribute names

At the start of the chapter we mentioned that dictionaries are there to benefit us. The spelling of an entry in the dictionary is not crucial because it is simply used for a mapping. For this reason we changed the attribute names listed on the MikroTik web page to fit in with the RADIUS convention. We did not specify `MIKROTIK_TOTAL_LIMIT` but rather used `Mikrotik-Total-Limit`. Sticking to a convention also helps us when specifying AVPs for a user.

Now that we know when and how to change the default dictionary configuration it is time to look more closely at the format of a dictionary file.

Upgrading FreeRADIUS

Newer versions of FreeRADIUS may also contain modifications and updates to existing dictionary files. It is advisable to create a backup of the directory containing the dictionary files before upgrading FreeRADIUS from which to restore them in the event that the upgrade process causes havoc amongst the existing dictionary files.

Upgrades may also change the permissions on certain directories and files that were adjusted after the initial installation. Make sure after the upgrade that the FreeRADIUS server starts up without errors to confirm everything went according to plan.

Format of dictionary files

There are two types of AVPs. The standard RADIUS attributes are called Attribute Value Pairs (AVPs) while those from a vendor are called Vendor-Specific Attributes (VSA). Although there are two types of AVPs we usually do not differentiate between the two and simply call them both AVPs. VSAs use RADIUS attribute type 26 (Vendor-Specific). The value of this AVP is used to wrap the vendor-specific attributes in turn. View the contents of the updated dictionary.mikrotik file to understand the content of a dictionary file. The following discussion will be based on it.

Notes inside the comments

Lines starting with # are treated as comments. Sometimes the comments contain valuable information that should be heeded to in order to avoid a broken system:

```
# -*- text -*-
#       http://www.mikrotik.com
#
#       http://www.mikrotik.com/documentation//manual_2.9/dictionary
#
#       Do NOT follow their instructions and replace
#       the dictionary in /etc/raddb with the one that they
#       supply. It is NOT necessary.
#
#       On top of that, the sample dictionary file they provide
#       DOES NOT WORK.  Do NOT use it.
```

Vendor definitions

A dictionary defining VSAs takes on the following format:

```
VENDOR          Mikrotik                          14988
BEGIN-VENDOR    Mikrotik
```

```
. . .

END-VENDOR        Mikrotik
```

A vendor definition must include the vendor's number at the start. Vendor numbers are assigned by IANA. You can get the existing assignments from the following URL:

```
http://www.iana.org/assignments/enterprise-numbers
```

Sandwiched between BEGIN-VENDOR and END-VENDOR are ATTRIBUTE and VALUE definitions.

Attributes and values

We will only cover basic attribute and value definitions in this chapter. However, FreeRADIUS includes a dictionary man page that contains more details:

`man dictionary`

Attribute definitions take on the following format:

```
ATTRIBUTE <name> <number> <type> [vendor|options]
```

Name field

Although the name field can be any non-space text it is best to follow the existing convention, which comes from the RFCs. This is what we've done with the new MikroTik attribute definitions. The name usually indicates the function of the number it maps to, for example Mikrotik-Total-Limit is used to limit the total bytes during a session.

Number field

The numbers are usually incremental and determined by a vendor or a standards organization like IANA. Each number has a special meaning to either the client or the server. This is why we have to get the latest numbers and their meanings from MikroTik. The only numbers you are allowed to assign yourself are those in the range between 3000 and 4000 as mentioned in the main dictionary file:

```
#
#        If you want to add entries to the dictionary file,
#        which are NOT going to be placed in a RADIUS packet,
#        add them here.  The numbers you pick should be between
#        3000 and 4000.
#
```

Type field

The `type` field can be one of a few pre-defined types. The following table lists these types with a short description:

Type	Description
date	32-bit integer value representing the seconds since 00:00:00 GMT, Jan. 1, 1970 (Unix epoch)
integer	32-bit integer value (values from 0 to 4,294,967,295)
text	1-253 octets containing UTF-8 encoded characters
string	1-253 octets containing binary data
ipaddr	4 octets in network byte order
ifid	8 octets in network byte order
ipv6addr	16 octets in network byte order
ipv6prefix	18 octets in network byte order
ether	6 octets of 'hh:hh:hh:hh:hh:hh' where 'h' is a hex digit, upper or lowercase
abinary	Ascend's binary filter format
octets	raw octets, printed and input as hex strings, for example 0x123456789abcdef

What would life be without exceptions! The `dictionary.wimax` file specifies a few non-standard data types. There is, for instance, a signed integer type called `signed`. This is different from the `integer` data type which is unsigned. The WiMAX VSAs also have a non-standard format, which is discussed in the comments of the `dictionary.wimax` file.

Optional vendor field

As an alternative to the exercise where we updated the MikroTik dictionary by sourcing a complete new file, we could simply have added the following to the dictionary file located under the FreeRADIUS configuration directory:

```
#Add New Mikrotik Attributes

ATTRIBUTE    Mikrotik-Wireless-PSK            16    string    Mikrotik
ATTRIBUTE    Mikrotik-Total-Limit            17    integer   Mikrotik
ATTRIBUTE    Mikrotik-Total-Limit-Gigawords  18    integer   Mikrotik
ATTRIBUTE    Mikrotik-Address-List           19    string    Mikrotik
ATTRIBUTE    Mikrotik-Wireless-MPKEY         20    string    Mikrotik
ATTRIBUTE    Mikrotik-Wireless-Comment       21    string    Mikrotik
```

The method to use for updating a dictionary is up to you. I prefer keeping all the attribute definitions of a vendor in a single updated dictionary file.

Value definitions

Values are defined to give human-readable options for attributes of type integer. This helps us to remember names instead of numbers. In the `dictionary.mikrotik` file the following values are defined:

```
# MikroTik Values
VALUE    Mikrotik-Wireless-Enc-Algo        No-encryption      0
VALUE    Mikrotik-Wireless-Enc-Algo        40-bit-WEP         1
VALUE    Mikrotik-Wireless-Enc-Algo        104-bit-WEP        2
```

This means for the `Mikrotik-Wireless-Enc-Algo` attribute we can specify any one of these three values instead of using the integer equivalent. If we, for instance, also want to enforce no encryption on Alice we can modify the users file to the following:

```
"alice" Cleartext-Password := "passme"
     Mikrotik-Total-Limit =10240, Mikrotik-Wireless-Enc-Algo = No-
     encryption
```

Value definitions are a great aid, which makes reading of attribute assignments much easier. Value definitions only apply to attributes of type integer.

Accessing dictionary files

Before we come to the end of the chapter there is a final important point that still needs to be mentioned. Although the files under `/usr/share/freeradius` are usually readable by everyone, the main dictionary configuration file located under the FreeRADIUS configuration directory may not always be. If you try to run `radtest` as a normal user and it refuses to start, check the access rights on the FreeRADIUS configuration directory as well as the dictionary file inside this directory.

To allow a normal user read access to files in a directory we set the execute permission of the directory. We take SUSE as an example:

`#> chmod o+x /etc/raddb`

To enable a normal user read access to the dictionary file, add read rights to it:

`#> chmod o+r /etc/raddb/dictionary`

Summary

Although dictionaries are not required for the RADIUS protocol they are a core part of the FreeRADIUS server. The following is a list of important points to remember about dictionaries:

◆ Do not modify the pre-defined dictionary files that are installed by FreeRADIUS.

◆ Check with an NAS vendor for any new supported RADIUS attributes in order to update the dictionaries.

◆ Updated dictionaries have to be sourced after the pre-defined dictionary files in order to have the latest supported attributes.

◆ Dictionaries are there for our benefit by mapping attribute names to AVP type numbers.

◆ Attributes of type integer can have value definitions that link a certain string to an integer value.

◆ Dictionary files located under /usr/share/freeradius are not automatically used by FreeRADIUS but they have to be specifically listed in the /usr/share/freeradius/dictionary file or in the dictionary file in the FreeRADIUS configuration directory.

Pop quiz – dictionaries

1. Isaac phones you in a state of shock. He followed the instructions from a hardware vendor to include their latest dictionary files with FreeRADIUS and now the FreeRADIUS server refuses to start. What can be wrong?

2. You are taking over from someone who left the company and are now responsible for managing and updating all the Linux servers. After you have updated the Linux server, FreeRADIUS refuses to start. If you try to start it in debug mode the following error is reported:

    ```
    /etc/raddb/users[11]: Parse error (reply) for entry bob: Invalid
    octet string "1" for attribute name "ChilliSpot-Max-Total-
    Gigawords"
    ```

    What may have caused this to happen?

3. You are working through the *FreeRADIUS Beginner's Guide* book and see that in *Chapter 7, Authorization* the author uses a private attribute called FRBG-Reset-Type of type string. This attribute can however only be one of four values (daily, weekly, monthly, or never). Is there a better way to do this?

12
Roaming and Proxying

The RADIUS protocol was designed with expandability in mind. If your initial RADIUS deployment only makes use of a local user store it is still possible to join a larger network of RADIUS servers without major changes to the configuration. The focus of this chapter is to help you integrate with other RADIUS servers.

In this chapter we shall:

- ◆ Discover the advantages and dangers of roaming
- ◆ See what a realm is and how it works in FreeRADIUS
- ◆ See how to proxy requests based on realms
- ◆ Explore ways to make a proxy setup more robust

So let's get on with it...

Roaming—an overview

Roaming allows you to use the same credentials in various localities to gain Internet access. There are two very common usages of roaming today. Let's see how they work.

Agreement between an ISP and a Telco

Consider the following diagram:

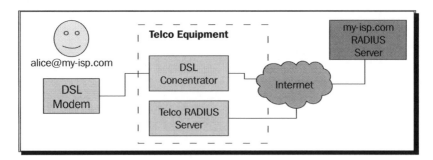

- ◆ Alice is a client of **my-isp.com**. My-isp.com does not have its own infrastructure.

- ◆ **my-isp.com**, however, has an agreement with the local **Telco**. The **Telco** allows clients from **my-isp.com** to connect to the Internet using the Telco's **DSL Concentrator** equipment.

- ◆ The local Telco's **DSL Concentrator** will first forward authentication requests to the **Telco RADIUS Server**.

- ◆ Because of the realm (**@my-isp.com**) these requests will be proxied to the **my-isp.com RADIUS Server**.

- ◆ The local **Telco RADIUS Server** in effect becomes just another client to the **my-isp.com RADIUS Server**.

Some of the advantages of this are:

- ◆ **my-isp.com** does not require its own infrastructure.

- ◆ **my-isp.com** can have multiple independent agreements with other infrastructure providers, for example, mobile phone operators or WISPs.

The dangers include:

- ◆ **my-isp.com** relies on third parties to provide part of the service.

Agreement between two organizations

To demonstrate this we will use two diagrams. The first one is where **alice@my-org.com** visits **your-org.com**:

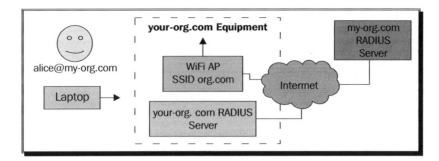

- This type of roaming is used in Eduroam. Both organizations install Wi-Fi access points with a common SSID (**org.com** in our case).

- When **alice@my-org.com** visits **your-org.com** she simply connects to the **org.com** SSID. This SSID is the same at **my-org.com** and **your-org.com**.

- The **Wi-Fi AP** then forwards her authentication request to the **your-org.com RADIUS Server**. This RADIUS server sees that **alice@my-org.com** is a user of **my-org.com** and proxies the request to the **my-org.com RADIUS Server**.

- The **your-org.com RADIUS Server** in effect becomes just another client to the **my-org.com RADIUS Server**.

The next diagram shows us what happens when **bob@your-org.com** visits **my-org.com**:

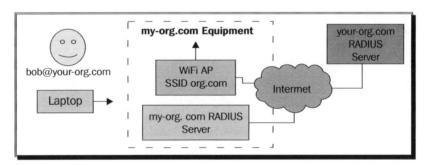

- **bob@your-org.com** is configured for connecting to the **org.com** SSID at **your-org. com**. As soon as he visits **my-org.com** the **org.com** SSID is ready and waiting for him to connect.

- The **Wi-Fi AP** forwards Bob's authentication request to the **my-org.com RADIUS Server**. This RADIUS server sees that **bob@your-org.com** is a user from **your-org. com** and proxies the request to the **your-org.com RADIUS Server**.

- The **my-org.com RADIUS Server** in effect becomes just another client to the **your-org.com RADIUS Server**.

The advantage of this is:

◆   Easy connectivity and an increase in productivity

Some of the dangers faced are:

◆   Vulnerable to misuse of network resources

◆   Potential security risks by allowing another organization to handle usernames and/or credentials of users in your organization

Now that we have a better overview of roaming it is time to get our hands dirty and see how proxying is done in FreeRADIUS in order to allow roaming. The rest of the chapter will be divided into two sections. We start with realms and after realms we discuss proxying.

Realms

Realms are used as a way to group users. The most common way to group them is by using the DNS name of an organization. This name is then separated from the user's name with a special character referred to as a delimiter. Again the most common delimiter is the '@' character although other characters can be used. The result is a username similar to an e-mail address (`alice@my-org.com`). Although the username may look like an e-mail address there is absolutely no requirement for it to be a valid e-mail address.

Other common conventions used for realm grouping includes user%realm, realm\user, or realm/user. These are, however, less popular.

Time for action – investigating the default realms in FreeRADIUS

In the following exercises we will learn about various aspects of realms. We will start with a clean installation of FreeRADIUS and change it subsequently to see how it handles various realm configurations:

 Ensure you have a default installation of a FreeRADIUS server.

1.   Edit the `users` file located under the FreeRADIUS configuration directory and make sure the following entry for alice exists:

```
"alice" Cleartext-Password := "passme"
```

2. Restart the FreeRADIUS server in debug mode and authenticate as alice. Observe the output of the FreeRADIUS server. The following should be part of the output:

```
[suffix] No '@' in User-Name = "alice", looking up realm NULL
[suffix] No such realm "NULL"
++[suffix] returns noop
```

What just happened?

We have done a normal authentication against the `users` file—nothing new here. We will, however, be focusing on a module inside the `authorize` section of the `sites-enabled/default` virtual server. This module identifies itself as the `suffix` module in the debug messages.

Suffix module

The `suffix` module is an instance of the `realm` module (`rlm_realm`). This module is defined in the `modules/realm` file under the FreeRADIUS configuration directory:

```
#    'username@realm'
#
realm suffix {
    format = suffix
    delimiter = "@"
}
```

This module is instructed to check if the `User-Name` AVP is in the form `username@realm`. There are also other instances of the `realm` module defined in the `modules/realm` file:

♦ **IPASS** looks for a username of the form `IPASS/username@realm`.

♦ **realmpercent** looks for a username of the form `username%realm`.

♦ **realmntdomain** looks for a username of the form `domain\user`.

NULL realm

There are three realms that have special meaning in FreeRADIUS. They are **NULL**, **LOCAL**, and **DEFAULT**. We can see from the debug output that the `suffix` module was actually looking for information on the realm called `NULL`. Because it could not find any information on the `NULL` realm it simply returned `noop`.

```
[suffix] No '@' in User-Name = "alice", looking up realm NULL
[suffix] No such realm "NULL"
++[suffix] returns noop
```

The `suffix` module groups any username that does not contain a suffix into the `NULL` realm. This means that any request without a realm will automatically be in the `NULL` realm. Since `alice` did not contain an `@realm`, the `suffix` module tried to get information on the `NULL` realm but could not get any and returned `noop`.

Enabling an instance of the realm module

As we've seen, `suffix` is simply an instance of the `realm` module. This instance is used during `authorization` (`Access-Request`) and also during `preacct` (`Accounting-Request`). Only `suffix` is enabled by default but we can enable any of the other defined instances, for example, `IPASS`. We can even declare our own named instance of the `realm` module and subsequently use it. The defaults, however, work just fine in most environments.

In the next exercise, we will see where the `suffix` module was looking for this realm called `NULL` that does not exist.

Defining the NULL realm

Realms are defined inside the `proxy.conf` file located under the FreeRADIUS configuration directory. Continuing with the previous exercise we will create our first realm.

Time for action – activating the NULL realm

Follow these steps to activate the `NULL` realm:

1. Edit the `proxy.conf` file under the FreeRADIUS configuration directory and change the following part from:

```
#realm NULL {
#       authhost            = radius.company.com:1600
#       accthost            = radius.company.com:1601
#       secret              = testing123
#}
```

to:

```
realm NULL {
#       authhost            = radius.company.com:1600
#       accthost            = radius.company.com:1601
#       secret              = testing123
}
```

2. Restart the FreeRADIUS server in debug mode and authenticate as alice. Observe the output of the FreeRADIUS server. The following should be part of the output:

```
[suffix] No '@' in User-Name = "alice", looking up realm NULL
[suffix] Found realm "NULL"
[suffix] Adding Stripped-User-Name = "alice"
[suffix] Adding Realm = "NULL"
[suffix] Authentication realm is LOCAL.
++[suffix] returns ok
```

What just happened?

We have created the special realm NULL and observed the change in the debug output of an authentication request.

Stripped-User-Name and realm

The `suffix` module found the NULL realm inside the `proxy.conf` file. If it finds a realm, two new attributes are added based on the value of User-Name, which is split into two components:

- ◆ **Stripped-User-Name**: This is just the username without the @realm, for example `alice`

- ◆ **Realm**: In the case of `alice` there is no realm and the `suffix` module uses the special realm NULL

The `suffix` module also decided what to do with the request and reported the following way:

```
[suffix] Authentication realm is LOCAL.
```

The `suffix` module automatically sets the realm; we can, however, at any time during the `authorize` phase decide to change it by simply using unlang and modifying the value of the Proxy-To-Realm attribute in the `control` attribute list.

Here we test the value of the User-Name AVP and when it is a required value, it will authenticate locally:

```
if(request:User-Name == 'my-org-test@your-org.com'){
    update control {
        Proxy-To-Realm := LOCAL
    }
}
```

This is a handy way to cancel or change a proxy request based on certain attributes.

LOCAL realm

The LOCAL realm as stated before is also one of the special realms. When we defined the NULL realm we did not specify an authost, accthost, or secret. When none of these are specified the special realm LOCAL will be used. The LOCAL realm is simply a way of saying "no proxying, continue, thank you". There is a realm LOCAL defined inside the proxy.conf file but it is more of a placeholder and it never is modified. Even when removing it from the proxy.conf file, the LOCAL realm is still available to the suffix module.

Actions for a realm

When defining a realm you can specify what action should be taken. This is determined by the use of directives inside the realm definition. There are three types of actions:

- Proxy this request to another RADIUS server or server pool, out on the Internet. This will be covered later in the chapter where we will be using the pool directive.

- Forward this request to a local virtual server by using the virtual_server directive. This is similar to forwarding it to another RADIUS server. The request will also be sent through the pre-proxy and post-proxy sections but, instead of going to an external server it goes to a local virtual server.

- Do not proxy this request, use the local server. When the realm definition does not contain any directives specifying external or virtual servers, the special realm LOCAL will be used. We've done this with the NULL realm.

Defining a proper realm

We will now investigate how FreeRADIUS reacts when we create a proper realm.

Time for action – defining the realm

The following steps demonstrate how to define a realm:

1. Add the following realm to the proxy.conf file located under the FreeRADIUS configuration directory:

    ```
    realm my-org.com {
    }
    ```

2. Restart the FreeRADIUS server in debug mode and authenticate as alice@my-org.com. Observe the output of the FreeRADIUS server. The following should be part of the output:

```
[suffix] Looking up realm "my-org.com" for User-Name = "alice@my-
org.com"
[suffix] Found realm "my-org.com"
[suffix] Adding Stripped-User-Name = "alice"
[suffix] Adding Realm = "my-org.com"
[suffix] Authentication realm is LOCAL.
++[suffix] returns ok
```

3. Edit the `my-org.com` realm to include the `nostrip` directive:

```
realm my-org.com {
    nostrip
}
```

4. Restart the FreeRADIUS server in debug mode and authenticate as `alice@my-org.com`. Observe the output of the FreeRADIUS server. Authentication should fail and the following should be part of the output:

```
[suffix] Looking up realm "my-org.com" for User-Name = "alice@my-
org.com"
[suffix] Found realm "my-org.com"
[suffix] Adding Realm = "my-org.com"
[suffix] Authentication realm is LOCAL.
++[suffix] returns ok
```

What just happened?

We have defined a real realm and investigated the results when the `nostrip` directive is used in the realm definition.

The `realm` module (of which `suffix` is an instance) will look for a realm in the `proxy.conf` file. If it is found and there is no `nostrip` option in the definition it will add the `Stripped-User-Name` and `Realm` attributes. However, if there is a `nostrip` option in the realm's definition it will only add the `Realm` attribute.

Modules that are involved with authentication (like the `files` module) check to see if there is a `Stripped-User-Name` attribute for a user. If one is found, they will use that value instead of the `User-Name` attribute's value to look for a valid user.

When we used the `nostrip` option there was no `Stripped-User-Name` attribute added and the `User-Name` was `alice@my-org.com`. This is why the authentication failed.

Rejecting usernames without a realm

A typical requirement when there is roaming between two organizations is to prevent the users from using their username without the realm name. Failing to do this may cause the username alice to work at my-org.com, but not at your-org.com. Forcing the username to be in the format alice@my-org.com will ensure that it works at both organizations. The next exercise shows you how to do this.

Time for action – rejecting requests without a realm

The following steps will demonstrate how to reject requests without a realm:

1. Edit the proxy.conf file under the FreeRADIUS configuration directory and ensure that the my-org.com realm does not have the nostrip directive (it was included in the previous exercise).

2. Edit the sites-enabled/default file and add the following unlang code just after the suffix entry in the authorize section. This will reject any requests with usernames without a realm:

```
if( request:Realm == NULL ){
    update reply {
        Reply-Message := "Username should be in format username@
domain"
    }
    reject
}
```

3. Restart the FreeRADIUS server in debug mode and try to authenticate as alice. The authentication request should fail.

4. Authenticate as alice@my-org.com. The request should pass.

What just happened?

We have managed to reject any authentication request where a username does not contain a realm.

We had to put the unlang code after the suffix module because it sets the Realm to NULL. We then perform a simple check for the value of the Realm attribute inside the request attribute list. If it is NULL we reject the authentication request with a relevant message.

DEFAULT realm

At the start of this exercise we said there were three special realms that the `realms` module (for example `suffix`) used:

◆ **The NULL realm**, if defined, is used for any user that does not have a realm in the username. The `Stripped-User-Name` attribute is set to the same value as the `User-Name` attribute. The `Realm` attribute will be set to `NULL`.

◆ **The LOCAL realm** is a realm that always exists and if `control:Proxy-To-Realm` is specified as `LOCAL`, no proxying takes place. The `LOCAL` realm is also used when a realm is defined without any external servers or virtual servers inside the realm definition. Another use for the `LOCAL` realm is to cancel a proxy request and handle the request locally.

◆ **The DEFAULT realm**, if defined, is used for any request that contains an unknown realm. The `DEFAULT` realm definition almost always includes the `nostrip` option in order to help the upstream server to differentiate between realms. This will typically be used when you are forwarding requests to an upstream server like the Eduroam servers. In short it matches all undefined realms that are received. See the following diagram for an explanation:

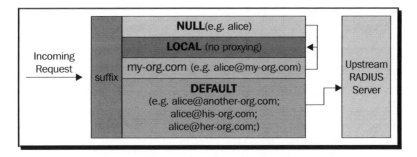

From the diagram we see that users with an unknown realm are grouped into the `DEFAULT` realm by the suffix module. From there, the request is usually forwarded upstream. This principle is similar to the TCP/IP protocol's default gateway.

Beware of creating endless loops

A common mistake that people make when two organizations configure roaming between them is for `my-org.com` to simply proxy unknown users to `your-org.com`. Then `your-org.com` in turn configures its servers to simply proxy unknown users to `my-org.com`. This will obviously create an endless loop! Take note of this and beware!

In closing

This brings us to the end of the first section on realms. There are three key points to remember about the work of the `suffix` module:

◆ It identifies a user's realm based on predefined realms in the `proxy.conf` file and sets the `control:Proxy-To-Realm` value accordingly.

◆ It adds a `request:Realm` attribute if the user is part of a pre-defined realm. This includes the special realms `NULL` and `DEFAULT`.

◆ If the pre-defined realm of a user does not include the `nostrip` option, the `suffix` module will add the `request:Stripped-User-Name` attribute.

Beware of old documentation

You may come across documentation instructing you to define a realm inside the `realms` file. It may also talk about options like `notrealm` and `hints` that can be used in a realm definition. The `realms` file and these options are not used any more. We now use the `proxy.conf` file to define realms. Read the comments inside the `proxy.conf` file to discover which options are currently allowed.

In the next section we will see how adding directives to a realm will cause it to forward requests.

Proxying

This section will also be hands-on like the previous section on realms. Our end goal is a similar setup to the one shown in the *Agreement between two organizations* section at the start of this chapter. This means that you will require two FreeRADIUS servers. We assume a default installation on both.

Time for action – configuring proxying between two organizations

We will start with the FreeRADIUS server for `my-org.com`:

1. Edit the `users` file located under the FreeRADIUS configuration directory and make sure the following entry for alice exists:

```
"alice" Cleartext-Password := "passme"
    Tunnel-Type = VLAN,
```

```
    Tunnel-Medium-Type = IEEE-802,
    Tunnel-Private-Group-ID = "100"
```

2. Edit the `proxy.conf` file located under the FreeRADIUS configuration directory and add a `home_server` entry for `your-org.com`. We assume it has an IP address of 192.168.1.106.

    ```
    home_server hs_1_your-org.com {
        type    = auth+acct
        ipaddr  = 192.168.1.106
        port    = 1812
        secret  = testing123
    }
    ```

3. Also add a `home_server_pool` section to the `proxy.conf` file that contains the `home_server` defined in the previous step:

    ```
    home_server_pool pool_your-org.com {
        type = fail-over
        home_server = hs_1_your-org.com
    }
    ```

4. Use this pool to proxy requests for the `your-org.com` realm:

    ```
    realm your-org.com {
        pool = pool_your-org.com
        nostrip
    }
    ```

5. Create a `LOCAL` realm for `my-org.com`:

    ```
    realm my-org.com {
    }
    ```

6. Edit the `clients.conf` file located under the FreeRADIUS configuration directory to allow requests from the `your-org.com` RADIUS server. We assume it has an IP address of 192.168.1.106:

    ```
    client your-org.com {
        ipaddr = 192.168.1.106
        secret = testing123
    }
    ```

This completes the required configuration for the `my-org.com` RADIUS server. The `my-org.com` RADIUS server will now do two things:

◆ Forward requests for the `your-org.com` realm to the `your-org.com` RADIUS server

◆ Accept requests from the `your-org.com` RADIUS server

We will now configure the `your-org.com` RADIUS server in a similar way:

1. Edit the `users` file located under the FreeRADIUS configuration directory and make sure the following entry for bob exists:

```
"bob" Cleartext-Password := "passbob"
    Tunnel-Type = VLAN,
    Tunnel-Medium-Type = IEEE-802,
    Tunnel-Private-Group-ID = "55"
```

2. Edit the `proxy.conf` file located under the FreeRADIUS configuration directory and add a `home_server` entry for `my-org.com`. We assume it has an IP address of 192.168.1.105.

```
home_server hs_1_my-org.com {
    type    = auth+acct
    ipaddr  = 192.168.1.105
     port    = 1812
    secret  = testing123
}
```

3. Also add a `home_server_pool` section to the `proxy.conf` file that contains the `home_server` defined in the previous step:

```
home_server_pool pool_my-org.com {
    type = fail-over
    home_server = hs_1_my-org.com
}
```

4. Use this pool to proxy requests for the `my-org.com` realm:

```
realm my-org.com {
    pool = pool_my-org.com
    nostrip
}
```

5. Create a `LOCAL` realm for `your-org.com`:

```
realm your-org.com {
}
```

6. Edit the `clients.conf` file located under the FreeRADIUS configuration directory to allow requests from the `my-org.com` RADIUS server. We assume it has an IP address of 192.168.1.105:

```
client my-org.com {
    ipaddr = 192.168.1.105
    secret = testing123
}
```

The your-org.com RADIUS server will now do two things:

◆ Forward requests for the my-org.com realm to the my-org.com RADIUS server

◆ Accept requests from the my-org.com RADIUS server

The stage is now set. Restart the two FreeRADIUS servers in debug mode and perform the following tests while carefully observing the debug output on both FreeRADIUS servers. We will use a table to list the tests to perform, servers on which to do it, and things that will be tested.

User to authenticate	Do on RADIUS server	What is tested
alice	my-org.com	Local user without realm
alice@my-org.com	my-org.com	Local user with realm
bob@your-org.com	my-org.com	Remote user with realm
bob	your-org.com	Local user without realm
bob@your-org.com	your-org.com	Local user with realm
alice@my-org.com	your-org.com	Remote user with realm

If both the servers were configured correctly all the Access-Requests should pass. If it does not work as intended, re-check the configuration and follow the debug output to try to determine where the request got rejected.

What just happened?

We have configured two RADIUS servers, each with the following functionality:

◆ Each server has its own realm.

◆ Each server will forward incoming requests (authentication and accounting) for users defined on the other server to that server.

The following section will be specifically looking at important points when proxying **authentication** requests. The section thereafter will discuss important points on proxying **accounting** requests.

Proxying authentication requests

To give another RADIUS server proxy rights to our server, we simply add it as a `client` on our server inside the `clients.conf` file. Users, as we have seen, are grouped together by defining a `realm`. The new part in this section is the definition of a `home_server` and a `home_server_pool`.

- ◆ A `home_server` and a `home_server_pool` are used to define the external RADIUS server(s) to which the various realms can send proxy requests.
- ◆ A `realm` contains a `home_sever_pool`.
- ◆ The `home_server_pool` in turn contains one or more `home_server` entries.

The following schematic shows how the `realm`, `home_server_pool`, and `home_server` sections can be used as individual building blocks to create many arrangements.

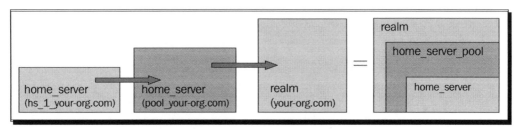

home_server

A `home_server` section defines a single server that is used to proxy certain types of requests to. In our sample setup we specified `auth+acct`. In essence it contains details that FreeRADIUS will use to act as a client to the specified home server. It can also contain optional directives that FreeRADIUS will use to determine fail-over and load balancing when this `home_server` is grouped in a `home_server_pool`. One `home_server` can be included in one or more `home_server_pools` or not included at all.

home_server_pool

A `home_server_pool` is used to group one or more `home_servers` together. The selection criteria of a `home_server` in a `home_server_pool` can either be done in fail-over mode (default) or load-balancing mode. Be sure to add only `home_servers` of the same `type` (for example. `auth+acct`) to a pool to ensure they will all be able to handle the requests forwarded to them.

Having these three building blocks gives tremendous flexibility and possibilities for different arrangements with minimum effort. There exists a lot of detailed information including sample configurations in the `proxy.conf` file under the FreeRADIUS configuration directory to help you to create alternative configurations.

The comments inside the `proxy.conf` file also mention an alternative way to define home servers for a specific realm by using the `authost`, `accthost`, and `secret` directives instead of the `home_server_pool` directive. These directives are part of an older way to define home servers and people are encouraged to use the newer way that offers more flexibility.

Flow chart of an authentication proxy request

The following diagram shows the difference in flow between a request that is proxied to another server and a request that is processed locally.

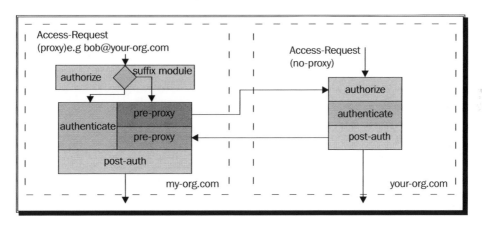

If we look at the debug output on the `my-org.com` RADIUS server when `bob@your-org.com` tries to authenticate, we can follow this flow. Let's discuss some highlights.

Suffix setting control: Proxy-To-Realm

During the `authorize` part, the `suffix` module identifies that `bob@your-org.com` belongs to the `your-org.com` realm and sets `control:Proxy-To-Realm` to `your-org.com`:

```
[suffix] Looking up realm "your-org.com" for User-Name = bob@your-org.com
[suffix] Found realm "your-org.com"
[suffix] Adding Realm = "your-org.com"
[suffix] Proxying request from user bob to realm your-org.com
[suffix] Preparing to proxy authentication request to realm "your-org.com"
++[suffix] returns updated
```

You will see that the output only states it is `Preparing to proxy authentication request`. This is because the proxying decision can still be changed or cancelled if other modules in the `authorize` section change the value of `control:Proxy-To-Realm`.

Pre-proxy section

Since `control:Proxy-To-Realm` was set to `your-org.com`, the request did not flow to the `authenticate` section, but went to the `pre-proxy` section instead. This section is, however, empty, which is why the following line is in the debug messages:

```
WARNING: Empty section.  Using default return values.
```

The `pre-proxy` section can be used as a last location to cancel or change the proxy request by modifying the `control:Proxy-To-Realm` AVP value. We see then how the request is sent to the home server of `your-org.com`.

Post-proxy section

When a reply is returned from the home server of `your-org.com` we see how this reply is then passed through the `post-proxy` section. This section will typically be used to remove AVPs returned by the home server of `your-org.com`. Thereafter the request passes through the `post-auth` section and the reply is returned to the original client.

```
rad_recv: Access-Accept packet from host 192.168.1.106 port 1812, id=184,
length=40
    Tunnel-Type:0 = VLAN
    Tunnel-Medium-Type:0 = IEEE-802
    Tunnel-Private-Group-Id:0 = "55"
    Proxy-State = 0x3330
+- entering group post-proxy {...}
[eap] No pre-existing handler found
++[eap] returns noop
Found Auth-Type = Accept
Auth-Type = Accept, accepting the user
+- entering group post-auth {...}
++[exec] returns noop
Sending Access-Accept of id 30 to 127.0.0.1 port 57020
    Tunnel-Type:0 = VLAN
    Tunnel-Medium-Type:0 = IEEE-802
    Tunnel-Private-Group-Id:0 = "55"
```

EAP and dynamic VLANs

In the previous section we saw three attributes returned from the `your-org.com` home server to the client of the `my-org.com` RADIUS server. These attributes are used for dynamic VLAN assignment. Dynamic VLAN assignment is done in some enterprise networks that use 802.1x on the LAN or WPA-2 on their Wi-Fi network. This helps to put each client inside a specified VLAN dynamically. The decision of which VLAN a user should belong to can be based on many things like privileges (for example students and professors) or on the type of device (for example VOIP phones).

> Watch out for the value of `Tunnel-Private-Group-Id`. This attribute's value is a `string` and not an `integer`. A VLAN can have a name in addition to a number. Some equipment will only take a VLAN name while other equipment requires the VLAN number. Be sure to check what your equipment needs before assigning a value.

The VLAN numbers used by `your-org.com` will not necessarily have the same privileges at or even be implemented by `my-org.com`. This is why in the next section we will modify the attributes returned from the home server at `your-org.com` so that they meet the requirements on the network at `my-org.com`. Before we modify the attributes, you can, as an optional exercise, use the **JRadius Simulator** program discussed in Chapter 10, *EAP* to test the proxying of EAP requests.

Have a go hero – testing proxying of EAP authentication

Test the proxying of EAP authentication between `my-org.com` and `your-org.com` by doing the same set of tests that was listed in the table earlier. You will notice that the reply AVPs will be missing when running tunneled EAP methods. To enable the return of reply AVPs in these EAP methods, be sure to change the following directive in the `peap` and `ttls` sections inside the `eap.conf` file located under the FreeRADIUS configuration directory from `use_tunneled_reply = no` to `use_tunneled_reply = yes`.

> The proxying of tunneled EAP methods never exposes the user details and passwords located inside the tunnel to the RADIUS servers that forward the request. This is more secure than other authentication protocols like PAP.

Removing and replacing reply attributes

Since you have no control over the AVPs that are returned from an external home server, it is simply good practice to manage these attributes and their values after they are returned to our server. In this exercise we will replace the dynamic VLAN detail returned from `your-org.com` with the dynamic VLAN detail used at `my-org.com` on the `my-org.com` RADIUS server.

Time for action – filtering reply attributes returned by a home server

The following actions have to be carried out on the `my-org.com` FreeRADIUS server:

1. Edit the `sites-enabled/default` file located under the FreeRADIUS configuration directory and uncomment the `attr_filter.post-proxy` line under the `post-proxy` section:

```
#   Uncomment the following line if you want to filter
#   replies from remote proxies based on the rules defined
#   in the 'attrs' file.
attr_filter.post-proxy
```

2. Edit the `attrs` file under the FreeRADIUS configuration directory and add the following entry before the `DEFAULT` entry:

```
your-org.com
    Reply-Message =* ANY,
    Tunnel-Type := VLAN,
    Tunnel-Medium-Type := IEEE-802,
    Tunnel-Private-Group-Id := "100"
```

3. Restart the FreeRADIUS server in debug mode and test the authentication for bob@your-org.com from the FreeRADIUS server at `my-org.com`.

4. The `reply` attributes will now always include the following, no matter what AVPs are returned by the home server of `your-org.com`:

```
Tunnel-Type:0 = VLAN
Tunnel-Medium-Type:0 = IEEE-802
Tunnel-Private-Group-Id:0 = "100"
```

What just happened?

We have implemented a filter for the reply attributes from the home server of `your-org.com`. To do this we made use of the `rlm_attr_filter` module. The module itself has plenty of documentation including a man page (`man rlm_attr_filter`) and a sample `attrs` file. Various instances of this module are defined in the `modules/attr_filter` file located under the FreeRADIUS configuration directory.

Attribute entries are of the form `<attribute> <operator> <value>`. Consult the man page when you are selecting operators. Selecting the correct operator is crucial for the filter to work as intended. We chose the `:=` operator, which will override the existing attribute if it exists or add the attribute if it does not exist. Suppose we had used the `==` operator instead of `:=`, then it would only return that particular attribute when the reply from the home server contains that particular attribute with the specified value. We have also used the `=*` `ANY` pattern for the `Reply-Message` AVP. This means that any value of `Reply-Message` should simply be forwarded.

Before we move on to the proxying of accounting requests we will briefly look at fail-over and load-balance configuration in a `home_server_pool`.

Status of the home servers

The creation of a `home_server_pool` allows us to specify a few home servers inside this pool. We can declare two types of pools. One will be to handle high loads better; the other will handle network outages better. With both of them, FreeRADIUS needs to keep track of the health of the home servers inside the pool. To specify how FreeRADIUS will check the health of a home server we use the `status_check` directive in a `home_server` declaration. Depending on the value of `status_check` there are other additional directives that will influence (or fine tune) the way in which a health check is done.

The three possible values for `status_check` are:

- **None**: Although this is the default, it is the least preferred. Only use it as a last resort.

- **Status-Server**: This requires that the home server support the receiving of `Status-Server` packets. Confirm that the home server supports it before specifying it. This is the preferred way of status checking.

- **Request**: FreeRADIUS will send `Access-Request` or `Authentcation-Request` packets to the home server to check its status. Use this if the home server does not support `Status-Server` packets.

Although we have only specified a single home server for `my-org.com` and `your-org.com`, we can still add the `status_check = status-server` directive to specify the preferred way of checking the health of a home server.

Time for action – using the preferred way for status checking

The following steps will demonstrate how to perform status checking:

1. Update the home_server definitions for my-org.com and your-org.com to include the following directive:

```
status_check = status-server
```

2. To see how FreeRADIUS sends Status-Server packets to a dead server simply shut down the FreeRADIUS server for your-org.com and keep on sending authentication requests for bob@your-org.com to the my-org.com server:

```
Marking home server 192.168.1.106 port 1812 as zombie (it looks
like it is dead).

Sending Status-Server of id 97 to 192.168.1.106 port 1812
Message-Authenticator := 0x00...

NAS-Identifier := "Status Check. Are you alive?"
```

3. Start the FreeRADIUS server for your-org.com again in debug mode and see how it answers to the Status-Server packets sent to it from the my-org.com server:

```
rad_recv: Status-Server packet from host 192.168.1.105 port 1814,
id=160, length=68

Message-Authenticator = 0x7b2f0a58666d532b2...

NAS-Identifier = "Status Check. Are you alive?"

Sending Access-Accept of id 160 to 192.168.1.105 port 1814
```

4. After a specified number of responses to the Status-Server requests, the FreeRADIUS server at my-org.com will mark the home server of your-org.com as alive again:

```
Received response to status check 16 (3 in current sequence)

Marking home server 192.168.1.106 port 1812 alive
```

This brings us to the end of the status server discussion. This was just a general introduction to gain more background. You are encouraged to read through the information in the proxy.conf file to help you configure and fine-tune the settings for fail-over or load balancing.

As a final word, remember that this fail-over and load balancing is used by the home_server_pool during proxying. FreeRADIUS itself also offers fail-over and load-balancing functionality through the use of unlang. The keywords redundant, load-balance, and redundant-load-balance are used to create fail-over and load-balancing configurations between different modules within FreeRADIUS.

Proxying accounting requests

To see what happens when the FreeRADIUS server at `my-org.com` receives an accounting request for bob@your-org.com we can use two of the files from Chapter 6, *Accounting* to simulate accounting:

- ◆ `4088_06_acct_start.txt`: This file can be used to simulate the start of a session.
- ◆ `4088_06_acct_stop.txt`: This file can be used to simulate the end of a session.

Modify these files and change `User-Name = 'alice'` to `User-Name = 'bob@your-org.com'`.

Time for action – simulating proxied accounting

Do the following on the FreeRADIUS server for `my-org.com`:

1. Change the directory to where the files are that you will use for simulating accounting for `bob@your-org.com` on the FreeRADIUS server of `my-org.com`.

2. Make sure FreeRADIUS runs in debug mode on the servers representing `my-org.com` and `your-org.com`.

3. Issue the following command on the `my-org.com` server:

```
$> radclient 127.0.0.1 auto testing123 -f 4088_06_acct_start.txt
```

This is to simulate the start of a session.

4. Issue the following command on the `my-org.com` server to end the previous session:

```
$> radclient 127.0.0.1 auto testing123 -f 4088_06_acct_stop.txt
```

5. Observe the debug output on both servers to see how the proxying of accounting requests happened by default.

What just happened?

We have simulated a typical accounting request that is proxied from one RADIUS server to the home server of another organization.

Flow of an accounting proxy request

The following diagram shows the difference in flow between a request that is proxied to another server compared to a request that is processed locally:

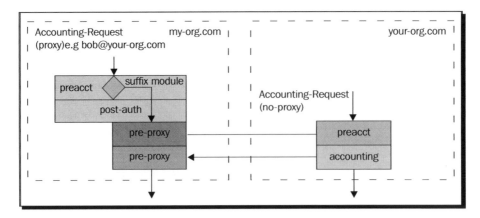

You will notice that the accounting is recorded on both servers by default. You can use unlang to create an `if` condition that will prevent the recording of accounting data in the forwarding server.

Updating accounting records after a server outage

A common question is how to handle requests to a home server that is down. When a home server is down or responding too slowly, you will see something like the following in the FreeRADIUS log file:

```
Tue Jul  5 19:13:16 2012 : Error: Rejecting request 2310 due to lack of
any response from home server your-org-1:1813
```

The principle that FreeRADIUS uses for this situation is to write a detailed log file on the local server and then use a virtual server with a listener on that log file to forward the requests when the home server is up again.

Before the 2.x release of FreeRADIUS this type of functionality was not part of the core and was usually done with the help of a program called `radrelay`. Now this functionality is built in. There are four sample virtual servers included under the `sites-available` folder under the FreeRADIUS directory that show possible ways to implement the functionality of writing to a detailed log and then creating a listener on those log files. The following list gives the name of the virtual server file and a brief description of its function.

- **buffered-sql**: De-couples the storage of long-term accounting data in SQL (slow) from "live" information needed by the RADIUS server as it is running (fast). It is used to speed things up.

- **copy-acct-to-home-server**: Enables duplication of information across a load-balanced or fail-over set of servers.

- **decoupled-accounting**: Similar to the `buffered-sql` configuration. Creates a virtual server for writing the details to a file and another virtual server to listen on this file.

- **robust-proxy-accounting**: Only writes the details when proxy requests to the home server fail. A listener for these failed requests will then attempt to forward them to the designated home server.

Have a go hero – implementing robust-proxy-accounting functionality

Take the `robust-proxy-accounting` file as an example and modify your own setup to make everything more reliable when network outages occur.

Summary

The creation of realms and setting up of proxying comes as a natural progression for any FreeRADIUS deployment that has to integrate into a larger network of RADIUS servers. Let's take a look at the important points from this chapter to remember:

- Realms are defined in the `proxy.conf` file and used to determine if a request has to be forwarded to an external home server.

- LOCAL, NULL, and DEFAULT are special realms. LOCAL always exists and is used to cancel proxying. NULL is used to group usernames without a realm and DEFAULT is used to group usernames from unknown realms.

- For an external home server to receive forwarded requests the server proxying the request has to be defined as a client on the home server.

- Realms defined with the `nostrip` option will cause the `suffix` module not to add the `Stripped-User-Name` AVP to the request. The `nostrip` option is usually chosen when forwarding requests to an external home server.

- When we proxy requests to other RADIUS servers it is important to filter the reply AVPs from those servers.

- When we wish to forward accounting data we can make use of the integrated radrelay functionality in FreeRADIUS to create a robust server that will be able to handle network outages.

Pop quiz – roaming and proxying

1. You work for a company called `my-org.com` that has just negotiated an agreement that will allow roaming between `my-org.com` and another company called `your-org.com`. You use FreeRADIUS and `your-org.com` uses Radiator. Will you be able to configure roaming despite having different RADIUS server software?

2. After you have configured and tested the roaming using EAP on the Wi-Fi network with a common SSID of **org.com**, a user from `your-org.com` visits `my-org.com`. He would like to know the EAP method used at `my-org.com` and would also like to load the CA of `my-org.com` in order to connect to the **org.com** SSID. Is this required?

3. `your-org.com` has upgraded its network and is implementing dynamic VLANs. Since then, when users from `my-org.com` visit them they can't get Internet access. What can be wrong?

4. A third company is joining the roaming agreement. After they have configured their FreeRADIUS server you see many requests forwarded to your FreeRADIUS for other realms also. What do you suspect they did on their side?

13
Troubleshooting

An efficient ICT Services department is almost invisible. Infrastructure just works as expected and users are blissfully unaware of the system layers that shield them from the underlying hardware. Even a little upheaval in the usually frictionless connectivity can seriously disrupt business operations and jeopardise business continuity.

It is the system administrator's responsibility to empower herself or himself with the skills and knowledge to limit disruptions and unwarranted blame. This final chapter should be used as a guide to diagnose and rectify things when FreeRADIUS does not work according to expectations.

In this chapter, we shall determine the following:

- ◆ Why FreeRADIUS would not start up
- ◆ Why FreeRADIUS may be slow
- ◆ Why FreeRADIUS would stop working
- ◆ Why FreeRADIUS would fail on a RADIUS client's requests
- ◆ Why a user would not authenticate

So let's get on with it...

Basic principles

Adhere to the principles established in *Chapter 3, Getting Started with FreeRADIUS* of the book in order to avoid unintended consequences. The rules were as follows:

◆ Do *as little as possible—the default configuration should work as is.*

◆ *Do not edit the default configuration files until you understand their purpose.*

◆ When you make changes, make a backup of the configuration beforehand and change one item at a time.

◆ Confirm that the changes work as intended by running FreeRADIUS in debug mode and carefully observing the output during various scenarios.

It is a good idea to create a backup of the FreeRADIUS configuration directory before you change anything. When one is under pressure, one tends to violate the principles advocating small changes or well understood configurations. Having a clean configuration to fall back on again can be a sanity check. The flip side is also true. Not having a clean configuration to fall back on means the one constant you should have relied on is now missing. You have been warned. The rest of this chapter contains common problems that you may encounter along with ways to trace and identify them.

Also make sure you have read through the FreeRADIUS FAQ at least once. It is called the FAQ for obvious reasons. The FAQ is located at the following URL: `http://wiki.freeradius.org/FAQ`.

FreeRADIUS does not start up

So you are eager to start this program called **radiusd**. You have logged in as root, type `radiusd` at the terminal prompt, hit *Enter* and you get the following:

`radiusd: command not found`

I know it sounds stupid, but make sure FreeRADIUS is actually installed, using this command:

`#> locate radius`

 Not all distributions include the `locate` command by default. On SUSE you probably first have to install it by running the following command:

`#> zypper in findutils-locate`

After you have established that FreeRADIUS is present but not starting, try to identify the server binary. On Ubuntu and Debian systems the binary is called `freeradius` and not `radiusd`. If you have the correct binary, start FreeRADIUS with the `-X` option to show debug messages that will help you identify problems. Some distributions, like CentOS, do not include the `/usr/sbin` directory in the root user's path. You then have to enter the absolute path together with the binary name in a shell in order for FreeRADIUS to start up.

The following list mentions common reasons why FreeRADIUS would not start up:

- Ports 1812 and 1813 are already in use.
- There is a problem with the configuration.
- A module or library is missing.
- FreeRADIUS connects to an external component that does not work as intended.

Who's using my port?

The culprit is usually another instance of FreeRADIUS that was started by the startup script during bootup. FreeRADIUS will then end with a message similar to the following one when you try to start it up. This means another program is using the UDP port that FreeRADIUS also would like to use:

```
Failed binding to authentication address * port 1812: Address already in
use
/etc/freeradius/radiusd.conf[240]: Error binding to port for 0.0.0.0
port 1812
```

The following command will show you all the UDP listeners on the machine:

```
#> netstat -uanp
```

Note that you have to be at the root to use the `-p` option of the `netstat` command. The `-p` option will show the process name that is using the listed ports. On my Ubuntu machine the following was returned:

```
Active Internet connections (servers and established)
Proto Recv-Q Send-Q Local Address           Foreign Address         State
PID/Program name
udp        0      0 0.0.0.0:68              0.0.0.0:*
605/dhclient3
udp        0      0 0.0.0.0:1812            0.0.0.0:*
1554/freeradius
udp        0      0 0.0.0.0:1813            0.0.0.0:*
1554/freeradius
udp        0      0 0.0.0.0:1814            0.0.0.0:*
1554/freeradius
```

You will notice FreeRADIUS also uses port 1814. This port does not listen for requests, but rather sends requests out, for example, during proxying when FreeRADIUS acts as a client to a realm's home server. To shut down the existing FreeRADIUS instance use the startup script with its `stop` option or the `killall` command. Here's how the two options are used on CentOS:

```
#> /etc/init.d/radiusd stop
#> killall radiusd
```

> If the output of the `netstat` command includes unwanted information, it is handy to pipe this output through the `grep` command to search for a certain phrase. The following command will only list the UDP ports used by the `freeradius` process:
>
> ```
> #> netstat -uanp | grep freeradius
> ```

Checking the configuration

FreeRADIUS has a `-C` option that is used to check the configuration. Starting FreeRADIUS with the `-XC` options will report if there was an obvious error in the configuration. This check is not foolproof and it may happen that FreeRADIUS passes this check but then still fails to start up. The debug message will, however, point to the problem most of the time.

FreeRADIUS uses the special keyword `$INCLUDE` inside configuration files to include other files but does not check to prevent recursive inclusion. This can result in FreeRADIUS recursively reading a file to include it in the configuration and eventually giving up. If this happens, the problem is usually with the last `include` line. Here is the output from a system that contains a broken `dictionary` file:

```
including dictionary file /etc/freeradius/dictionary
Errors reading dictionary: dict_init: /usr/share/freeradius/
dictionary[57]: Couldn't open dictionary "/usr/share/freeradius/
dictionary.compat": Too many open files
```

Finding a missing module or library

Finding a missing module is not always a matter of simply installing a FreeRADIUS package that contains this missing module. As FreeRADIUS allows us to define various instances of a module by giving a name to subsequent instances of the module, any name can appear in a virtual server section to represent a module instance. We do not necessarily know the function of this instance or the module that this instance is derived from.

To prevent this in future, it is good practice to give a hint of which module is used in the instance name of the module that is used. The `attr_filter` instances defined by default serve as excellent examples, like `attr_filter.access_reject`.

If a missing module is not required, it can be commented out in the configuration file. The debug output indicates which file, section, and also the line a missing module is listed on, for example:

```
/etc/freeradius/sites-enabled/default[160]: Failed to find module "frbg".
/etc/freeradius/sites-enabled/default[62]: Errors parsing authorize
section.
```

If the missing module is required, check whether it is not included in additional FreeRADIUS packages that are not installed yet. Finally, you can try to compile FreeRADIUS from source by ensuring that all the required development libraries are included to create this module during the compilation of FreeRADIUS. Older releases of Ubuntu for instance did not include support for EAP-TTLS and this was the route you had to take in order to include EAP-TTLS support with FreeRADIUS.

If you have compiled FreeRADIUS using the `configure`, `make`, `make install` pattern, you may get the following error when trying to start FreeRADIUS:

```
radiusd: error while loading shared libraries:
libfreeradius-radius-2.1.10.so: cannot open shared object file: No
such file or directory
```

This is because the operating system does not yet know about the existence and location of the newly installed libraries. If you run the `ldconfig` command it should be fixed.

Fixing a broken external component

Some modules rely on external components to do part of their work. The way FreeRADIUS reacts when there are problems with these external components differs between modules. Let's discuss three possibilities:

FreeRADIUS refuses to start

The `perl` module calls an external Perl script. This script is loaded into memory during startup along with the Perl runtime. However, if the external Perl script contains errors, FreeRADIUS will not start. The location of the error inside the external Perl script will be shown in the debug output.

> FreeRADIUS does not test the execution of the Perl script during startup. The Perl script is only executed when the `perl` module is called to service a request. During this execution the Perl script can also fail.

FreeRADIUS runs despite the display of an error message

The `sql` module will create a connection to the database during startup. If the database server is down, FreeRADIUS will still start up but will report it in the log files or the debug output. Here is a snippet from the log file that shows FreeRADIUS could not connect to the MySQL database:

```
Tue May 17 19:21:02 2012 : Info: rlm_sql_mysql: Starting connect to MySQL
server for #0
Tue May 17 19:21:02 2012 : Error: rlm_sql_mysql: Couldn't connect socket
to MySQL server radius@localhost:radius
Tue May 17 19:21:02 2012 : Error: rlm_sql_mysql: Mysql error 'Can't
connect to local MySQL server through socket '/var/lib/mysql/mysql.sock'
(2)'
Tue May 17 19:21:02 2012 : Error: rlm_sql (sql): Failed to connect DB
handle #0
```

Be sure to check the log files of a production system regularly in order to identify potential problems like these.

When FreeRADIUS connects to a database on an external server, ensure there is no firewall blocking access from the FreeRADIUS server to the database server. Some databases like MySQL also allow you to specify a host along with the username and password that a database user can connect from. These problems can be difficult to trace since everything seems OK while all the services are running. Unfortunately, one small component like the closing of a required port on a firewall can render FreeRADIUS in a broken state.

FreeRADIUS only reports a problem when answering a request

The `ldap` module does not check if the LDAP server is working fine during startup. Any problems with this external component will only be discovered when the `ldap` module is called to service a request. The log file will then report on the failure as follows:

```
Tue May 17 22:59:36 2012 : Error: rlm_ldap: cn=binduser,ou=admins,ou=rad
ius,dc=my-domain,dc=com bind to 127.0.0.1:389 failed: Can't contact LDAP
server
Tue May 17 22:59:36 2012 : Error: rlm_ldap: (re)connection attempt
failed
```

Also keep in mind that an external component can fail at any time. To minimize the impact of such a failure, you can use the redundant functionality that FreeRADIUS includes as part of unlang.

Using the startup script

After you have confirmed that FreeRADIUS can start from the terminal, also ensure that it starts fine using the start up script. Run a `tail -f` on the FreeRADIUS log file while starting the service up through the start up script.

```
#> tail -f /var/log/radius/radius.log
```

Finally make sure that FreeRADIUS will survive a reboot. Refer to *Chapter 2, Installation* to see how to activate the start up script on each distribution.

FreeRADIUS is slow

If your deployment of FreeRADIUS does authentication and accounting for many users, you have to make sure it performs as expected. You can start with a baseline speed test, which can be used as a reference in future. To do speed testing, the **JRadius Simulator** is ideal and easy to use.

Time for action – performing baseline speed testing

The following steps will demonstrate how to perform speed tests:

1. Install and configure **JRadius Simulator** using *Chapter 10, EAP* as a guideline.

2. Test the response time of FreeRADIUS by increasing the values of the *Requester Threads* and *Requests per Thread*, observing at what value FreeRADIUS reaches a saturation point.

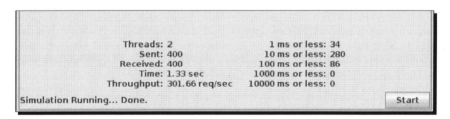

```
         Threads: 2                   1 ms or less: 34
            Sent: 400                10 ms or less: 280
        Received: 400              100 ms or less: 86
            Time: 1.33 sec        1000 ms or less: 0
      Throughput: 301.66 req/sec  10000 ms or less: 0
 Simulation Running... Done.                              Start
```

3. Test the duration of typical transactions that will be done on your FreeRADIUS server. If you are, for instance, part of Eduroam, you can record the duration of the various EAP methods that you support. You can also test the speed of accounting requests.

What just happened?

You have performed a baseline speed test on FreeRADIUS by making use of the **JRadius Simulator** program.

FreeRADIUS performs well in isolation. However, when FreeRADIUS utilizes external components or servers to service requests, performance may degrade because of the synchronous nature of requests. The next section will help you to maximize the performance of the FreeRADIUS server itself as well as the external components like files, LDAP, and SQL servers.

Tuning the performance of FreeRADIUS

The list of items in this section is taken from the following URL:

```
http://freeradius.org/radiusd/doc/tuning_guide
```

The URL offers a handy checklist that you can use in order to increase the performance of FreeRADIUS.

Main server

- Scalable authentication mechanisms like LDAP or SQL are better with large number of users and/or big volume of requests.

- Enable `noatime` on all the FreeRADIUS log files or better yet on the FreeRADIUS log directory. You can either mount a whole filesystem using the `noatime` mount option in the `/etc/fstab` file or if you have an ext2-type filesystem you can add the `A` attribute using the `chattr` command.

  ```
  #> chattr -R +A /var/log/freeradius/
  ```
  ```
  #> lsattr /var/log/freeradius/
  ```

- The `noatime` will disable the recording of the last time that the file was read, which results in an increase in performance.

- Do not use the `detail` and `radwtmp` (files) modules. They will slow down your accounting. The `detail` module can, however, be used in an alternative setup to de-couple the SQL accounting, which in turn can speed things up.

- Use the `users` file to only set default profiles. Do not place any users there. Keep it as small as possible. Always set default attributes in the `users` file and don't fill the user entries in LDAP/SQL with default values. In general the LDAP/SQL user profiles should only contain user attributes not catered for by default profiles.

- Tune the thread pool parameters to match your size requirements. Set `max_requests_per_server` to zero to avoid server thread restarts.

- Increase the timeout (10 seconds) and retries (5–7) in the Network Access Servers (NAS) for accounting. That way you won't lose any accounting information. If you use Mikrotik, it will definitely increase the timeout value since the default is only 100 microseconds.

- Use well-tuned Fast Ethernet connections to minimize latency.

- Ensure the operating system always has the latest patches installed.

There are also tips specific to some modules that can be used to make things faster.

LDAP Module

- Tune the `ldap_connections_number` in the `modules/ldap` file under the FreeRADIUS configuration directory to be larger than the average number of simultaneous user authentication requests.

- On the LDAP server, try to maximize caching. In particular, always enable indexing of the `uid` attribute (equality index) and the `cn` attribute (equality index – the `cn` attribute is used to search for groups). Make the LDAP server entry/directory cache memory sizes as large as possible. In general, try allocating as much memory as you can afford to your LDAP server.

- Put default profiles in LDAP. User entries should only contain non standard values in order to remain small and maximize the gains of caching the user default/regular profiles.

SQL Module

- Tune the `num_sql_socks` in the `sql.conf` file under the FreeRADIUS configuration directory to be larger than the average number of simultaneous authentication/accounting requests.

- Use the `sql` module in the `session` section instead of the `radutmp` module. It works much quicker.

- Create a multi-column index for the `Username` and `AcctStopTime` attributes especially if you are using `sql` for double-login detection. In the MySQL shell you can enter the following to do this:

```
mysql> use radius;

mysql> ALTER TABLE radacct ADD INDEX myIndex (username,
acctstoptime);
```

- If you are using MySQL and you do a lot of accounting, try using `InnoDB` for the `radacct` table instead of `MyISAM`. You can use the following command from the MySQL shell to determine the current engine:

```
mysql> show table status from radius LIKE 'radacct';
```

- To change the MySQL table's engine issue the following command:

  ```
  mysql> use radius;
  mysql> alter table radacct ENGINE = InnoDB;
  ```

- Add `Acct-Unique-Session-Id` in the `accounting_stop` query. Especially if you have a lot of access servers or your NAS does not send very random `Session-Ids`. That way you will always have one candidate row to search for, instead of all the rows that have the same `Acct-Session-Id`.

- Use the EXPLAIN statement in MySQL to evaluate the SELECT statements used by FreeRADIUS to help with the creation of indexes.

Now that our server is fine-tuned, we can make it even more reliable and faster by using the redundant and load-balancing functionality built into unlang.

Redundancy and load-balancing

The following is a list of keywords that unlang offers to create redundancy, load-balancing, or a combination of both:

- **redundant**: A `redundant` section is specified inside the `authorize` or `accounting` sections of a virtual server. This section can only contain a list of modules. If a module in the list fails, the next module in the list will be tried until one passes.

- **load-balance**: A `load-balance` section is also typically specified inside the `authorize` or `accounting` sections of a virtual server. Like the `redundant` section it can also only contain a list of modules. The modules, however, have to be of the same type (for example: `ldap` or `sql`) in order for the load balancing to work fairly. To handle the request, a module in the list is chosen at random.

- **redundant-load-balance**: There is a combination of `redundant` and `load-balance`.

Most enterprises have more than one LDAP server. When you are using the `ldap` module, it just makes sense to have a more solid deployment by utilizing the redundant and load-balancing functionality. The following snippet from the `authorize` section should speak for itself:

```
redundant-load-balance {
      ldap1   # 50%, unless ldap2 is down, then 100%

      ldap2   # 50%, unless ldap1 is down, then 100%
}
```

The FreeRADIUS Wiki contains two pages that show more complex possibilities for redundancy and load-balancing. The following are the links:
`http://wiki.freeradius.org/Fail-over`
`http://wiki.freeradius.org/Load_balancing`

Things beyond our control

Unfortunately, some RADIUS deployments include network portions that are not under our control. The fact that the FreeRADIUS server is running at top speed with a super-fast backend will make no difference if the connection between the client and the FreeRADIUS server is unreliable or slow. Using networking troubleshooting commands like `ping` and `traceroute` will be a good start in trying to determine if there is a latency problem with the client sending requests to the server and the server responding to these requests in return. If there is nothing you can do about the latency, you may look at increasing some timeouts in the configuration of the server or the client.

Having a working and fast system is no guarantee that FreeRADIUS will never crash. The next section discusses a way to let FreeRADIUS bounce back after it has died.

FreeRADIUS dies

Wouldn't it be nice to have a dedicated process that constantly watches another process and the moment it dies, simply restarts this dead process. The **deamontools** package contains such a program called `supervise`. If you want to minimize downtime, the following URL describes in detail how to incorporate a check on the `radiusd` process using the `supervise` program:

`http://freeradius.org/radiusd/doc/supervise-radiusd.txt`

After you have discovered that FreeRADIUS has died unexpectedly, go through the various system log files in order to try to determine what has caused this to happen.

Up till now, we have discussed problems that can prevent FreeRADIUS from starting and performing, and also how to keep it running. The rest of the chapter will look at common problems when clients interact with a running FreeRADIUS server.

Client-related problems

A user connects to a RADIUS client; the RADIUS client in turn connects to the RADIUS server. If a client does not seem to be able to connect with the server check the following first:

- ◆ Does FreeRADIUS knows about this client? Check the FreeRADIUS log file for lines like the following:

  ```
  Wed May 18 17:53:57 2012 : Error: Ignoring request to
  authentication address * port 1812 from unknown client
  192.168.1.103 port 39881
  ```

- ◆ Is the client allowed through the firewall running on the FreeRADIUS server? To check the firewall rules use the following command (requires root access):

  ```
  #> /sbin/iptables -L -n
  ```

If these initial checks have passed, run FreeRADIUS in debug mode in order to do proper troubleshooting. The debug messages will show when a request is received and how it is processed. These debug messages are verbose, containing lots of detail making it easy to follow.

Unfortunately, when you run FreeRADIUS in a production environment it is not always easy to first stop the FreeRADIUS server and then start it in debug mode in order to do troubleshooting. The second problem you will experience is to identify requests from the problem client, among all the other requests also going to FreeRADIUS. To help with both these problems, we can make use of the control-socket virtual server in combination with the raddebug program.

Another option is virtualization. Today most big enterprises are moving to a virtualized environment. This makes troubleshooting and testing new configurations much easier. A copy of the production virtual server can be used for tests or configuration changes. This minimizes disruptions in the production environment.

Testing UDP connectivity to a RADIUS server

Most people are familiar with using **telnet** to test connectivity to a specified TCP port. Unfortunately, we cannot use the **telnet** test on FreeRADIUS because it runs over UDP instead of TCP.

Testing for UDP connectivity with programs such as **netcat** and **nmap** does not really give a clear indication of whether one can connect to the UDP port or not. It is much more efficient to use a RADIUS client program like radtest or radclient to test the UDP connection. These client programs will also report on a wrong shared secret as follows:

```
rad_recv: Access-Reject packet from host 192.168.1.42 port 1812, id=62,
length=34
```

```
rad_verify: Received Access-Reject packet from home server
192.168.1.42 port 1812 with invalid signature!  (Shared secret is
incorrect.)
```

The control-socket virtual server

FreeRADIUS features a `control-socket` virtual server that allows you to control a running server. This virtual server is enabled by default on SUSE and CentOS but not on Ubuntu. The comments inside the virtual server have the following to say:

> *HIGHLY experimental! It should NOT be used in production environments.*

There is actually a second problem. The fact is this virtual server is so handy that you just have to bend the rules on this one! This virtual server allows the following programs to connect to the FreeRADIUS control socket:

- ◆ `radmin`: This is a FreeRADIUS Server administration tool that connects to the control socket of a running server, and gives a command-line interface to it.

- ◆ `raddebug`: This is a shell script wrapper around `radmin` that automates the process of obtaining debugging output from a running server. It does this without impacting service availability, unlike using `radiusd -X`.

Both of these programs include their own `man` pages for a more detailed description on how to use them.

 There is a security warning attached when activating the `control-socket` virtual server in read/write mode (required for `raddebug` and `radmin`). For me the convenience of `raddebug` outweighs the added risk.

Time for action – using the control-socket and raddebug for troubleshooting

As stated before, the `control-socket` virtual server is not enabled on Ubuntu and the default install on SUSE and CentOS requires a few adjustments before we can use the control socket with `raddebug`.

CentOS

Do the following on CentOS in order for `raddebug` to be useable:

1. Confirm that the `control-socket` virtual server is enabled by checking if it is listed under the `sites-enabled` directory:

```
#> ls /etc/raddb/sites-enabled
```

2. Edit the `control-socket` virtual server file and ensure `mode` is specified as `mode = rw` at the bottom of the `server` section.

3. Ensure the `radiusd` user is part of the `root` group:

```
#> /usr/sbin/usermod -a -G root radiusd
```

4. Restart FreeRADIUS using the start-up script:

```
#> /etc/init.d/radiusd restart
```

SUSE

Do the following on SUSE in order for `raddebug` to be useable:

1. Confirm that the `control-socket` virtual server is enabled by checking if it is listed under the `sites-available` directory:

```
#> ls /etc/raddb/sites-enabled
```

2. Edit the `control-socket` virtual server file and ensure `mode` is specified as `mode = rw` at the bottom of the `server` section.

3. SUSE by default runs FreeRADIUS as `root` so there will be no requirement to add the `radiusd` user to the `root` group to fix the permissions. If you are, however, running FreeRADIUS as user `radiusd` instead of `root`, remember to add `radiusd` to the `root` group.

4. Restart FreeRADIUS using the start up script.

```
#> /etc/init.d/freeradius restart
```

Ubuntu

Do the following on Ubuntu in order for `raddebug` to be useable:

1. Enable the `control-socket` virtual server:

```
$> sudo su
#> cd /etc/freeradius/sites-enabled
#> ln -s ../sites-available/control-socket ./
```

2. Edit the `control-socket` virtual server file and ensure `mode` is specified as `mode = rw` at the bottom of the `server` section.

3. Ensure the `freerad` user is part of the `root` group:

   `#> usermod -a -G root freerad`

4. Restart FreeRADIUS using the start up script.

   `#> /etc/init.d/freeradius restart`

Using raddebug

The `raddebug` program is a real life-saver in production environments. Let's imagine we have a production environment with an Access Point having an IP of 192.168.1.103 trying to authenticate a user. We do not know that the shared secret is wrong but we will soon find out!

1. Ensure you are the root user on the FreeRADIUS server that has the `control-socket` activated and configured as described previously. Purists may frown on being root in order to use `raddebug`. This, however, proved to give the least problems across all distributions.

2. From a terminal issue the following command:

   `#> raddebug -t 300 -i 192.168.1.103`

3. (If you use CentOS you have to use the following command before the `raddebug` command in order to prepare the $PATH variable: `export PATH=$PATH:/usr/sbin)`

4. Send an EAP authentication request from the host with the IP address of 192.168.1.103 but use a wrong shared secret.

5. Observe the output on the terminal running `raddebug`:

   `Received Access-Request packet from host 192.168.1.103 port 41450, id=18, length=63`

   `Cleaning up request 5 ID 18 with timestamp +253`

6. Run a `tail -f` on the FreeRADIUS log file to observe the output to the log file:

   `Thu May 19 21:20:47 2012 : Error: Received packet from 192.168.1.103 with invalid Message-Authenticator! (Shared secret is incorrect.) Dropping packet without response.`

7. Fix the shared secret and do another EAP authentication request. The output from `raddebug` should now show the transaction as it goes through:

```
Received Access-Request packet from host 192.168.1.103 port 34008,
id=22, length=63
NAS-IP-Address = 192.168.1.103
User-Name = "alice"
EAP-Message = 0x0200000a01616c696365
```

What just happened?

We have used the `raddebug` command to selectively watch the debug output for requests from a client with the IP Address of 192.168.1.103.

Remember the log output

The `raddebug` command only reports the debug messages and not the error messages. The error messages will still be logged to the FreeRADIUS log file. This is different compared to when we start FreeRADIUS in debug mode. When we start FreeRADIUS in debug mode the error messages as well as the debug messages are reported in the terminal. For this reason we use the `tail -f` command on the log file to also see what is reported there.

Spotting a mismatched shared secret

It is easy to spot a mismatched shared secret when you look at the `User-Password` attribute inside an `Access-Request` that uses PAP. The value of this AVP will contain all weird characters instead of the password of the user. Here is a sample of one from the debug output:

```
User-Password = "(*t\303v\230_\264\t;\211\221\343\024\343$"
```

However, in our exercise we used EAP and not PAP. With EAP you have to take a different approach to detect a wrong shared secret. Recent implementations of RADIUS on the client side include the `Message-Authenticator` AVP in the request. This AVP adds extra security to the RADIUS protocol and is also a quick way for FreeRADIUS to confirm if the shared secret is correct or not. If FreeRADIUS picks up from the value of `Message-Authenticator` that the shared secret is wrong, it will simply report it and ignore the packet. This is what we have experienced during the exercise.

Client implementations with a wrong shared secret that do not include the `Message-Authenticator` AVP can be extremely difficult to detect on the server when they do not use the PAP authentication protocol. A client definition inside the `clients.conf` file under the FreeRADIUS `configuration` directory can make use of `Message-Authenticator` compulsory with the following directive:

```
require_message_authenticator = yes
```

For more information on the Message-Authenticator AVP and other suggested improvements to the RADIUS protocol you can look at **RFC 5080**.

Always try to use a RADIUS client that includes the Message-Authenticator AVP. This makes the RADIUS protocol more secure and also makes it easy to detect a wrong shared secret. Also take note that although FreeRADIUS supports a shared secret of up to 31 characters not all the client devices can support a shared secret of that many characters. These devices may not always inform you of this limitation leading to confusion when things do not work correctly.

Options for raddebug

There are two convenient options available to the raddebug command as follows:

◆ -u name: This option lets you specify a username that will be used to filter requests on. Only requests with User-Name == name will be displayed.

◆ -i ipv4-address: This option lets you specify the source IP Address of the client to filter requests on. Only requests from Packet-Src-IP-Address == ipv4-address will be displayed.

There is also a -c option available that allows you to create more complex conditions. The conditions are created using unlang syntax.

Raddebug auto termination

The raddebug man page mentions that by default it will terminate after ten seconds. This duration varies between systems and is usually much longer. In the exercise, we have increased the duration to 300 seconds (5 minutes). The man page also mention that the -t 0 option will let it run forever. However, this did not work on any of my servers.

If there's no output from raddebug

If you do not get any output from raddebug make sure the user that runs the FreeRADIUS server, for example, radiusd is a member of the root group and that you have restarted the FreeRADIUS server after making it a member of the root group. When you run FreeRADIUS as root, it will not be required.

Some tips when defining clients

New clients defined in the `clients.conf` file are NOT loaded with the `SIGHUP` signal. You have to restart FreeRADIUS before they become available. If you define the clients in an SQL table, the same applies. However, there is a virtual server called `dynamic-clients` that can be used as a reference to support new clients without restarting FreeRADIUS.

If you decide to create a script that will automatically restart FreeRADIUS whenever there are new clients configured, remember to do a configuration check (`-C`) before you actually restart the server. Failing to do so can be problematic when configuration errors that cause the server not to start up are introduced.

The next section will look at possible problems when users authenticate through the RADIUS clients discussed in this section.

Authenticating users

Various authentication protocols are supported by FreeRADIUS. They vary in complexity with PAP being the simplest and EAP the most complex.

Editing the users file

If a user store consists of the `users` file, remember that you have to send the running FreeRADIUS process a `SIGHUP` signal before the latest changes to the `users` file to become effective.

```
#> kill -1 `cat /var/run/radiusd.pid`
```

If you do not know what the `SIGHUP` signal is, it has a long history that is explained on this Wikipedia page:

`http://en.wikipedia.org/wiki/SIGHUP`

FreeRADIUS uses it in following (modern) way:

Daemon programs sometimes use `SIGHUP` as a signal to restart themselves, the most common reason for this being to re-read a configuration file which has been changed.

The FAQ page on the FreeRADIUS Wiki includes a basic script that you can use to automate the committing of changes to the `users` file. Please note that the information on the FAQ should be used as a guideline and may require additional tweaking depending on the distribution. Also take heed not to simply send a `SIGHUP` (or restart) without checking the configuration first. You are, however, also encouraged to rather use dynamic user stores like LDAP and SQL.

Using raddebug

The `raddebug` command is your friend when it comes to tracing authentication problems in a production environment. The `-u` option lets you view only debug information for a specified user.

When passwords change

Most enterprises have a password policy that enforces regular changes of user passwords. When FreeRADIUS utilizes these user stores, there is a potential of users locking their accounts by using software that keeps on trying authenticating with an expired password.

A well-written supplicant will prompt the user to supply a password if the stored username and password fail to authenticate a user. The iPad and the iPhone contain a shining example of such a supplicant. Unfortunately, the Windows environment can contain a variety of supplicants and they are not always written with this scenario in mind.

When you run `raddebug` with the `-u` option while asking the user to try to authenticate you should be able to troubleshoot password problems fairly easy.

It is not always only the supplicant that misbehaves. Some Wi-Fi Access Points will 'cache' the credentials of clients that have previously authenticated successfully. If these clients disconnect and connect again to the Access Point, the Access Point will simply forward the previous credentials (which it successfully connected with) to the RADIUS server. If these credentials have changed in between connections, you're in for a surprise, because the AP does not ask the supplicant for the latest credentials but simply forwards a previous session's to the RADIUS server.

Password length

A problem that may come up sooner or later is where a user with a very long password authenticates fine on one RADIUS client but not on another. This problem is usually then related to the RADIUS client that truncates the password. This is similar to the problem we have explained with the shared secret where certain NAS clients have a limit on the shared secret's length.

EAP problems

As stated at the start of this section, the EAP protocol is the most complex of the authentication protocols. There are many places where things can go wrong but if you stick to logical troubleshooting principles even the biggest problem should at least be identifiable.

The CA certificate

Ensure that the CA certificate contains the Object Identifiers (OIDs) required by Microsoft. If they are not included you are likely to experience problems with Microsoft clients. There is a README included with FreeRADIUS that has extensive detail on generating and using certificates in the correct manner. On SUSE and CentOS the README is located under the /etc/raddb/certs directory. On Ubuntu it is located under /usr/share/doc/freeradius/examples/certs.

If you use Internet Explorer to download and install a new Root CA on Windows 7, be sure to launch Internet Explorer with the **Run as administrator** option in order to place the CA in the correct store after it is downloaded. On some installs of Windows 7, this was the only way to get the new CA to be listed with the existing CAs in the supplicant's CA selection control. When we did not take this route, the certificate was imported but it did not show in the supplicant's CA selection control.

Identify where a problem is located

If a user experiences problems connecting, try to determine if it is supplicant related or account related. The situations can be described as follows:

◆ If it is supplicant related, another user will also experience problems connecting using the same supplicant but with their own credentials.

◆ If it is account related, the same user will also experience problems connecting from a different supplicant on a different device.

If you are using raddebug to help with the troubleshooting remember to either ensure that the User-Name used in the outer identity is the same as the User-Name specified in the inner tunnel and use this with the -u option or to create a custom condition than will accommodate both by using the -c option.

Problems with proxying

The proxying process can be split into two components as follows:

◆ Determining the realm and home server of a user
◆ Forwarding the request to the home server of a user

When you are troubleshooting a proxy problem, ask yourself in which of the two components the problem occurs. The forwarding of a request to a home server can be simulated by using the radtest or radclient programs from the proxying server.

Many problems in practice are related to network problems. These problems are sometimes hard to detect. Latency, for instance, can be fine when you test the speed during off-peak hours, however, during peak hours the network will become so congested that problems start to arise. Because there are so many variables in the equation, it may be good to implement a proper monitoring system or include the components that are part of a proxying setup in an existing monitoring solution.

Online resources

The following table lists some handy URLs along with a short description of their content. Most of these URLs are also listed elsewhere in the book but this table groups them together in a single location.

URL	Description
`http://freeradius.org`	The FreeRADIUS project's home page.
`http://wiki.freeradius.org`	The Wiki for the FreeRADIUS project, which is used as the main source of documentation.
`http://wiki.freeradius.org/pages`	The Wiki is a living and growing entity. This URL lists all the wiki pages available for our consumption.
`http://freeradius.1045715.n5.nabble.com`	User-friendly searchable front-end to the FreeRADIUS mailing lists.
`http://freeradius.org/radiusd/doc/`	Miscellaneous documentation, some of which is not included in the Wiki.
`http://deployingradius.com/`	Contains some handy information on various things related to FreeRADIUS. Some may be out-dated by now.

The URLs listed should be the first to consult. Beware of older documentation or less trustworthy sources of documentation since they can be either dated or outright wrong, leading to much frustration.

Using the mailing list

The primary way to get help on issues that you cannot solve yourself is by using the FreeRADIUS mailing list (`freeradius-users@lists.freeradius.org`). The mailing list is searchable, which allows you to also search through previous discussions that have the search phrases you supplied.

Stick to the rules stipulated on this URL:

```
http://freeradius.org/list/users.html
```

Don't be overly sensitive when someone gives you a blunt response to a posted question. Remember that this support costs nothing and the people responding do so out of free will. They do us a favor by helping us to solve our problem. Also post back if a suggestion has either solved your issue or put you on the right track to solving it.

Summary

Good troubleshooting skills consist of a combination of disciplines that one learns to master over time. When you experience problems with FreeRADIUS you should take a logical approach to identify and fix the problem. This includes the following:

- Don't panic.
- Ask yourself what has changed recently.
- Make a complete backup of the configuration before you make any changes.
- Remember the log files.
- Remember debug mode.
- Remember the FAQ.
- Introducing a deliberate error is sometimes helpful to see how something behaves if it is broken and compare this to something that does not behave it should.
- Google is your friend (GIYF).
- Don't be afraid to post on the mailing list but stick to its rules.

Pop quiz – troubleshooting

1. You are newly employed by a firm that uses a mixture of Ubuntu and Debian servers. Coming from a SUSE environment you used to type in the following command to confirm that FreeRADIUS is running:

   `ps -aux and not pa -aux`

   When you run this command on a the primary FreeRADIUS server it shows there is no process called `radiusd`. Why is this?

2. Since last week, the LDAP server configured in the `ldap` module has became unstable. This server, however, is lightning fast compared to the other two LDAP servers that are available. For this reason you never even bothered to use them. What can you do to allow FreeRADIUS to first try the fast LDAP server and if it is down try the other slower ones?

3. Bob runs a Windows XP machine with a special supplicant that supplies EAP-TTLS/PAP functionality. He first connects through a WPA-enabled Wi-Fi AP and then changes his password on the backend. This backend is also used by FreeRADIUS. Not long after this his account is locked. What may have caused this to happen?

4. You have battled for two days trying to solve a proxying issue on FreeRADIUS. After you have posted a cry for help on the mailing list explaining just what you think of their piece of software, you get a response informing you are not welcome on the mailing list any more. Why did this happen?

Pop Quiz Answers

The answers to the pop quizzes from each chapter are provided here for your reference. How did you score?

Chapter 1

Pop quiz – RADIUS knowledge

1. A NAS device is a Network Access Server which controls access to the network and its resources.

2. A session starts directly after successful authentication and ends when the connection is terminated.

3. RADIUS uses UDP protocol. Port 1812 is used for authentication and port 1813 for accounting.

4. A shared secret.

5. An `Access-Request` packet

6. A `Disconnect-Request` packet is initiated by the RADIUS server and received by the RADIUS client.

7. The type, length, and value.

8. The name of the realm is freeradius.org.

Chapter 2

Pop quiz – installation

1. The `radiusd` binary is renamed to `freeradius` on Ubuntu and Debian Linux.

2. This happens when there is already an instance of FreeRADIUS running. To fix this, you should stop the current running one using the start-up script. The instance which is running now was started through the start-up script.

3. `freeradius2-mysql`.

4. Ensure he uses `zypper` instead of `yast -i` to install the required libraries.

Chapter 3

Pop quiz – clients.conf

1. Each client section has a short descriptive name between the keyword indicating the section's name, for example, client in this case and opening bracket.

2. This is not recommended since it has security implications.

3. There is a virtual server called `dynamic-clients` which can be used as a pattern to handle clients with unknown IP addresses.

4. `Message-Authenticator` may be missing. Set the `require_message_authenticator` directive to `no` to compensate for this.

5. Yes, the `ipv6addr` directive is used to specify the IPv6 address.

6. False, more characters will make it more secure. Also avoid recognizable words.

7. The simultaneous use checks done by FreeRADIUS may not be accurate, allowing a user multiple sessions even when it's been limited.

Chapter 4

Pop quiz – authentication

1. The use of PAP on its own can be a security risk, but when tunneled through TLS it is very secure.

2. These users are probably authenticating with CHAP. CHAP requires that the passwords be stored in cleartext. Most RAS servers allow you to select the authentication protocols which it supports. Configure the RAS server to use only PAP.

3. You can encrypt the passwords by using the `smbencrypt` program and use the value of NT hash for the `NT-Password` AVP.

Chapter 5

Pop quiz – user stores

1. The value of the `read_groups` directive in `sql.conf` was probably set to `no` by the previous administrator; changing it to `yes` will activate reading of the group tables for all users.

2. The `freeradius-postgresql` package needs to be installed first. This package contains the required set-up files as well as the PostgreSQL-specific FreeRADIUS module.

3. No, you do not authenticate against an SQL database or text files, but rather use them to store credentials. Password verification is then done by an authentication module using the data stored in the text file or the SQL database. (If he's non-technical just tell him no problem, can be done.)

4. Connect to the server through a secure connection and add access control to the directory to restrict access to the `userPassword` attribute.

5. No, this is not true! You can still use the 'bind as user' method, which limits you to PAP authentication. The `nspmPassword` attribute, which is available when Universal Password is enabled, allows MS-CHAP authentication since `nspmPassword` is formatted in a way that allows FreeRADIUS to get a user's password in cleartext (Remember that you have to connect to the LDAP server using SSL/TLS and the user you bind with needs to have enough rights to read this attribute).

6. Ensure that the user or group under which FreeRADIUS runs has read access to this directory.

7. Confirm that all the services have started up after the reboot, especially `smbd`, `nmbd`, and `winbind`.

Chapter 6

Pop quiz – accounting

1. Take a look at the firewall rules of the router connected to your server as well as the server itself. Ensure both UDP port 1812 and 1813 are open for the Telco's servers.

2. Those people were most likely connected to the Wi-Fi tower that is now down. According to FreeRADIUS they still are connected and it limits the simultaneous sessions for them. Use `radzap` to close their orphan sessions.

3. It can be that the time zone or time on the captive portal is not correct. You are encouraged to use Network Time Protocol (NTP) to make sure the time is synchronized between all the NAS devices and the FreeRADIUS server.

4. No, this is what happens with reset values other than never for data-based counters. The `sqlcounter` module should only be used for time-based counters.

Chapter 7

Pop quiz – authorization

1. It may be that the NAS does not support the AVP that is returned to throttle the bandwidth. There may also be a mismatch of the AVP's units. The counter for instance expects the value to be Kbit/s instead of bit/s.

2. Perl should be used instead of Bash for better speed. If you use the `perl` module, the Perl interpreter along with the Perl script will be loaded into memory when FreeRADIUS starts up.

3. Additional attributes that are used internally by FreeRADIUS should be defined in the dictionary file, which is located under the FreeRADIUS configuration directory.

4. The internal attribute list is known as the control list. To reference the `Auth-Type` attribute you can use `control:Auth-Type` inside conditional statements and `%{control:Auth-Type}` inside a double-quoted or back-quoted string.

5. This code defines a policy called `rewrite_calling_station_id`. The policy code searches for MAC addresses that contain delimiter characters of : or - and rewrites them to be delimited with the - character.

Chapter 8

Pop quiz – virtual servers

1. Create a new virtual server in the `sites-available` directory. Configure and specify a separate SQL database for this new virtual server. Link this virtual server to the `sites-enabled` directory. Define the VPN server as a client in the `clients.conf` file and use the `virtual_server` directive to force the use of this new virtual server for RADIUS requests.

2. The `buffered-sql` virtual server under the `sites-available` directory can be used as a template to work around the slow SQL response.

3. This is because the authenticate section does not contain a `Auth-Type PERL {...}` sub-section. Usually the `Auth-Type` will be set by a module or by unlang inside the authorize section. The authenticate section then requires a sub-section for the `Auth-Type` to handle its values.

Chapter 9

Pop quiz – modules

1. The `files` module is configured by the `files` file in the modules sub-directory under the FreeRADIUS configuration directory. Check if the `usersfile` directive does not point to a file different from the default of `users`.

2. Yes, you can split the `users` file. You have to create two named files sections that point to the separate files. These named sections can now be included inside the `authorize` section of the virtual server. By doing this FreeRADIUS will make use of different instances of the `files` module, each with its own configuration.

3. In CentOS the `perl` module is packed separately and has to be specifically installed before it can be used.

4. When we refer to the named section of the `ldap` module as `ldap_new_department` it gives an indication what type of named module is involved (`ldap`). If we simply call it `new_department`, there is no real indication as to the type of module we refer to.

Chapter 10

Pop quiz – EAP

1. Ignore the links; you may even go as far deleting them for sanity's sake. EAP works as is on a new installation. The less you change on the EAP configuration the better.

2. The EAP-TTLS/PAP method makes use of the `inner-tunnel` virtual server instead of the `default` virtual server when authenticating users. Make sure you also specify the use of the `ldap` module in the `inner-tunnel` virtual server. These virtual servers are independent from each other.

3. No, when you bind as a user you need to send the user's cleartext password to the LDAP server. When you use PEAP/MSCHAPv2 there is no way to get a cleartext password out of the transaction.

4. No lies here! The Universal Password feature allows the `ldap` module to get passwords in cleartext from the LDAP server. There are a few rules to follow in order to get this password. The connection to the LDAP server has to be a secure connection with a special privileged user binding to it to run the queries. The `password_attribute` also has to be specified in the `ldap` configuration. See the `ldap` configuration file for more details.

5. Use the iPhone Configuration Utility to create a `.mobileconfig` file. Distribute this file from a web server.

Chapter 11

Pop quiz – dictionaries

1. Not all instructions from vendors on updating the dictionary files are correct. Advise Isaac to revert to the backup of the working configuration (he did make a backup, right?) and rather follow the comments inside the dictionary configuration files that come with FreeRADIUS.

2. The previous administrator had probably made changes to the pre-defined FreeRADIUS dictionaries and these dictionaries were replaced during the update of FreeRADIUS. There is no real way to determine all the changes the previous person may have made. It does, however, seem that the Chillispot dictionary was changed because the complaint is about the `Chillispot-Max-Input-Gigawords` attribute. A good start to solving this problem will be to contact the previous administrator or to visit the CoovaChilli website and locate the latest supported attributes and then update the dictionary according to best practices.

3. Yes there is. We can change the type of `FRBG-Reset-Type` to `integer` instead of `string` and create value definitions to specify the four values that this attribute is allowed to have.

Chapter 12

Pop quiz – roaming and proxying

1. Yes, configuring roaming between RADIUS servers is not dependent on certain RADIUS server software. If the server software sticks to the standards in the RFC it should work easily.

2. No, you can inform the visitor from `your-org.com` that he should be able to simply connect using the profile for the `org.com` SSID without making any changes. The EAP requests to `your-org.com` will simply be proxied to the RADIUS server at `your-org.com`.

3. The Dynamic VLAN assignment is most likely done through a RADIUS server that returns specific AVPs to specify the VLAN a user should be in. The administrator of the RADIUS server at `your-org.com` has probably neglected to assign a default VLAN to visitors from `my-org.com`.

4. They most likely configured the special `DEFAULT` realm to forward requests from unknown realms to the RADIUS server at `my-org.com` instead of creating a dedicated realm for `my-org.com`.

Chapter 13

Pop quiz – troubleshooting

1. On Debian and Ubuntu the FreeRADIUS server binary is called `freeradius` instead of `radiusd` when you install the standard FreeRADIUS package.

2. You can create named instances of the `ldap` module that will use the slower servers. Then you can replace the `ldap` entry in the `authorize` section with a redundant section that lists the module using the fast LDAP server first and thereafter `ldap` module instances using the slower ones.

```
#ldap
redundant {
    ldap
    ldap.slow1
    ldap.slow2
```

```
}
```

If you use the 'bind as' authentication method for LDAP you also need to change the Auth-Type LDAP in the authenticate section to the following:

```
Auth-Type LDAP {
      redundant {
          ldap
          ldap.slow1
          ldap.slow2
      }
}
```

3. The supplicant on Bob's machine is probably designed badly. While his password was changed on the backend, his supplicant kept on attempting to connect by sending the previous password. The backend detected a potential intrusion and locked the account. If the supplicant was well written it would have popped up a dialog box for Bob to supply his credentials. If this is not the problem, it may be that the access point to which Bob connects forwards credentials stored from a previously successful session to the RADIUS server.

4. This happens when people do not follow proper netiquette as specified in RFC 1855 or when they do not stick to the rules of the mailing list specified in this URL:

    http://freeradius.org/list/users.html

Index

dynamic-clients module 212
dynamic VLANs 265

E

EAP
about 22, 215
authenticator 215
backend authentication server 215
components 216
conversation 218
module, configuring 223, 224
inner identity 229
inner-tunnel virtual server, configuring 228
issues 291
outer identity 229
Public Key Infrastructure 226
Public Key Infrastructure, creating 226
supplicant 215
testing, on FreeRADIUS with JRadius Simulator 220
unused EAP methods, disabling 232
using, on client 225
EAP authentication
proxying, testing for 265
EAP components
about 216
authenticator 216
backend authentication server 217
supplicant 217
EAP conversation
about 218
EAPOL-Packet 219
EAPOL-Start 218
EAP Method
gtc 223
leap 223
md5 223
mschapv2 224
peap 224
tls 224
ttls 224
eap module
configuring 223
user store 224

EAPOL-Packet
about 219
code field 219
type field 219
workflow 219, 220
EAPOL-Start 218
EAP-TTLS 227
EAP-TTLS/PAP 225
echo command 165
echo module 212
eDirectory LDAP server
connecting, Universal Password used 224
Eduroam 225
enabled virtual servers
including 186, 187
Post-Auth-Type, handling 187
using 185, 186
environment variables 177
ethernet switches 7
existing setup
consolidating, virtual server used 191
expiration and linelog modules
using 203, 205
Extensible Authentication Protocol. *See* **EAP**
Extensible Authentication Protocol (EAP)
protocol 67
extensions, RADIUS
about 21
Dynamic Authorization extension (RFC5176) 21
EAP (RFC3579) 22
external component issues, FreeRADIUS 277, 278

F

fail keyword 155
fakeroot command 42
files module 200
FRBG-Avail-Bytes attribute 168
FRBG-Reset-Type attribute 168
FRBG-Start-Time attribute 168
FRBG-Total-Bytes attribute 168
FRBG-Used-Bytes attribute 168
freerad 44

reply attribute 231
reply-name directive 143
Request Authenticator 14
requests
  rejecting, without realm 256
reset directive 143, 146
reset_time.pl script
  about 170
  contents 170-172
Response Authenticator 14
restrictions
  about 151
  implementing 152
return code
  obtaining, if statement used 153-155
return codes, modules 211
RFC2865 10
RFC2866 10
RFC 2903 8
RFC 5080 289
RFCs 8
rlm_expiration documentation 206
rlm_sqlcounter
  using 144-146
roaming
  benefits 248-250
  overview 247
robust-proxy-accounting functionality
  implementing 271
rpmbuild command 39
rpm-build package 36
rpm systems 58

S

Secure Hash Algorithm 79
SecureW2 225
session
  about 8
  ending 129, 130
  orphan session 130
  starting 128, 129
  terminating, at specified time 141, 142
session database
  SQL, using as 135-137
session section
  about 137

checkrad feature 138
SHA password 79
shared secret 11
SIGHUP signal 290
simultaneous sessions
  limiting, for user 135-137
single database
  used, for running multiple counters 144
SLA 9
SLES
  about 37
  Red Hat Package Manager (RPM), building on
    37-39
SMD5 password 78
software
  building, from source 34
software repositories 28
source
  software, building from 34
source RPM package 36
speed tests
  performing 279, 280
SQL
  using, as session database 135-137
sql_counter module 167
sqlcounter module 144
SQL database
  about 123
  advantages 95
  preparing 175
  uses 96
sql module 162, 200, 278, 281, 282
SQL statements
  using, as variables 162
SSHA password 80
SSL/TLS 68
start-up script
  using 279
stop option 276
sudo apt-get update command 40
suffix module
  about 251, 253
  key points 258
supplicant 217
SUSE
  about 28, 31, 37
  bug 176

firewall, configuring 33
raddebug command, used for troubleshooting 286
SUSE bug 176
SUSE README file 87
switch statement 153
symbolic link 184
system-config-securitylevel-tui utility 32
system users
about 86, 87
activating 88
stips 90

T

TACACS+ 24
tail command 288
tape archive. *See* **TAR file**
TAR file 34
Telco, agreement with ISP
about 248
advantages 248
disadvantages 248
telnet 284
traceroute command 283
Triple A Framework. *See* **AAA**
troubleshooting
about 274
basic principles 274
FAQs, URL 274
type attributes
about 187
Acct-Type 188
Auth-Type 188
Authz-Type 188
Post-Auth-Type 188
Session-Type 188
type directive 195

U

Ubuntu
about 28, 40, 87
bug 176
debs, installing 40, 41
raddebug command, used for troubleshooting 286

Ubuntu bug 176
UDP connectivity
testing, to RADIUS server 284
UDP listeners
displaying 275
UDP port 1812 126
UDP port 1813 126
unlang
about 152
command substitution 165
conditional statements 153, 154
custom attributes, defining 167, 168
data counter, creating with 167
default values, setting for variables 163, 164
feature 153
keywords 155
load-balance section 282
redundant-load-balance section 282
redundant section 282
regular expressions 166
variables 161-163
unlang code
adding, to virtual server 175, 176
unlang, keywords
fail 155
noop 155
ok 155
reject 155
unquoted string 155
unused EAP methods
disabling 232
update keyword 155, 161
user
User-Name AVP 229
usernames
rejecting, without realm 256
users
about 54
authorizing, with if statement 154
authorizing, with logical expressions 157, 158
data usage, limiting for 167
DEFAULT user 56
file module 54
Framed-IP-Address 57
Login-Time 57
operators 56

Thank you for buying
FreeRADIUS Beginner's Guide

About Packt Publishing

Packt, pronounced 'packed', published its first book "*Mastering phpMyAdmin for Effective MySQL Management*" in April 2004 and subsequently continued to specialize in publishing highly focused books on specific technologies and solutions.

Our books and publications share the experiences of your fellow IT professionals in adapting and customizing today's systems, applications, and frameworks. Our solution based books give you the knowledge and power to customize the software and technologies you're using to get the job done. Packt books are more specific and less general than the IT books you have seen in the past. Our unique business model allows us to bring you more focused information, giving you more of what you need to know, and less of what you don't.

Packt is a modern, yet unique publishing company, which focuses on producing quality, cutting-edge books for communities of developers, administrators, and newbies alike. For more information, please visit our website: www.packtpub.com.

About Packt Open Source

In 2010, Packt launched two new brands, Packt Open Source and Packt Enterprise, in order to continue its focus on specialization. This book is part of the Packt Open Source brand, home to books published on software built around Open Source licences, and offering information to anybody from advanced developers to budding web designers. The Open Source brand also runs Packt's Open Source Royalty Scheme, by which Packt gives a royalty to each Open Source project about whose software a book is sold.

Writing for Packt

We welcome all inquiries from people who are interested in authoring. Book proposals should be sent to author@packtpub.com. If your book idea is still at an early stage and you would like to discuss it first before writing a formal book proposal, contact us; one of our commissioning editors will get in touch with you.

We're not just looking for published authors; if you have strong technical skills but no writing experience, our experienced editors can help you develop a writing career, or simply get some additional reward for your expertise.

Cacti 0.8 Network Monitoring

ISBN: 978-1-847195-96-8   Paperback: 132 pages

Monitor your network with ease!

1. Install and setup Cacti to monitor your network and assign permissions to this setup in no time at all

2. Create, edit, test, and host a graph template to customize your output graph

3. Create new data input methods, SNMP, and Script XML data query

4. Full of screenshots and step-by-step instructions to monitor your network with Cacti

Zabbix 1.8 Network Monitoring

ISBN: 978-1-847197-68-9   Paperback: 428 pages

Monitor your network hardware, servers, and web performance effectively and efficiently

1. Start with the very basics of Zabbix, an enterprise-class open source network monitoring solution, and move up to more advanced tasks later

2. Efficiently manage your hosts, users, and permissions

3. Get alerts and react to changes in monitored parameters by sending out e-mails, SMSs, or even execute commands on remote machines

Please check **www.PacktPub.com** for information on our titles

Zenoss Core Network and System Monitoring

ISBN: 978-1-847194-28-2   Paperback: 280 pages

A step-by-step guide to configuring, using, and adapting this free Open Source network monitoring system - with a Foreword by Mark R. Hinkle, VP of Community Zenoss Inc.

1. Discover, manage, and monitor IT resources

2. Build custom event processing and alerting rules

3. Configure Zenoss Core via an easy to use web interface

Learning Nagios 3.0

ISBN: 978-1-847195-18-0   Paperback: 316 pages

A detailed tutorial to setting up, configuring, and managing this easy and effective system monitoring software

1. Secure and monitor your network system with open-source Nagios version 3

2. Set up, configure, and manage the latest version of Nagios

3. In-depth coverage for both beginners and advanced users

Please check **www.PacktPub.com** for information on our titles

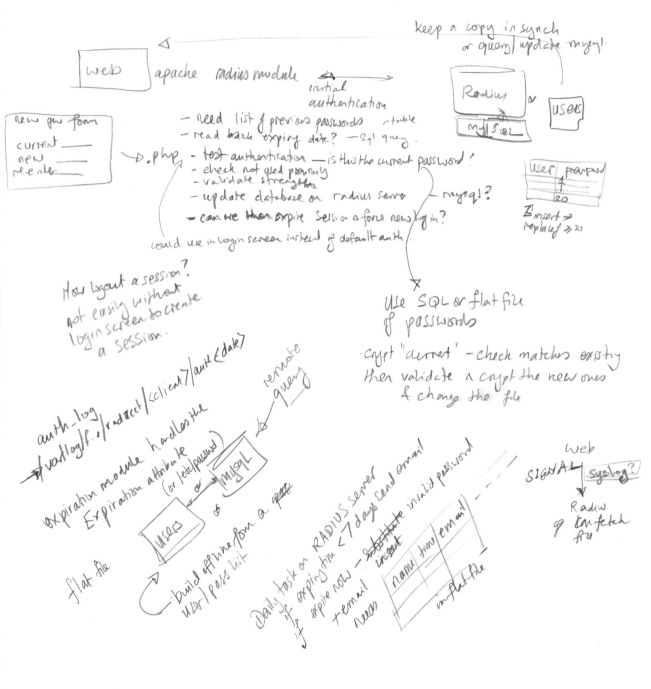

keep a copy in synch
or query/update mysql.

web | apache radius module →
initial
authentication

Radius | or | users

mysql

new pw form
current ____
new ____
re-enter ____

→ .php

- need list of previous passwords →table
- read back expiry date? — sql query.
- test authentication — is this the current password?
- check not used previously
- validate strength
- update database on radius server — mysql?
- can we then expire session a force new login?

could use in login screen instead of default auth.

User | prevpwd
1
20

Σ insert →
replay/ ≥ 20

How logout a session?
not easily without
login screen to create
a session.

Use SQL or flat file
of passwords

Crypt "current" — check matches existing
then validate & crypt the new ones
& change the file

auth_log
/varlog/f../radacct/<client>/auth[date]

remote query

expiration module handles the
Expiration attribute
(or else[passwd])

→ users | of | or | MySQL

flat file

- build off line from a file
user/pass list

Daily task on RADIUS server
if expiring in < 7 days send email
if expire now — substitute invalid password
+ email insert
need

name time email

in flat file

web
SIGNAL | syslog?

Radius
g to fetch
file

Printed in Great Britain
by Amazon.co.uk, Ltd.,
Marston Gate.